Louisa Anne Meredith was the wife of one of the early settlers in Van Diemen's Land. Both she and her husband Charles delighted in the natural world and it is this delight coupled with Louisa's exquisite observations that bring to life the bush and the days of settlement in Van Diemen's Land. Her account of the long journey across the land with her husband, her baby, a nurse and a servant is unforgettable. Their amusement at the trials occasioned by an attempt to keep an opossum as a pet and her recount of a hunting party's encounter with a Tasmanian tiger are just two of the many precious glimpses of life in the mid nineteenth century. Louisa's description of the floods and destruction they caused, struggles with and by aborigines and the trials of establishing gracious homes and gardens in an often tempestuous and treacherous land is essential reading for anyone who seeks to achieve an understanding of those early days.

MY HOME IN TASMANIA

HOBARTON.

FROM A SKETCH BY THE BISHOP OF TASMANIA.

MY HOME

IN

TASMANIA,

DURING A RESIDENCE OF NINE YEARS.

By Mrs. CHARLES MEREDITH.

Adventure Bay.

Combining two volumes
VOLUME ONE

LONDON:
JOHN MURRAY, ALBEMARLE STREET.
1852.

First Edition Published: John Murray, London, 1852.
This Facsimile Edition: Glamorgan Spring Bay Historical Society,
                        Swansea, Tasmania
Copyright © Glamorgan Spring Bay Historical Society, 2003

Acknowledgements

We are grateful to the Allport Library and Museum of Fine Arts, State
Library of Tasmania for permission to use the cover photograph of Louisa
A Meredith and to the Glamorgan Spring Bay Council for its sponsorship
and support .

The Society was motivated by a widespread demand that this valuable
text be made available once more. This work brilliantly details the land
and inhabitants of Tasmania in the early years of settlement. The style of
presentation, similar to Louisa Anne Meredith's original publication, is
one which should ensure her inspiring work is affordable for most
readers.

National Library of Australia Cataloguing-in-Publication data:
    Meredith, Louisa Anne, ca. 1812-1895
    My Home in Tasmania, During a Residence of Nine Years

    ISBN 0 646 42586 2
    1. Meredith, Louisa Anne, 1812-1895. 2. Tasmania - Social
    life and customs - 1803-1851. 3. Tasmania - Description
    and travel. I. Title.

    994.602

Printed in Australia by McPherson's Printing Group,
Maryborough, Victoria

PREFACE.

My gossiping " Notes and Sketches of New South Wales" met with a reception so cordial and flattering, and so far beyond my own expectations, that a grateful acknowledgment, in the shape of a second series, became the natural and inevitable result. The delay in its appearance has been reluctantly prolonged from year to year, as our erratic life, and the exacting duties of the present, precluded attention to a task which, however congenial, had only reference to the future (for, after the completion of a work here, fully a year must elapse ere any intelligence of its further advancement reaches the writer); and this circumstance, so unfavourable to any literary work, may per-

haps excuse the desultory character of the present one. Could any of my readers have marked
the fitful and uncertain progress of my notes—
sometimes amidst a Babel of busy tongues, loud
on the relative merits of humming or peg-tops—
or, more often, in brief intervals between lessons
in history, geography, or arithmetic—when, turning from the mighty records of Rome and Greece,
of Cæsar and Lycurgus, I have essayed to continue the memoir of a pet opossum; or, after
setting an "ugly" sum in multiplication, have
laid down slate and pencil to finish the descriptive portrait of some delicate bush flower—they
would less marvel at omissions and discrepancies
committed, than that many more probable blun-
ders had been avoided; and would kindly lay
aside the severity of criticism in judging so unpretending a work.

The risk of typographical errors in a work
which must of necessity go through the press
without its author's correction or revision, is un-
avoidably great; but the comparative rarity of
such mistakes in my former volume, published
under the same adverse circumstances, encourages
me to hope that the present may be as fortunate.

Lest the minute, perhaps trifling, detail, entered into in some parts, may seem inclining towards the egotistical, I should perhaps remark that I have been induced to adopt a more personal narrative, and to identify ourselves with the simple realities around us, just as events truly occurred, instead of generalizing my observations, because I have found, from my own feelings in the perusal of works of somewhat similar character, that the interest of such unvarnished histories is proportionally enhanced, according to the degree of identity preserved by the narrator; and, acting upon this hint from experience, I have unscrupulously practised the plain matter-of-fact candour and "individuality" which we ourselves like to find in the narratives of other dwellers in new countries.

The great amount of misconception and the positive misrepresentations relative to the present social condition of this colony, now prevalent, not in England only, but wherever the name of Van Diemen's Land is known, also determined me to enter more into domestic details than otherwise I might have thought it pleasant or desirable to do. No general descriptions would so well tend to show the truth, as the veritable chronicle of every-day life, in our solitary yet cheerful country homes, that stand all day with open doors, and all night without a shutter or bar or bolt to the windows; as innocent of lawless intrusion as dwellings of a like isolated and lonely character would be in any part of Britain—indeed, much more so; and why our really peaceful lives should be represented at home as invested with such terrors by day and perils by night, as might beseem the heroes of old romance in their most doughty days, I am wholly at a loss to conjecture, and can only hope that my humble efforts in the cause of truth may avail in dispelling at least some portion of the evil clouds that at present sully and overshadow our good name.

I cannot refuse myself the pleasure of here repeating my grateful and sincere thanks to our highly-esteemed friend, the Bishop of Tasmania, whose kind voluntary offer of his valuable aid, as my illustrator, has enabled me to present some of our lovely scenes to my readers in a form so well worthy of their own beauty, and so immeasurably enhancing the interest of my written descriptions. It is likewise right to remark, that beyond a knowledge of the localities mentioned, his Lordship has no acquaintance whatever with the contents of my MSS.; for my errors, be they few or many, I am alone responsible.

Of my own trifling sketches, I am perfectly aware that in their accuracy rests their sole merit: that they are rigidly faithful, I can honestly vouch; and as, in weaving a garland, small and insignificant flowers, worthless in themselves, ofttimes aid the general effect, so I am induced to hope, that my little drawings may peep pleasantly out from nooks and corners of the book, which would otherwise remain unoccupied.

I beseech the august body of British critics to receive my unfeigned thanks for the unmixed meed of approval and praise vouchsafed to my last appearance in print (and many former ones). Not one dissentient voice mingled in the pleasant sounds of kindly welcome which so delightfully echoed even into our far-away solitude here, and, like a singing summer breeze, spread over the peaceful current of my tranquil happy life a bright sunny ripple of surprise and joy; for from the generous reviewer of the mighty " Quarterly," to the passing notices of provincial papers, every pen seemed dipped in honey to greet my unpretending little tome of womanly gossip.

Some of the Sydney papers, I have been told, kindly took considerable pains to prove the correctness with which I had formerly estimated their elegance and ability; but as I have never myself met with any of their characteristic effusions, I still remain in blissful unconsciousness of the amount of my obligation to them.

Riversdale, Great Swan Port,
Van Diemen's Land, July 18th, 1850.

CONTENTS.

CHAPTER I.

PAGE

Departure from Sydney.—The "Sir George Arthur."—An Arrest. — Colonial Craftsmen.—Opposite Neighbours.—"Dick."—Hippolyte Rocks.—Cape Pillar.—Tasman's Island.—Cape Raoul . 1

CHAPTER II.

Night Alarm.—Squall.—Storm Bay.—Lose Topmasts.—Approach to Hobarton. — Cast Anchor. — Mount Wellington. — Scenery round Newtown. — Gardens. — Hobarton Society.—Theatre.— Melodramas 17

CHAPTER III.

The Hunt.—Public Amusements.—Public Decorum and Morality. — Prisoner Population. — "Assignment System." — "White Slavery." — Magistrates. — "Probation System."—Experience in Prisoner-Servants. — Their Length of Service. — Their Attachment and Good Faith 33

CHAPTER IV.

Journey to Swan Port.—Restdown.—Richmond.—"The Grand Stand."—Colonial Roads.—Pic-nic Dinner.—A "Sticker-up."— Jerusalem.—Native Names.—Halt in the Forest.—Free Roads. —Road-Gangs.—Transit over Gullies.—Eastern Marshes. — An Invasion.—Lonely Houses.—Organ of Locality . . . 49

CHAPTER V.

Journey continued.—Pic-nic Dinner.—Ascent of the Sugarloaf.— Gum-Tree Forests.—Rest on the Mountain.—Descent.—Night Quarters.—Sea Coast.—"Rocky Hills."—Oyster Bay.—Isle des Phoques.—Maria Island.—Probation Gang.—Waterloo Point. —Journey's End 68

CHAPTER VI.

Cambria. — Hedges.—View.— Garden and Orchard. — Fruits.— Flowers.—Rabbits. — Black Swans. — Christmas Day.— Pic-nic Parties.—Sponges.—Shrubs and Shells 87

CHAPTER VII.

PAGE

Bush Fires.—Their Use.—Diamond Bird.—Robin.—Blue-Cap.—
Cormorant.—Gulls.—Islands in Bass's Straits.—Pied and Black
Red-Bills.—Blue Crane 107

CHAPTER VIII.

Excursion to the Schoutens.—Scenery.—Kelp Forests.—Fishing.
—White Beach.—Rivulet.—Gully.—Lace Lichen.—Ferns.—
Echoes.—View.—Dinner on the Beach.—Return   .   .   . 117

CHAPTER IX.

Swan Fort Conchology.—Peculiarly-formed Arca.—Banks of
Oyster-Shells.—Living Oysters.—Sea-Hares.—Land Shells.—
Mutton Fish.—Beauty-Snails.—A Volute.—Corallines.—Star-
Fish.—Sponges   132

CHAPTER X.

Our New Home of " Riversdale."—Colonial Housewifery.—Female
Servants.—Progress at Spring Vale.—A Dead-wood Fence.—
Buildings.—Site and Plans.—Materials.—Timber.—Lightwood
Tree.—Stone.—Clearing Fields.—Green Marshes.—Honey-
suckle Tree.—Wattle Tree.—Brushy Pine   152

CHAPTER XI.

Home Occupations.—The " Weeping Gum " Tree.—Household
Duties.—Society.—Snakes.—Quail.—Wattle-Birds.—Walks.
—Wild Flowers.—Acacias.—" Wattling."—Parasite Creepers.
—Native Mistletoe.—Clematis.—Comesperma.—A " Dry Path."
—The First Stack.—Melancholy Accident.—Losses   .   .   . 168

CHAPTER XII.

The Aborigines of Van Diemen's Land.—Their First Murders of
the Settlers.—" Mosquito."—Murders at Swan Port.—The Murderers chased.—A Native Shot dead.—Warning by Native
Women.—Murder of Robert Gay.—Native Woman wounded.
—John Raynor.—Attack on Buxton's Cottage.—Burning and
Murders near Jericho.—Murder of the Hooper Family.—Murders
at St. Paul's Plains.—Erroneous Impressions.—Aborigines Removed   188

CHAPTER XIII.

PAGE

Joyful Removal to Spring Vale.—Improvements. — Clearing and Burning.—Great Flood.—The Half-drowned Man.—Two to be Extricated.—The Rescue.—The "Big Pool."—The Sweet Bay.— Black Cockatoos.—Pied Magpies.—Black Magpies . . . 219

CHAPTER XIV.

Garden-making. — Walks and Rides. — Native Raspberry.—Old Don and the Kangaroo. — Tasmanian Quadrupeds. — Forest Kangaroo. — Brush Kangaroo. — Joey and Beppo.—Wolloby. — Kangaroo-rat. — Bandicoot. — Porcupine. — Wombat. — Its Haunts 238

CHAPTER XV.

The "Devil."—Native Cat.—Tiger-cat.—Native Tiger, or Hyena. —In at the Death.—Musk-rat.—Platypus.—Opossum Mouse. —Kangaroo Mouse 261

LIST OF ILLUSTRATIONS TO VOL. I.

HOBARTON	Frontispiece.
ADVENTURE BAY	Title-page.
ENTRANCE TO PORT ARTHUR	Page 1.
TASMAN'S ISLAND AND CAPE PILLAR	,, 14.
CAPE RAOUL	,, 17.
CAMBRIA	,, 87.
WEEPING GUM-TREES AND OLD FORGE	,, 168.
SPRING VALE COTTAGE	,, 219.
PORCUPINES	,, 238.

NINE YEARS IN TASMANIA.

ENTRANCE TO PORT ARTHUR.

CHAPTER I.

Departure from Sydney.—The "Sir George Arthur."—An Arrest.—
Colonial Craftsmen.—Opposite Neighbours.—"Dick."—Hippolyte
Rocks.—Cape Pillar.—Tasman's Island.—Cape Raoul.

THE concluding paragraph of my gossiping chronicle of experiences in New South Wales mentioned
our departure from Sydney on our way to Van
Diemen's Land; and I now resume the slender
thread of my story where I then broke off *.

* Notes and Sketches of New South Wales, during a Residence in
that Colony from 1839 to 1844. London. Murray, 1849.

VOL. I.   B

I return to the morning of our embarkation,
when, in a straggling procession, including the
baby, the new nursemaid, the old pointer, and
sundry of our goods and chattels on trucks and
hand-barrows (the main body having been previously shipped), we proceeded to the jetty, and
bade adieu to the friends who came " to see us
out of sight." I must confess that I felt less regret than I could have believed possible, at leaving
a country which had been my home for above a
year; and if a wistful thought did stray back to
the bright and beautiful gardens, the lovely wild
flowers, the delicious fruits, and the deep blue sky
of the ever-brown land, such a thick hot cloud of
dust, flies, mosquitoes, and other detestabilities,
rose in imagination before me, as threw a veil
over all such charms; and I parted from them
with a stout heart, full of hopefulness for the
future, and rejoicing, above all things, to take our
baby-boy into a more temperate climate, where the
fair promise of his infancy might have some prospect of being realized in a life of health, strength,
and intelligence.

His good kind-hearted nurse (who, being married, could not leave the colony with us) stood

sobbing most piteously as her little charge was
borne away in the arms of a stranger, whose domestic ties were as yet unformed, she being a
starch, prim spinster, desirous of seeing as much
of the world as possible, and of showing it a very
tasteful wardrobe in return.   I, too, grieved to lose
my old servant, for she was as cheerful, willing,
earnest, and simple a creature as I ever knew;
albeit not perhaps the most dainty waiting-woman
in the world—for, to hear her footsteps in the
house, one might fancy some tame elephant was
pacing about, and I had often found reason to
rejoice that all the rooms at Homebush were on
the ground-floor—but she was so affectionate and
good, that I should have been well pleased if her
heavy footsteps could still have followed our own.
She had odd quaint notions and expressions, too,
that were very droll, uttered as they were with
such earnest seriousness.   She told me once, that
her former master "was a very learned gentleman,
a great scholar—*so* clever at preaching and doc-
toring, and talking languages of foreign parts.
Indeed, ma'am, he did serve his time at Cam-
bridge College for a parson, only he didn't never
take no sort of sitiwation after."

The vessel had dropped down the stream, and
was anchored some distance below the town; and
when, at the end of our long pull, we came along
side, the aspect of the "Sir George Arthur" was
anything but inviting.   (Why will people persist in
giving male names to ships?)   She, that is, "Sir
George," had been employed in the coal-trade between Sydney and the mines at Newcastle, on the
Hunter River, and bore as evident marks of her
sooty calling as ever did an old coal-boat on the
Birmingham Canal; whilst the air sweeping round
her wafted over us a veritable coal-smoke odour,
full of murky reminiscences of the good old town.
There she lay—as ugly, ill-shapen, slovenly, dirty,
black, disreputable-looking a tub as ever sullied
the bright blue waves of old Neptune.   However,
as our present lot was cast in her—no other vessel
for Hobarton offering at the time—we went on
board the mis-shapen craft, which seemed to have
been built as much as possible after the model
of a brewer's vat.   The deck was as dirty as
the rest, and my cabin, which was tolerably large
and convenient, so swarmed with wood-lice that
I soon began to have a tolerably vivid idea of
another of the plagues of Egypt, that of flies

having been fully realized during our sojourn in Sydney.

Whilst we were at dinner, a slight disturbance arose from the abrupt entrance of certain subordinate members of the legal profession in search of some considerate friend, who no doubt wished to spare them the pain of parting, and had therefore quietly shipped himself without the ceremonies of leave-taking, unless taking French leave may be so considered; but the affectionate interest of such friends is not easily eluded, and the poor young man was finally compelled to forego his humane intentions, and return to shore with his *friends,* despite the most vehement protestations that he was somebody else.

I had hoped to have been able to remain on deck until we had fairly passed through those great gates, the North and South Heads, and could look back on the grand entrance to Port Jackson which had so delighted me a year before; and many were the subtle deceptions I practised on myself as to the real nature of the indescribable symptoms which were gradually and horribly creeping over me—but all would not do; the approaching misery made a stride with every roll and lurch of the vessel, and a positive leap when she "went about." My love for the picturesque waned most lamentably, and I stowed away my sketch-book as an useless incumbrance: cliffs, woods, snow-white beaches, and blue waves were at a deplorable discount, and all sea scenery was so distasteful to me, that I retreated to my berth.

Servants who are engaged to go a sea voyage always declare themselves quite indifferent to sea-sickness—"never were the least ill all the way from England"—and so protested my new maid; but she proved after all to be quite as poor a sailor as myself. I was compelled, therefore, to make some exertions in taking care of my little boy, who appeared happily unconscious of the prevailing indisposition.

Having a fair and sufficient wind, we expected to have made a quick passage; but, owing to the vessel being (in strict accordance with the usual colonial style of that period) only half-rigged, and wanting top-gallant and studding sails, she progressed very slowly. A singular disinclination to finish any work completely, is a striking characteristic of colonial craftsmen, at least of the "currency," or native-born portion. Many of them who are clever, ingenious, and industrious, will begin a new work, be it ship, house, or other erection, and labour at it most assiduously until it is about two-thirds completed, and then their energy seems spent, or they grow weary of the old occupation, and some new affair is set about as busily as the former one, which, meanwhile, lingers on in a comfortless, helpless, useless condition, till another change comes over the mind of the workman, and he perhaps returns to the old work, to which, if a house, he does just enough to enable the impatient proprietors to occupy it; or if a ship, for it to go to sea in a half-fledged condition, which is rarely improved afterwards.

The thoughtful kindness of an old friend of Mr. Meredith's had supplied us with some new novels, as suitable provision for the voyage, and when the horrible sea-sickness had subsided into its second stage of half-dead, half-dreamy, and wholly deplorable stupor and helplessness, I lay and beguiled the weary time by the fictitious miseries of the heroines; though, as their narrated afflictions all happened on dry land, I fear my sympathy was of a very niggardly order, perhaps closely verging on the envious.

Unlike our snug apartment in the "Letitia," our present rooms were entered from the mess-cabin, the upper portion of the sliding door and a window frame beside it being fitted with Venetian shutters, which, as they could not by any device be induced to shut close, were a perpetual annoyance, and kept my ingenuity constantly at work, devising stratagems to complete the concealment they refused to afford,—but we could not block them wholly, for want of air.

My opposite neighbours naturally attracted some of my attention and interest, as I lay contemplating the outer world of the mess-cabin through the chinks in my shutters. The lady had, like myself, been invisible for some days, but her indefatigable lord was all that time a prey to the most alarming excitement, darting constantly in and out of her cabin in a most distracting manner, and keeping the slide-door vibrating to and fro like a pendulum. Any one who has ever seen a boy with a live mouse in his hat, covered over with an outspread handkerchief, and remembers the nervous twitchings up of the corner to peep in, and the spasmodic hiding-up again, lest the mouse should jump out, may imagine the daily process of my

worthy neighbour " over the way." Fifty times a
day would he dart out, shove the door violently to
—at the imminent peril of his fingers—and after
making various stages of one, two, and three
yards towards the companion stairs, rush fran-
tically back again, and bolt the door inside in
a most decided manner, always limiting the aperture to the smallest possible space that he could
thrust himself through, and doing all with the
greatest noise possible, until my sufferings from
these shocks became so intense, that I could
not help pitying those of the young wife to
whose solace and benefit they were especially
dedicated.

In a berth a little beyond this abode the master
of the vessel, the " captain," who had remained there
invisible for some days, whether really indisposed, or
only indisposed to do his duty, I cannot determine ;
but certain it is, that he refused to go on deck, or
to take any part in the command, further than by
receiving and giving messages in his cabin.   The
crew were an idle unruly set, not more than one or
two among them knowing anything of seamanship,
and those very little ; and the owner of the whole
concern being on board, chose to stand at the wheel

himself a part of each day, and with a knowing wink to such of the passengers as he took into his confidence, informed them that " the captain's orders *was*, that the wessel should be steered south half west, but I 've kep' her away a point or two to the west,"—which accounted for our being rather close in-shore, and must have contributed greatly to assist the invisible captain in determining the ship's position and course. We were fortunate in having had fine weather hitherto.

In condemning the idleness of the crew and servants on board, I must make one memorable exception. There was a smart, active, good-natured boy, about ten or twelve years old, who, if ever ubiquity fell to the lot of mortal form, possessed that property ; he was everywhere, doing everything for everybody, and apparently in at least three places at the same time :—

" Dick ! take Mr. Smith some hot water."

" Dick ! Mr. Jones wants his coat brushed."

" Dick ! bring a light in the cabin."

" Dick ! go and swab the deck."

" Dick ! peel them 'taturs for cook."

" Dick ! you lazy scoundrel—steward says you 've not cleaned his knives."

"Dick! go and water the sheep" (a whole flock formed part of the cargo).

"Dick! go and help reef topsails."

"Dick! feed the geese."

"Dick! take these bones to my dog," &c., &c., &c.

The cry of Dick—Dick—Dick—resounded all day long, and poor Dick seemed really to execute all the multifarious orders given him, with the most unflinching alacrity and good humour. One day Mr. Meredith inquired of the owner, if the ubiquitous Dick was an apprentice in the ship. "Why, no," drawled forth the broad burly personage addressed; and then he added, with a slow smile overspreading and widening his ample countenance, —"No—he aint a 'prentice, he's a nevy o' mine, as come aboard for a holiday!"

Alas! for poor relations!

I began to make a "rule-of-three" statement of the question—if in a cruize for a holiday, Dick has harder work and rougher usage than any other creature on board, required the amount of Dick's sufferings at school?—but my heart failed me—I could not work the sum; and I comfort myself in the thought, that whatever vagrant propensities might attack Dick in subsequent holidays, he would not be likely to indulge them by a voyage with his uncle.

As we neared Cape Pillar, on the tenth day of the voyage, I made an heroic effort to leave my berth, and went on deck for the first time since passing the Heads. Shortly after I had taken my place (on a comfortable steady hen-coop), and had begun to enjoy my return to the upper air and the exhilarating scene around me, a great sensation seemed to arise in the small community—servants ran about and knocked up against each other in the orthodox way of people who wish to show that they have no time to lose—then they dived into the cabin in an agitated and important manner—presently they reappeared, one with a cushion, another with a basket, a third with a cloak—and after spreading these about, all again plunged violently below. Another charge accomplished the conveyance on deck of an umbrella, a pillow, a shawl, a book, and another umbrella. Then came, in more slow and stately fashion, bobbing up gradually and fitfully out of the companion, a large easy chair, in and about and round which, as the nucleus of the whole, the other movables were carefully disposed, and both umbrellas opened ready for active service.

Finally, after another pause, heralded by a servant, half carried by her vigilant spouse, and followed by two more servants, came the pretty young lady herself, thickly veiled and folded in multitudinous envelopes. She was presently seated in the easy chair, her feet raised on a second chair, and the two umbrellas so carefully arranged that she became again invisible, and my valiant resolve of tottering across the deck, to offer her the common civilities natural between such partners in calamity (our respective husbands being on the most amicable passenger terms) was fairly and finally extinguished. I felt wholly unequal to the perilous task of storming such a citadel of exclusiveness, and remained faithful to my hen-coop and more accessible acquaintances.

It was a most beautiful afternoon, sunny and pleasant, with a fair breeze, and, as we sailed along the picturesque coast of Tasmania, the deep bays, rocky headlands, and swelling hills, formed a charming panorama, which I roughly and hastily sketched as we glided past. The white-cliffed Hippolyte Rocks, commonly called by colonial seamen the "Epaulettes," rising squarely, like masses of neat masonry above the sea, had exactly the appearance

of a fort, and I almost expected to discern a flag
floating over them, or to be startled by the flash
and boom of a cannon from their snow-white walls;
but a flight of sea-birds rising from the summit
was the only token of living residents that the
formidable rocks displayed.

The southern promontory of Fortesque Bay appeared to be entirely composed of upright basaltic
columns, some of them standing alone, like tall
obelisks, but the greater number forming groups of
mimic towers and chimneys. The coast rises considerably towards the south, where the mountain-
range terminates abruptly in the Cape Pillar, a
grand basaltic precipice, or rather an assemblage
of precipices, which, seen from the sea, every
moment assume some new and more picturesque
aspect. Separated from the mainland only by a
strait of half a mile in width is Tasman's Island,
a scarcely less striking feature in this most grand
scenery than the Cape Pillar. Like it, the island is
composed of basaltic columns, though on a less
stupendous scale, but exceedingly fantastic in form,
particularly on the southern side, where the taper
spires and pinnacles seem a part of some ancient
Gothic edifice, some " Lindisfarne" or " Tintern"

TASMAN'S ISLAND AND CAPE PILLAR.

FROM A SKETCH BY THE BISHOP OF TASMANIA.

of bygone glory; whilst, as we gained a broader
view of the cape, it assumed the appearance of a
fortification—a wall and seaward tower at the north-
east end being singularly well defined. When
parallel with the strait, we gained through it a fine
view of another high basaltic promontory, Cape
Raoul, the entrance to Port Arthur being between
the two; but this was soon lost, and the island
seemed to fold in, as it were, with the westerly
cliffs of the cape, until in a south view they formed
one towering stupendous mass of dark rocks, most
richly tinged with the changeful rose-colour, and
purple, and gold of the sunset's glorious hues,
which shone forth in still greater lustre from
contrast with the deep chasms and ravines which
were in almost black shadow, and with the white
crested billows of the blue sea, that dashed their
glittering spray high over the broken crags. It was
a scene never to be forgotten! I have heard much
of the grandeur of the "North Cape" at midnight; but I would not lose my memory of Cape
Pillar at sunset for all the icy glitter of that more
renowned scene.

One great omission in my meagre descriptive
sketch I must here supply, and insert the "figures,"

which well sustained their share in the beauty of the scene. These were a very elegant-looking (but I have no doubt a very dirty and disagreeable) little schooner, which, as she kept still closer in-shore than our shapeless unwieldy vessel could do, gave that life and interest to the sea portion of our view, which a sailing vessel always affords; distance lending enough of enchantment to romancify the veriest tub that ever swam, if her sails look white in the sunshine; and the swarming clouds of "mutton-birds" continually rising from the sea, where they had floated unobserved, or flying, dipping, swimming, and diving all around us—these would alone have furnished me with ample amusement; as it was, I felt quite busy with so much to enjoy, and only seemed to fear that I could not look about with enough energy to observe everything.

CAPE RAOUL.

CHAPTER II.

Night Alarm.—Squall.—Storm Bay.—Lose Topmasts.—Approach to
Hobarton.—Cast Anchor.—Mount Wellington.—Scenery round
Newtown.— Gardens. — Hobarton Society. — Theatre. — Melo-
dramas.

I HAD been asleep some hours that night, when I
was awakened by a strange and terrific noise; and
instantly knew, though I had never heard the sound
before, that it was the violent flapping of a sail
blown out of the ropes. Another and another
quickly followed, and buffeted about with a noise
like thunder; and the added hubbub of voices and

hurried footsteps on deck told me that some serious disaster had occurred. I thought, with fear and trembling, of the iron-bound coast which I had seen so near to us at sunset, and for once found no comfort in my husband's attempts to reassure me, when I knocked at the bulk-head of his cabin to know what was the matter, but helplessly wept over my sleeping baby, expecting each moment some fearful crisis; nor did my instinctive terror much exaggerate the peril we were in. The captain of the vessel had scarcely been seen out of his berth since the day we sailed, and with only half a crew, and those very ignorant of their duty, it may well be imagined that the ship could not at any time be properly worked; but on this particular night, although bad weather had been anticipated, only one man and a boy composed the "watch;" and both these were shut up in the caboose drinking coffee, when a violent squall struck the vessel, with all her canvas set, blew the sails from the bolt-ropes, and threatened to end our voyage somewhat speedily on the rocks of Cape Raoul, where several vessels with every soul on board had perished before. The night was dark, with a dense fog, and the cliffs were *only a mile to leeward*.

I believe we owe our lives, so far as mortal aid availed, to the promptitude and skill of one of the passengers, Captain Millett (master of an American merchantman), who, when the squall struck the vessel, rushed on deck, and gave all the necessary orders and assistance to restore something like discipline amidst the confusion and riot on board.

At last, for I thought that dreadful night was interminable, the morning dawned;—we were in Storm Bay, which I shall ever think very accurately named;—the weather dark, thick, and squally, with incessant rain. The vessel's deck was so ill-joined that the dirty water dripped through the chinks all over my bed; and, as I lay reading, something dark fell into the border of my cap: thinking it a drop of mud, I snatched off the cap and gave it to the servant, when, to my horror, I discovered that it was an enormous * centipede which had fallen upon me, a hideous, many-jointed, many-legged green creature, about three inches long, with a forked tail, and a railroad rapidity of progression. My horror in this instance was soon changed to thankfulness that the dangerous reptile had fallen

* Enormous *here*, but I am told these amiable-looking creatures thrive best in India, and there grow to the length of a foot or fourteen inches, and as thick as one's finger!

where it did; for my happy little child, on whom it might have dropped, lay sleeping close beside me, and the bite of the centipede is often more venomous and painful than even the sting of a scorpion.

As the weather got slightly better, I went on deck, but all around was very dreary; the fog hung about, and wind and rain came in fitful gusts. Whilst I sat, vainly trying to make out something of the surrounding scenery, Mr. Meredith and several of the other passengers remarked to the captain, who had " turned out" at last, that another squall was coming; and indeed I could distinctly see the ruffled and foaming water rapidly approaching the ship.

" The masts will go, unless you take in sail," said some one, growing nervous at the apathetic supineness of the captain, who, lazily gazing aloft, and then resettling himself on a hen-coop, muttered that he " didn't know—didn't think they would," and accordingly no change was made.

" *You* had better go below," said my husband, leading me to the companion, and before I had reached the cabin, there was a loud crash—the rattle of falling rigging and blocks knocking about, quickly followed by a repetition of the same sounds,

as the main and mizen topmasts successively went
over the side. Such an accident a few hours before would probably have been fatal; but now,
being in smooth water, it was only productive of a
little bustle and discussion.

The bad weather and total discomfort of the
latter portion of our voyage prevented my enjoying
the fine scenery of the Derwent, as we approached
Hobarton, sailing past Bruni Island and Iron-pot
Island Lighthouse.

The situation of the town is the most beautiful
that can be conceived—on the rising banks of the
noble Derwent, with green meadows, gardens, and
cultivated land around it, interspersed with pleasant
country residences and farms; and, above and beyond all, the snowy mountain peaks soaring to the
very clouds. At length we cast anchor. The rattle
of the chain-cable must always be a welcome sound
at such a time, but perhaps our recent hair-breadth
scapes lent a still pleasanter tone to its rough
music, which at the moment eclipsed, in my estimation, the choicest concerto ever composed; and
we immediately went ashore, most thankful and
delighted to step once more on land.

The great difference between Sydney and Hobarton struck me as forcibly during my first ten minutes' walk as after a longer acquaintance; and, in point of pleasantness, I must certainly award the palm to the latter. It is a much smaller place than Sydney, but its home-like English aspect at once won my preference.

Our next fortnight passed happily among relatives whom I had not seen since childhood, and in a cool breezy climate, that reminded us of April in England; the weather was too showery to admit of so much out-door amusement as I could have wished; still, the cool moist greenness everywhere was most refreshing and cheering to me; the little gardens before and between many houses in the middle of the town, with their great bushes of geraniums in bloom, were all full of sweet English spring flowers, looking happy and healthy, like the stout rosy children that everywhere reminded me of HOME; so different to the thick white complexions and tall slender forms so prevalent in New South Wales. The houses, too, at least the few I entered during our short sojourn, were more snug than showy, as if the English attribute of comfort more especially belonged to them. In the streets, carriages and equestrians were less numer-

ous than in Sydney, and I found that here it was
not only believed possible, but positively "fashionable," for ladies to walk about; an improvement
upon Sydney customs, which is in a great measure
attributable to the climate. The shops were numerous and good, and the buildings neat and substantial, chiefly of brick, but many of the newer
ones of cut stone. Some of the more suburban
streets, or rather the suburban ends of them, consisting of good detached houses standing in nice
gardens, and adorned by verandas covered with
lovely plants, are very pleasant, commanding fine
views of the harbour; and from every point I
visited, Mount Wellington (or Table Mountain)
forms the crowning glory of the landscape. Rising
immediately behind the town to the height of 4200
feet, with its summit of basaltic columns covered
with snow more than half the year, its aspect is
one of ever-varying, but never-decreasing grandeur.
Whether it was wreathed in fleecy vapours, dark
with rolling clouds, or stood out clear and sunlit
against the blue morning sky, I was never weary
of gazing on this magnificent object.

A stream flowing from the mountain through a
picturesque ravine and valley, supplies the town

with water, turning a number of mills of various kinds in its course. To a botanist, Mount Wellington must be a treasury of gems, many rare and beautiful plants inhabiting its wild and almost inaccessible glens and ravines. The ascent of the mountain is long, and was formerly very fatiguing; but the formation, for a considerable distance, of a road passable for horses, has greatly reduced the difficulty. Several unfortunate persons who at various times have imprudently attempted the ascent without a guide, have never returned, nor has any vestige of them ever been discovered; most probably they have fallen into some of the deep chasms and fissures, and, if not killed instantly, have lingered awhile, and died of starvation. The view from the summit is described as surpassingly grand and beautiful, as indeed it must be, from its great altitude and the varied and picturesque scenery around.

I have been frequently told that the real Waratah is found on Mount Wellington, and have since seen several specimens of the flower mistaken for it— very different and inferior indeed to my gorgeous favourite of the Blue Mountains. The Tasmanian Waratah is a shrub or bushy tree, with handsome dark-green foliage, and bright red flowers of loosely-clustered trumpet florets, scarcely so large as an English woodbine.

We passed the chief part of our sojourn at Newtown, in the environs of Hobarton, where many of the wealthier merchants, government officers, and professional men have tasteful residences. The church and the Queen's Orphan Schools are large and handsome buildings; in the latter, children of both sexes are clothed and educated *.

The scenery around Newtown is the most beautiful I have seen on this side the world—very much resembling that of the Cumberland Lakes: the broad and winding estuary of the Derwent flows

* The children received into the Queen's Orphan Schools are those of prisoners, male or female, undergoing probation or sentence, orphans, and children deserted by their parents; the former are admitted by order of the Comptroller-General of Convicts, the latter through the Colonial Secretary, with the authority of the Lieutenant-Governor. The prisoners' children are paid for by the British Government, the orphans and deserted children by the Colonial Government. There are usually between 400 and 500 children in the schools; when old enough, they are apprenticed as servants or to some useful trade. They are superintended and instructed by the following officers—a superintendent, at 500*l.* per annum; a chaplain, at 50*l.*; a physician, at 150*l.*; a purveyor, at 120*l.*; a teacher of psalmody, at 50*l.*; a schoolmaster, at 150*l.*; a matron, at 50*l.*; a Roman Catholic master, at 35*l.*; a matron of female school, at 130*l.*; a schoolmistress, at 60*l.*; a Roman Catholic schoolmistress, at 60*l.* The expense of each child, including maintenance, clothing, pay of officers and servants of every description, and repair of buildings, averages from 10*l.* to 12*l.* per annum.

between lofty and picturesque hills and mountains, clothed with forests, whilst at their feet lie level lawn-like flats, green to the water's edge. But the most English, and therefore the most beautiful things I saw here, were the hawthorn hedges; those of sweetbriar, which are, I think, more general, did not please me half so well, not having so much of common country home life about them.

It seemed like being on the right side of the earth again, to see rosy children with boughs of flowering "May," and to feel its full luscious perfume waft across me. Let no one who has always lived at home, enjoying unnoticed the year's bounty of rainbow-tinted blossoms, fancy he knows the full value of English flowers, or the love that the heart can bear for them. I thought I always held them in as fond admiration as any one could do, but my delight in these hawthorn hedges proved to me how much my regard had strengthened in absence; and as I recalled to mind the wide brown deserts I had lately left, with their miles of "post and rail," or more hideous "log" and "deadwood" fences, and then took an imaginary glance over the green hawthorn hedges and elm-shaded

lanes of my own beautiful native land, I heartily
wished that all dwellers in her pleasant country
places could only know and feel what a paradise
they inhabit!

I am often glad that I spent the first year of my
antipodean life in New South Wales, for now many
things which I should not have observed had I
arrived here in the first instance, are sources of
great delight to me, as being so much more English
than in the larger colony, and I could fancy myself
some degrees nearer home.

In the Tasmanian gardens are mulberries, cherries,
currants, raspberries, strawberries, gooseberries,
apples, pears, quinces, medlars, plums of all kinds,
and peaches in abundance, growing well and
luxuriantly. Our forest trees, too, thrive admirably
here, and walnuts, filberts, and hazelnuts are
becoming much more common. Vines also succeed
in sheltered aspects, but not better than in many
parts of England; the summer-frosts to which this
climate is liable frequently cut off plants which in
Britain can be grown with certainty. Even potatoes
are, in some districts, considered a very precarious
crop from this circumstance, and, except in situations near the sea-shore, are often nipped by the

c 2

frosts at night, although the weather in the day-time is as warm as in an English June.

The Government Gardens here, although not comparable with those at Sydney, are finely situated on the sloping shore of the Derwent, and charmed me by their verdant and shady aspect. They are— for I must again repeat my oft-used term of praise —they are *English*-looking gardens, not rich in glowing oranges, scarlet pomegranates, and golden loquats, nor stored with the rare and gorgeous blossoms of India, but full of sweet homely faces and perfumes. Great trees of a lovely blush rose were in full bloom at the time of my visit, looking so like the rose-trees of olden days at home, that I could scarcely believe them the growth of the opposite side of the world.

The domain adjoins the gardens, and is laid out in pleasant drives among the groves of native trees. We witnessed there the ceremony of laying the first stone of a new Government House, on a spot commanding views of the Derwent and the surrounding beautiful scenery. A collation was provided on the occasion by the Lieutenant-Governor and Lady Franklin, in a pretty rustic lodge near the site of the new mansion, and some

of the guests availed themselves of the presence of
an excellent military band to have quadrilles on the
grass, or rather in the dust, for the turf was something of the scantiest.

At the period of which I am writing, Hobarton
was certainly not in advance of Sydney in point of
society or intelligence, and the constant efforts of
Sir John and Lady Franklin to arouse and foster a
taste for science, literature, or art, were more often
productive of annoyance to themselves, than of
benefit to the unambitious multitude. The coarse
and unmanly attacks made in some of the public
papers on Lady Franklin, whose kindness and
ability, even if not appreciated at their full value,
ought at least to have met with gratitude and
respect, were most disgraceful. Unhappily the
perpetual petty squabbles and quarrels which seem
to form an indispensable part of all small com-
munities, and were especially rife in this little frac-
tion of a world, occupied its attention too exclusively
to admit of any great interest being felt in subjects
not immediately connected with individual success
or advantage. That there might always be found
exceptions to this rule is most true, but their good
influence, like the light of a few stars in a clouded

sky, only served to make the surrounding intellectual gloom more apparent.

Among the young ladies, both married and single, in Tasmania, as in Sydney, a very "general one-ness" prevails as to the taste for dancing, from the love of which but a small share of regard can be spared for any other accomplishment or study, save a little singing and music; and Lady Franklin's attempts to introduce evening parties in the "conversazione" style were highly unpopular with the pretty Tasmanians, who declared that they "had no idea of being asked to an evening party, and then stuck up in rooms full of pictures and books, and shells and stones, and other rubbish, with nothing to do but to hear people talk lectures, or else sit as mute as mice listening to what was called good music. Why could not Lady Franklin have the military band in, and the carpets out, and give dances, instead of such stupid preaching about philosophy and science, and a parcel of stuff that nobody could understand?"

The performances at the neat little theatre in Hobarton are of a better order than the colonies can generally boast, and most romantic and heart-stirring are the titles of the melodramatic pieces usually

represented there. I often regretted our distance
from town when I saw such announcements as
"THE MAID OF GENOA, or THE BANDIT MER-
CHANT, with the celebrated BROAD-SWORD COMBAT
and HIGHLAND FLING *in the Second Act;*"—the
introduction of apparent anomalies being made
much on the pump-and-tub principle of the im-
mortal Crummles.   Sometimes half a page of a
colonial paper is filled with startling hints of each
scene, plentifully peppered with stars, dashes, notes
of exclamation, and gigantic italics, quite distracting
to read in a quiet country home, amidst peaceful
woods; and to know the while, that people in town
may go and " sup full of horrors " with " The Convict Captain, or the Nun of Messina;"—have their
very heartstrings lacerated by "The Broken Dagger,
or the Dumb Boy of the Pyrenees;"—and sit in
petrified and agonizing terror to behold the woes of
the "The Bandit's Victim, or the Black Caverns
of St. Bruno!"

Perhaps it is scarcely fair to send forth such
agitating advertisements into far away nooks of the
forest, where their temptations are all unavailing.
But wonderful is the serenity with which repeated
disappointment enables the mind to endure even

such privations! Recently one or two of Shakspeare's tragedies and some good modern plays have been got up very respectably, and last year the announcement of a pantomime sounded cheerily in our ears, like a faint echo of our childhood's laughter; but we afterwards found that its subject was wholly made up of local and personal allusions. The superior success of melodramas over the higher order of dramatic representations, affords an evidence as to public taste which needs no comment. The frightful amount of *snobbishness* which prevails here among those who might really well dispense with the feverish terror of being said or thought to do anything " ungenteel " or " unfashionable," is adverse to the interests of the theatre; and accordingly the patronage vouchsafed by the alarmed exclusives is lamentably small.

CHAPTER III.

The Hunt.—Public Amusements.—Public Decorum and Morality.—
Prisoner Population.—" Assignment System."—" White Slavery."
—Magistrates.—" Probation System."—Experience in Prisoner-
Servants.—Their length of Service.—Their Attachment and Good
Faith.

As balls must infallibly be popular in a place where
everybody dances, so must races claim a large share
of patronage where everybody rides, or is in some
manner interested in the quality and value of horses;
and accordingly Hobarton, Launceston, Campbelltown, Oatlands, and other places in the colony,
have their annual meetings, where " cups," " ladies'
purses," " town plates," " sweepstakes," and such
like exciting prizes, are gallantly striven for, and
fairly won, often by gentlemen-riders, and horses
worthy of them.

Hunting is also a favourite diversion, and occasionally the newspapers put forth most grandiloquent
narratives purporting to be communications from

" correspondents," detailing the exploits of the
" field," which usually consist of galloping over a
rough country after two or three couple of hounds
(a kind of "scratch pack"), which drive before
them a poor tame deer, one of the few imported into
the colony, and placed at the disposal of the hunt,
by owners more liberal than humane.   When the
poor creature is completely exhausted, it is rescued
from the hounds for future torments, and again and
again chased to the very verge of existence, by the
noble and Christian worthies who enjoy the cruel
sport.   Perhaps I may be told that deeds quite as
cruel are considered "sport" at home, and encouraged by the highest sanction; but that does not
in the least convince me that all the bad habits of
an old country should be scrupulously transplanted
to a new one, whilst so many of the good ones remain forgotten; and assuredly the absurd custom of
hunting, with all the show and pretence of earnest
pursuit, a gentle tame creature that can scarcely be
driven away, would be "more honoured in the
breach than the observance."

One of these cruel exhibitions occurred only a
week before our arrival, as I am informed by a person who shared the "sport" with about sixty others,

which ended in the poor tame stag being worried to death by the dogs, its antlers having caught in a low tree, and entangled it: knowing that its longer life would but have led to greater sufferings, I rejoice that it was killed.

A kangaroo is sometimes hunted as a substitute for the old country fox, and, being a wild and swift creature, is said to afford excellent sport.

The dingo of New South Wales, so generally hunted there, is, I rejoice to say, wholly unknown in Tasmania.

Public balls, concerts, regattas. and horticultural shows, are also frequent, and attended fully, and most respectably. I know of no place where greater order and decorum is observed by the motley crowds assembled on any public occasion than in this most shamefully slandered colony: not even in an English country village can a lady walk alone with less fear of harm or insult than in this capital of Van Diemen's Land, commonly believed at home to be a moral pest-house, where every crime that can disgrace and degrade humanity stalks abroad with unblushing front.

The unfounded assertions which have been made and believed in England for some years respecting the moral and social condition of this colony, are most astonishing : how, why, and from whom they have originated, I am at a loss to conjecture; but that they are, for the most part, cruelly, scandalously false, I know.

Not in the most moral circles of moral England herself is a departure from the paths of propriety or virtue more determinedly or universally visited by the punishment of exclusion from society, than in this "Penal Colony;" nowhere are all particulars and incidents of persons' past lives more minutely and rigidly canvassed, than in the "higher circles" of this little community; and nowhere are the decent and becoming observances of social and domestic life more strictly maintained. One fact, familiar to hundreds here, may well illustrate this assertion. I select this particular instance, because the parties have now left the colony, and whilst in it occupied a prominent station. A lady, the wife of a military officer of high rank, had for some years held that place in society to which her husband's influential position, and her own right as a gentlewoman, entitled her. She was visited and courted, and might select her own associates from the best families here, until, one unlucky day, there came to the colony a person who professed to be intimately acquainted with this lady's " birth, parentage, and education," and somewhat officiously proceeded to set forth in various companies a narrative of some long-past error of her early youth; whether false or true, no one paused to ascertain, nor to ask themselves who, amongst them all, could, if similarly attacked, withstand such (possibly) unfounded assertions. Her correct and unblemished conduct during her sojourn here availed nothing; but one and all of her former devoted friends fell away, and refused to hold any further communion with her. Is it possible to believe that this could have been the case, were moral feeling in Van Diemen's Land at the low ebb generally represented ?

A residence here for the last nine years, and an intimate acquaintance during that time with the habits and usages of the higher and middle ranks, as well as of the free labouring population of the country places, may, I think, in some measure qualify me to judge how far the sweeping condemnations of the few, are borne out by the demeanour of the many; and now, in all honest faith and truth, I declare them to be every whit as unjust to the people of Tasmania as they would be if cast upon those of the same rank in England. And as, in days of yore, the doughty champion of slandered virtue flung into the lists his mailed gauntlet, or the glorious Bombastes hung aloft his invincible boots, even so, in these modern days of more wordy, but not less mortal strife, do I gently lay down my black silk mitten in the cause of fair and wronged Tasmania!

Nor will I quit the subject thus entered upon, without a few words on behalf of those whose friends are too few in number to allow the silence of one willing voice, however feeble, when aught *can* be said for them. I allude to the numerous prisoners of the Crown, now forming so large a portion of our population, and respecting whom so much discussion has of late arisen, and so little truth been elicited. It was not my purpose to touch upon this matter so early in these pages, because at the time of which I am writing, I had not had the opportunities of forming an opinion which I have since had; but having alluded to the subject, it is perhaps best to anticipate the lapse of time so far, and briefly glance over the general question.

The transportation of British criminals to Van Diemen's Land was, as is well known, continued for many years (and until 1842) under the " assignment system ;" the prisoners brought in each ship being " assignable " to private service as soon as they arrived. The greater portion of them, therefore, were immediately removed and distributed among different masters in distant places, and with small probability that they would again be brought in contact with their former partners in crime—thus effecting at once the first great step towards reformation, in the breaking up of old and evil connections and associations.   The majority became speedily engaged in various ways, chiefly in pastoral or agricultural pursuits, or clearing land ; nearly all their fellow-labourers being persons of a like class, but in whom at least a partial improvement had already taken place ; and with these they too went on, labouring in occupations or trades they did understand, or learning those they did not. They had huts to live in (which were so far superior to the wretched cabins of many labourers at home that they kept out wind and rain), as much fuel as they chose to cut for themselves, abundant rations of good and wholesome food, and a certain allowance of clothing, boots, and bedding, fixed by Government.

After serving thus for three, four, or five years, according to the length of their original sentence, they were, if well-conducted and recommended, allowed a "ticket-of-leave," which enabled them to quit their first master, if so disposed, and hire themselves for wages to any one else in the colony who was eligible as an employer of convicts; the police magistrate of the district granting them a "pass" or certificate of permission to proceed to any other specified place. This stage of their punishment appears to have been attended with great success, restoring to them, as a reward for past amendment, enough of independence to arouse their feeling of self-respect and encourage them to continue improving, whilst it reserved power in the hands of the authorities for future rewards or punishments. So manifest are the advantages of this part of the system, that the settlers prefer ticket-of-leave men as servants to any other class, and if the periods of their being such were allowed to arrive sooner and be of longer duration, the change would in most cases benefit the men materially, and tend, by habituating them to the good

conduct they then practise, to render more safe
and certain their ultimate reformation.

After remaining the allotted number of years in
the ticket-of-leave class, the deserving convicts
usually received a " conditional pardon," which
permitted them the range of the Australian colonies; and to some was granted a " free pardon,"
which generally found them fully prepared to keep
and value the liberty it bestowed.

To this system it has of late been fashionable to
attach the term " white slavery," and other oppro-
brious epithets. Although doubtless susceptible of
great improvement, (as what human scheme is not?)
the results were in the main highly satisfactory,
and precisely what the Home Government and all
humane persons desired they should be, namely,
the conversion, in five cases out of six, of idle
unprincipled outcasts into industrious trustworthy
servants, and the redemption of thousands, who
(not strong enough in good to resist evil entirely,
yet with the better impulses of their nature far
over-balancing the worse) would, if they had remained at home, after a first offence, have been reduced in their degradation to suffer the contagious
influence of spirits more wicked than themselves,

and so have sunk gradually but surely downwards to the lowest depths of vice. Here, removed from the first crushing grief of disgrace, and seeing before them the prospect of rising again, and of building for themselves a new character above the ruins of the old, all the latent good in them springs into action; and, in very many instances, a life of honest industry and an old age of decent comfort have succeeded a youth of vice and crime.

For this system to produce its full amount of good in the men, there must needs be the requisite qualifications of common sense, probity, and humanity in the masters; and to ascertain and decide who are and who are not really eligible as such, requires greater diligence and more impartiality than Government agents are often found to possess. Bad masters and severe dishonest magistrates have devoted more men to live as bushrangers, and to die on the scaffold, than any inherent depravity of their victims. When the choice of persons to fill the solemn and responsible offices of justices of the peace was guided, as it *was* here, not by worth, fitness, or respectability, but by their very reverse— when servility became the requisite qualification for the man who should be pleasing to a governor—

wretched indeed was the prospect of the unfortunate
prisoner dragged before such a magistrate, and
little indeed had *justice* to do with the proceedings,
which wholly depended on the venal character of
the man's master, not of himself. If his master
was a useful tool of the governor, he might fix the
precise punishment he chose to have inflicted; if,
on the other hand, he was an honest unpurchase-
able person, his servant, however guilty, was either
dismissed unpunished, or removed from his service.
Such things, and worse than these, were of daily
occurrence, but are happily now far less frequent;
and I believe the lingering remnants which are
still found only need exposure to insure removal.

In 1842 the old method of " assignment " was
replaced by the " probation system;" and the
prisoners, instead of being taken into private service
direct from the ship, were subjected to a proba-
tionary period of (supposed) hard labour and instruction, which appears to have been *intended* by
the Home Government to advance their reformation,
to render them more useful afterwards as servants,
and to benefit the colony meanwhile by the great
amount of labour available for the execution of
public works. These were good intentions, but

the officers appointed to carry them out failed signally in their task; some from determined perversity and unpopularity, some from inability, and more from distaste and inattention: and then the herding together of hundreds of criminals of all classes and grades in notorious idleness, made those who were really bad tenfold worse—and even men naturally willing and diligent lapsed into apathetic drones; so that, when they became eligible for service, they were found far less useful and promising than those used to be who were assigned direct from the ships.

To all persons connected with the colony, this will appear an useless repetition of things as familiar as one's alphabet; but I do not write for colonial readers—I can tell *them* nothing that they may not equally well discover for themselves, if disposed to take the pains. I write to communicate such information to general readers in England as I believe many are deficient in, and, not being ambitious of seeming learned myself, would rather repeat many things that everybody knows, than omit one which some require to learn. I wish to convey to others the veritable impressions made on my own mind by the condition and character

of the convict population here, and I could not do
so intelligibly without some slight sketch of their
general position.

I have now lived above nine years in the colony,
the wife of a " settler," and the mistress of a
" settler's " home, and during that time we have
been served by prisoners of all grades, as ploughmen, shepherds, shearers, reapers, butchers, gar-
deners, carpenters, masons, blacksmiths, shoemakers,
house-servants, &c., &c., and (with one or two
exceptions) served as well and faithfully as we
could desire. What more could be said by any
farmer's wife at home? Are all English labourers
blameless? I can only call to mind one instance
of known dishonesty among our many men-servants
(that of a groom who stole some wine), and I
believe that acts of petty theft are far less common
among them than among the generality of servants
at home. Many persons here could and would, if
required, give the same evidence which I now do;
but I prefer adducing a few facts from my own
knowledge, as proof that transportation to these
colonies *is*—always excepting the probation system
—productive of reformation to many who otherwise
would, in all probability, have been utterly lost.

Five, ten, and fifteen years are common periods for prisoner-servants to remain in the same service, before and after their conditional pardon; and I lately heard of one who has for *twenty-eight* years lived with another master in a situation of great trust.

My husband's father, Mr. George Meredith, and himself, have now on their estates five old servants, four of whom have been in their family since 1826, and one since 1825, the latter being until lately overseer on a large agricultural farm. One of the four before-named was once an overseer for many years, and now rents a farm and flock from my husband—his wife having joined him eighteen or twenty years ago, with their family, now grown up and married; the second was in like manner gradually promoted from one post to another till he married, became a superintendent, and then a tenant; the third, a good workman in an useful trade, has received a free pardon, is now also a tenant of my father's, and working for himself; and the fourth, after being employed, since he became free, in whaling, sawing, splitting, and divers other avocations, has, for the last eight years, been cook and "major domo" in our own house, where his faithful attachment and incorruptible honesty are appreciated as they deserve. At the very time I am writing, he and a "ticket-of-leave" gardener are the only male persons in our lonely house (Mr. Meredith being absent in town), and I feel no more, perhaps even less, fear of attack or molestation, than I should in the middle of London: firstly, because I have no idea that robbers will come; and, secondly, because I know that, if they did, I and my children would be defended to the uttermost by *these very prisoner-servants;* and I think it must be very evident, that the country cannot be the den of horrors it has of late been painted, where a female only *so* protected can sit in her quiet country house, forty miles from the nearest village, with doors and windows left open the whole day through, and sleep safely and peacefully at night, without a bar or bolt or shutter to a single window, every room being on the ground floor.

I have only particularised a *few* instances of long service, but I could enumerate numbers of men who have lived in the same family ten, fifteen, eighteen years, as trusted and respected servants; some who have grown old and died on the same establishment. Surely such distinct indisputable facts as these are more worthy of credence, and a safer guide to the truth, than the vague generalizing denunciations now so commonly dealt forth by the slanderers of the colony. If I were to note all the corroborative evidence that occurs to me, I should fill my little book with it; in no place that I ever knew at home are houses and families left so totally unprotected and in such perfect safety as here. In a lone cottage, seven miles from our own, there lives, at this very time, a lady, an educated gentlewoman, and her four young children—the eldest only eleven—without even a man-servant in or near the place, all being with their master on a distant farm: all the neighbouring settlers have numerous prisoner-servants, yet she lives undisturbed.

I will now quit this subject for the present, assured that if my counter-statement has no other good effect, it will at least enable my friends to journey on with me more pleasantly than if haunted by those frightful anticipations for my personal safety which the reports of the croakers must have awakened.

CHAPTER IV.

Journey to Swan Port.—Restdown.—Richmond.—"The Grand Stand."
—Colonial Roads.—Pic-nic Dinner.—A "Sticker-up."—Jerusa-
lem.—Native Names.—Halt in the Forest.—Free Roads.—Road-
Gangs.—Transit over Gullies.—Eastern Marshes.—An Invasion.
—Lonely Houses.—Organ of Locality.

OUR final destination was Great Swan Port, at the
head of Oyster Bay, on the east coast. We commenced our journey thither by a short stage, first
crossing the Derwent in the ferry-boats, ourselves
in one, and our horses and vehicle in another.
Colonial country roads are not calculated for four-
wheeled carriages; Mr. Meredith therefore purchased
in Hobarton a broad, stout, colonial-built conveyance, an ingenious variety of the gig species, with
a seat behind for a servant, which seemed fully
capable of enduring all the trying exertions of the
journey.

We drove from the ferry to Risdon (properly, I
believe, Restdown), a very lovely spot, and the resi-

dence of one of my husband's oldest and most valued friends (T. G. Gregson, M.L.C.). I had not seen so beautiful a view, since I left England, as that commanded by the windows of his dining-room. Mount Wellington is here, as in Hobarton, the chief object in the landscape, whilst the broad bright Derwent, enlivened by sailing and steam-vessels, and skirted by green slopes and meadow-like flats, adds greatly to the beauty of the scene. The greater verdure of the forest trees in Van Diemen's Land, than of those in New South Wales, here struck me forcibly.

We lingered so pleasantly with our kind friends, that it was not until the afternoon of the following day that we set forth to make another short stage, and this was a very pleasant one, being for the most part over a fine, newly-made Government road. From the summit of Grass Tree Hill we had a most beautiful view of the town and harbour, bright in the full radiance of the afternoon sun.

Great numbers of the singular "grass trees" (*Xanthorrea arborea*), of all ages and growths, short, tall, straight, and crooked, each with its long tressed head of rushy leaves, gave a peculiar cha-racter to the steep and rocky hills between which we passed, and created an amusing variety in the otherwise monotonous near scenery.

We proceeded to Richmond, a place named, I imagine, in true Antipodean fashion, from its utter lack of all likeness to its charming old-country namesake. It is a squarely-planned township, situated in a flat valley, with a neat square-towered church and square formal houses dispersed about its incomplete streets. A very square many-windowed inn, seeming very new, very roomy, and very empty, looked at us as we passed with as imploring an expression as might be assumed by an inn of its great pretensions and stony dignity; but fortunately we were not destined to test its capabilities, having accepted the proffered hospitality of the then police magistrate of Richmond, who, being a geologist and a virtuoso, afforded us an agreeable evening in the examination of his various collections. Many of the limestone fossils I saw here were new to me, but as their possessor purposed forwarding a characteristic collection either to the British Museum or the Geological Society, the *savans* at home are doubtless acquainted with them ere this.

Our friend's gatherings in the paths of science

being somewhat extensive, the room in which my
maid slept was plentifully stored with choice and
rather bulky fossil specimens, and I had no easy task,
next morning, in striving to compose the feelings of
the terrified and indignant damsel, who declared she
" had lain all amongst skillintons and dead men's
bones, as bad as vaultses under churches." She had
not observed the horrors over night, but was quite
positive they *were* " death's-heads and cross-bones,"
for she had had such " horrid odorous dreams."
At length I succeeded in calming her perturbation,
and she resumed the charge of the " young
Erkerluss" (Hercules), as she termed my bouncing
baby.

On setting forth, our kind host directed us to
proceed along a new road, or rather track, for some
distance, our beacon being " the grand stand" on
the racecourse, which was shortly to appear on our
left hand. As we drove on, I carefully looked
about for at least a humble imitation of the buildings usually erected for such purposes—some neat
little summer-house affair, perhaps, with a white
roof stuck aloft on white posts—but no such thing
appeared. At length, Mr. Meredith, from his
knowledge of the country, was convinced that our

route would be wrong, if pursued further in the direction we were then going; and on looking around again most intently, we discovered a small post-and-rail *pen*, of common split timber, neither smoothed nor painted, but bearing a tolerably near resemblance to a temporary pigstye, and this was "The Grand Stand!" I afterwards remembered having seen the one at Paramatta, which, though far superior to this, was only calculated to hold some half-dozen persons, and was framed in the same rough and unpolished style.

The road now became quite colonial, that is, execrably bad, and the scenery too monotonous to divert my attention for a moment from the misery of the rough jolting we suffered, and from my cares lest every shock should disturb or hurt my baby, whom I dared not trust in the maid's arms for fear she might drop him out whilst saving herself from one of the incessant jolts, which threatened fractures and dislocations at every step.

In the afternoon we reached a solitary public-house, where we purposed resting for an hour, but finding a large party of rather riotous guests already in possession of its wretched little rooms, we hastened on for a short distance, and paused on the

next hill, where the horses were tethered to graze,
and we soon made a fire to grill our cold meat and
warm baby's food ; and so, under the shade of some
sombre gum trees, had a pleasant pic-nic sort of
repast, far more to my taste than a sojourn in the
unpromising dingy little hostel we had left.

Here I was first initiated into the bush art of
"sticker-up" cookery, and for the benefit of all
who "go a-gipsying" I will expound the mystery.
The orthodox material here is of course kangaroo,
a piece of which is divided nicely into cutlets two
or three inches broad and a third of an inch thick.
The next requisite is a straight clean stick, about
four feet long, sharpened at both ends. On the
narrow part of this, for the space of a foot or more,
the cutlets are spitted at intervals, and on the end
is placed a piece of delicately rosy fat bacon. The
strong end of the stick-spit is now stuck fast and
erect in the ground, close by the fire, to leeward ;
care being taken that it does not burn. Then the
bacon on the summit of the spit, speedily softening
in the genial blaze, drops a lubricating shower of
rich and savoury tears on the leaner kangaroo cutlets below, which forthwith frizzle and steam and
sputter with as much ado as if they were illustrious

Christmas beef grilling in some London chop-house
under the gratified nose of the expectant consumer.
"And gentlemen," as dear old Hardcastle would
have said, if he had dined with us in the bush,
"to men that are hungry, stuck-up kangaroo and
bacon are very good eating." Kangaroo is, in fact,
very like hare.

On this occasion, however, as our basket was
town-packed, our "sticker-up" consisted only of
ham. The evening of this day we reached Jerusalem, and, not having any friends in the holy city,
took up our quarters at one of the caravanserais,
where we were as little uncomfortable as we could
expect to be in a place of such limited accommodation. Jerusalem is a township of far less imposing aspect than Richmond, and the neighbouring
scenery is very uninteresting.

The absurdity of giving to new little settlements
like this the names of old-world places of renown,
always seems to me excessive. Not far away from
the new Jerusalem are Jericho and Bagdad; whilst
English town and country names abound, and the
plain farmhouses of settlers are often called after
some of the most magnificent palace-seats of English nobles, making the contrast, which cannot fail

to occur to one's mind, ludicrous in the extreme.
I know only three native names of places in this
island—Ringarooma and Boobyalla on the north
coast, and Triabunna on the east.   In New South
Wales many of the settlers have had the good sense
and taste to preserve the aboriginal names, which
are always significant (when understood), and for
the most part singularly musical in sound.   Such
are Paramatta, Wooloomooloo, Illawarra, Wollon-
gong, Wollondilly, Mittagong, Maneroo, Tuggera-
nong, Mutmutbilly, Yangalara, and many more;
whilst some few, it must be owned, are more grotesque than euphonious, for instance, Jerriconoram-
wogwog, Jininjininjininderry, and Jinjulluk.   Yet
even these are preferable to the reiterated old
names, and at any rate excite no ridiculous comparison between great old things and little new
ones.

Our onward road from Jerusalem was worse than
any we had hitherto traversed, being deep loose
sand mingled with stones of all sizes, and great
masses of rock, over which we bumped and jumped
and jolted most perseveringly for some miles; the
horses being sufficiently tired in dragging us along
at a slow foot-pace, and through as uninteresting a

tract of country as can well be conceived. Forests of straggling dingy gum-trees (*Eucalyptus*) were here and there mingled with an equally dingy growth of wattle and honeysuckle-trees (*Acacia* and *Banksia*) ; the ground bore very little herbage, but was chiefly covered with coarse, harsh, reedy plants, some of which are called "cutting grass," from the extremely sharp edges of the leaves, which cut like glass; so sharp, indeed, that we have had dogs severely hurt in running through them : other and more numerous kinds are less mischievous.

A large tussock of this grass I have often found a very pleasant resting-place, as, by bending sideways a portion of the upper leaves, and seating oneself upon them, they form an elastic cushion, well backed by the remaining upright leaves, and very preferable to a seat on a log, which usually swarms with ants : it is prudent to *poke* the tussock with a stick, before sitting down on it, as snakes are not unfrequently found coiled within.

On such a primitive kind of ottoman I very gladly rested awhile at our usual mid-day halt in the forest, whilst the smoke of our gypsy fire curled sluggishly upward in the still air, and the horses eagerly rolled themselves in the damp marsh grass that skirted the tiny spring which had made us fix upon this spot for the halt of our little caravan.

Tall gaunt-looking gum-trees, with many straggling far-spreading branches and scanty foliage, towered high above, with streamers of loose bark hanging from all parts of them, sometimes five or more yards long, and waving rustlingly to and fro. At least a fifth part of the trees had either died of natural decay, or been blown down, and lay in all directions; their massive trunks, broken branches, and withered leaves, together with many years' accumulation of fallen bark (which these trees shed annually) covering the earth, and scarcely allowing the lesser plants to struggle up amongst them. A few common shrubs grew here and there with pretty but scanty blossoms; and, beside the precious little spring, a gleam of real green brightened the dreary place, and the few poor reeds and shrubs so fortunate as to dwell within its blessed influence, shot up tall and lithe and verdant, amidst that dry, sapless, lifeless-looking forest.

I was pleased to see some fern here, very similar to the common forest-fern or brake at home; but, instead of growing tall and spreading, it seemed

stunted and crisped with drought, its leaf-tips all
brown and brittle, and the stems hard and shri-
velled.

We journeyed on through this seemingly endless
region of standing and prostrate gum-trees, frequently walking to spare our poor child the motion
of the carriage, and having continually, when driving, to turn aside into the uncleared "bush," to
travel round some enormous tree which had fallen
across the beaten track. How little do the good
people in England, whom I have heard grumble
outrageously at the sixpences extorted from them
by the turnpikes—how very little do they know the
value of the roads they so grudgingly help to maintain! If they could possibly enjoy, as we did, the
delight of making a journey of 120 miles upon
one of these free roads, I think turnpikes would
ever after beam upon their charmed eyes as the
loveliest objects in the landscape, the ever welcome
tokens of level roads and easy drives, of Macadam
and civilization.

In the district around Hobarton, and on the
direct route to Launceston, the roads are reasonably
good, and when the probation system rendered the
services of so many thousands of convicts avail-

able to the local Government for the execution of
works of public utility, it was generally hoped that
in time our colonial highways would be considerably mended, but such expectation has been signally disappointed. Gangs of many hundreds of
men have been located about the island in various
places, but, as it would appear, with the most careful determination on the part of their directors
that their labour should *not* be beneficial to the
colonists. Roads were begun, it is true, but generally in such directions as were rarely traversed,
and if one over a more frequented part of the country was commenced and carried on successfully for
some time, the gangs were almost invariably removed from it when a little further labour would
have rendered it essentially serviceable to the
neighbourhood. I know positively of more than
one instance where a road between two districts
was in the course of formation, which, had it been
carried through, would have greatly enhanced the
value of certain large properties; but because the
owners of these were obnoxious, upon political
grounds, to the officer then in charge of the convicts, the work was stopped when within a short
distance of the proposed terminus (a portion of the

road was left unfinished and wholly impassable), the prisoners' barracks were dismantled and allowed to go to ruin, and the gang removed to a distance, most probably to be kept in idleness; for, as the officer had uncontrolled power, and rather a lengthy list of private feuds, it became extremely difficult to plan a road, in any quarter, which should not either directly or indirectly benefit some of the objects of his undying and vindictive dislike; and hence the very small amount of good effected by a very large amount of power—hence the number of unfinished, almost useless roads and expensive stations and barracks, built at the cost of the Home Government, and left to go to ruin, all over the island—and hence the unpopularity and ultimate failure of the probation system.

A common bush-road cleared of trees and stumps, the latter being too frequently left in the ground, is, if on firm smooth soil, by no means unpleasant, but where rocks intervene, or deep gullies, or the broad stony ford of a river, or a low tract of bog or marshy clay — which the least traffic in wet weather beats up into a slippery tenacious batter-pudding consistency—these, in consequence of no means being adopted for rendering them moderately passable, become serious impediments, and with such obstacles our colonial bush-roads are replete.

How some of the yawning "gullies" and ravines were passed on our journey, is an enigma to me to this day; for sometimes their banks were so precipitous, that I could with difficulty descend one side and scramble up the other on foot. How the carriage was lowered down and dragged up again, I cannot divine; but my husband and brother, and the good horses, managed it in some mysterious way amongst them, and regularly overtook me as I and my servant walked on before with the child; who, after sleeping through the first three days' easy stages with most exemplary and philosophical indifference to the jolting, now began to intimate that his patience was exhausted, and put in his protest against carriage nursing most determinedly. Still, it was pleasant and comforting to think that we *might* have been far more miserable! and, when growing really weary, distressed, and vexed at our many petty troubles, I used to silence my inward murmurs by the query—

" *Would you prefer going by sea ?* " and instantly
the all-powerful charm of the dry land reconciled
me to all present or future annoyances that our
journey might present.

Our resting-place, on the fourth evening of our
slow and tiresome pilgrimage, was the house of a
settler at the "Eastern Marshes," who, from being
the only resident in the neighbourhood, or for miles
around, must have his well-known hospitality tried
by most of the travellers on this dreary route.
Judging from the number we met, these are, fortunately for him, not very numerous; during two
days we had only seen two shepherds and their
dogs.   Our worthy host was an old acquaintance of
Mr. Meredith's, and our weary group received every
attention and comfort he could possibly provide us;
and truly it is no small trial for a quiet little household to be invaded at a moment's notice, or rather
with no notice at all, by a whole family party,
hungry, thirsty, tired, hot, cold, sick or sleepy, as
the case may be, but always troublesome to an incalculable extent, and turning the house upside
down to make up cradles for children, and "shake-
downs" for gentlemen, and causing, however reluctantly, multifarious orders to go forth for hot

water, cold water, towels, carpet-bags, blankets,
driving-boxes, mutton-chops, brandy, milk, slippers,
boiled eggs, dry wood, bread and butter, and tea,
within half-an-hour driving the bewildered serving-
woman nearly beside herself, and making the distracted master glad to escape to the stable to superintend the arrangements for the quadrupedal part of
the invading army. Luckily our present kind entertainer was a bachelor, and ourselves not very
exacting guests. When there is a wife in the case,
I am always trebly grieved at occasioning such a
domestic disturbance, being tolerably well able to
sympathize in her sufferings. Yet it is not un-
common for such compulsory guests (especially
residents in towns), to lay the flattering unction to
their souls, that they confer the greatest imaginable
favour on an establishment, by turning it inside out;
at the same time avowing their conviction that
"people in the country are *always* so delighted to
see *anybody;*" which is not exactly the correct
construction to put upon the almost universal spirit
of kind hospitality which prevails among settlers
in the Bush, whether rich or poor; the simplicity
and regularity of their lives and occupations rendering such interruptions far more serious than people

accustomed to lounge and idle away their days in town can understand. How great a delight it is to welcome to the solitary home in the wilderness, some old and valued friend, and to see the well-known face mingle its silent tales of bygone years with all the newer interests and affections of the present time, can only be known when enjoyed! I believe, in truth, that to appreciate fully and completely the blessings of happy homes, children, friends, and books, a trial of lonely bush-life for a few years is indispensable. Such partial solitude does the spirit good.

I really think that, after seeing the truly lonely houses which we often find in these colonies, I should be puzzled to know where a lonely house could be placed in England! I have in former days seen what I then imagined such, and have read, with an admiring conviction of its truth, my friend Mr. Howitt's eloquent description of "lone country houses" in general, and of some very fearfully lone ones in particular; but I verily begin to disbelieve the whole theory, and am almost prepared to assert that there is not, and cannot be, a lone house in England, and that there is nobody now living who ever lived in or saw such an one there!

Now this homestead on the Eastern Marshes might with some semblance of truth be invested with the ghostly and robbery qualifications of a " lonely house : " it stands all alone by itself, on an extensive tract of low marsh land, which, even at the time of our visit in November *, was all splashy with water, and alive with unimaginable legions of frogs. Beyond the marsh, the forest land, or, to use the settlers' universal term, the "Bush," commences, and spreads away over miles and miles of inhospitable country used for nothing but sheep-runs, usually called sheep-*walks* at home, but in these young countries we are in such haste to " advance" and " go ahead," that, among all other fast things, we must needs have fast sheep, or talk of them as if they were fast, which does as well. Mountains, hills, valleys, ravines—all are wild and trackless as they were thousands of years ago, except where a rude fence of brushwood indicates the boundary-line of different properties, or the narrow thread of a sheep-path winds away amidst the fallen trees and spreading reed-tussocks. No road passes by or anywhere near the place, at least

* November here, corresponding with May in England, is a warm dry month.

none that I could espy: those travellers who go
there, find their way by means of some occult
science like divination, appertaining, I presume, to
the organ of "Locality" in its most perfect deve-
lopment, but which I still venerate in the blindest
ignorance ; for all forests here, and all parts of
them, are to me so exactly alike, that the power of
knowing which is the right way to turn round one
of many thousand similar trees seems, to my un-
practised comprehension, to border on the miraculous.

CHAPTER V.

Journey continued.—Pic-nic Dinner.—Ascent of the Sugarloaf.—Gum-
Tree Forests.—Rest on the Mountain.—Descent.—Night Quarters.
—Sea Coast.—"Rocky Hills."—Oyster Bay.—Isle des Phoques.—
Maria Island.—Probation Gang.—Waterloo Point.—Journey's
End.

LEAVING the Eastern Marshes the following morning, we again pursued our way through the Bush,
over as wretched roads as heretofore, and by noon
had reached the foot of the Sugarloaf Mountain, a
most formidable part of our journey.

A high and rugged mountain-tier wholly encom-
passes the fertile district of Great Swan Port on the
land side, rendering it imperative upon us to scale
it at some point; and, after much deliberation and
many inquiries as to what bridges were broken—
such bridges too! a Welsh pony would scarcely
trust them in their best days—and what gullies
were altered by floods, and what new fences now
crossed old roads—whether such as could be pulled

down to pass through (the putting up again after passing, being a point of honour with respectable travellers, who do as they would be done by), and where certain slip-rails were to be found, and where we must " look out for the bull-dog that was always loose," and other pleasant little items of preliminary information essential to be acquired ;—after all was canvassed, the Sugarloaf route was decided on as the best. My readers will be kind enough to imagine, if they journey with me to the end, what the other routes must be. There was an alternative proposed, of " taking the Thumbs for it"—a part of the ridge with three hummocks called the " Three Thumbs" being sometimes traversed instead of the Sugarloaf ; but the latter was finally preferred.

Here then, at the foot of the mountain, we first forded, and then halted beside a beautiful picturesque stream, which, with the whole scene, strongly reminded me of spots in North Wales, or on the Wye above Rhaiddyr—dear old names ! how pleasant it is to write them once again, and how almost impossible to believe that thirteen long years have passed over my head since I wrote about them first ! Huge rocks here and there interrupted the course of the bright little river, round which it gurgled and foamed in true trout-stream style; shrubs and trees hung over and dipped into its clear dark shady pools, that reflected in dancing pictures the high and frowning mountain-peaks around; exquisite flowering plants, one a tree-veronica with bright polished foliage, and a profusion of lovely sprays of ultra-marine eye blossoms, grew close beside us, as we spread our repast on the broad flat mossy stones, and with our wine cooling in the river, and our little cups brim-full of the crystal water, we were fast growing luxurious in our notions, when, as if to realize more fully my Welsh mountain reminiscences, a cloud, which I had once or twice glanced at somewhat suspiciously, poured down upon us in a veritable mountain-shower; but it soon passed over, and the sun shone out brightly, making all the little twinkling diamond drops in the flowers glitter and dance as if in enjoyment of our temporary discomfiture.

Luncheon being finished, and knives, forks, cups, and "table service" packed up, I set off, as usual, in advance, with the child and nurse, to climb the mountain on foot; the road being too distinct to be mistaken even by so obtuse a bush-traveller as myself. We plodded on and on, sometimes pausing to listen for the horses or carriage behind, and then

hastening on again, to walk as far as possible before
it overtook us, in mercy both to the poor horses
and to the child. A most fearful ravine soon
yawned before my feet, far deeper and steeper and
wider than any yet passed, and with only a crazy
bridge of long thin poles thrown across and turfed
over. Many of the poles were broken, and most of
the turf fallen away, so that it was little more than
a net-work of holes; even I could not step lightly
and quickly over without risk and fear, and I
paused some minutes on the edge, hoping the carriage party would come, that I might know if they
attempted to cross, and whether this seeming impossibility would be accomplished, as so many
others had been; but hearing nothing approach, we
again proceeded on the steepest part of the ascent.
Here the road winds to and fro along the ridge of
the mountain, and most unaccountably passes nearly
over its peak, much in the same style as Major
Mitchell's Blue Mountain track. A wide extent of
hills and vales, or rather ravines, spread far around
and beneath, all robed in dim-hued forests, which
in the distance looked brown and rusty, and the
nearer portions only displayed the skeleton forms of
the universal gum-trees in a more gaunt and un-

pleasing aspect—so gaunt and grim and gnarled were they, with such vicious twists and doublings in their gray-white trunks—such misshapen caricatures of arms and legs scrambling all abroad; such odd little holes and clefts, making squinting eyes and gaping mouths in elvish faces, with scratchy scrubby-looking wigs of dry leaves; and they had altogether so disreputable and uncanny an aspect, that if they had incontinently joined over my head in a Walpurgis dancing party, it would only have seemed a natural and suitable proceeding.

Here and there portions of the rocky cliffs that overhung the road assumed strange and picturesque forms, sometimes draped with creeping plants, or clasped around in a rugged embrace by long-armed forest tree roots, knotted over them like mighty cables. I was growing very weary, and the utterly helpless loneliness of the situation I had so indefatigably walked into, began to impress me with no very cheerful feelings, for there was no human being within call, save my frightened maid, to have offered us assistance, had any of the bushrangers, then said to be numerous in the colony, chanced to pounce upon us. Even the worst of these desperadoes are, however, generally respectful and humane towards females. Nevertheless, I grew "horribly afeard," and my efforts to assume an air of courageous indifference were, I have no doubt, most grim and lamentable failures. To return, at all events, would have been useless folly, and to stand still nearly as bad; so on we climbed, still up, up, up, along that ever-turning and, as it seemed, never-ending ascent, and it was not until we had got close to the brow of the mountain that Mr. Meredith and the "caravan" reached us.

A rest on the summit was as needful for the poor horses as it was welcome to me, and a cup of sparkling water from a spring close by was deliciously cool and refreshing to my parched lips as I sat panting "on a log."

And now began the worst part of the day's journey; having with a world of trouble succeeded in getting to the top of the hill, naturally the next thing to be done was to get to the bottom again. We young-country folks never adopt your mean middle courses, or go sneaking round a hill half way down; if a thing *is* to be done, we do it manfully, in the most difficult possible manner, and if people *must* go over mountain-tiers, why of course they

like to make much of the treat, and go as high up
as they can! At least such seems to be the principle on which all mountain-roads are laid out in
this country.

The road by which we had ascended was a
"made" one, and tolerably good; but from the
opposite side the pioneers of the wilderness seemed
to have shrunk aghast, and left their task in sheer
despair. The descent, as I viewed it, seemed all
but perpendicular. I know that people skilled in
theories and calculations say that an angle of 75°
is the steepest ascent that a man can walk up; but
as no one that I know of has ascertained the precise degree of slope for bodies to roll down, I cannot in this instance recognise the rule. Certain it
is, that our descent of the hill-Sugarloaf might be
likened to that of flies creeping down a real one,
and the whole broadside of the mountain being
thickly strewn with loose sharp stones, was rendered doubly dangerous to traverse. My year's
inactivity in New South Wales had spoiled my good
old English habits of walking, and I was too much
exhausted to crawl further on foot, so I was compelled to cling to the carriage—I cannot say I sat in
it, but crouched on the foot-rug, clasping baby in

one arm, whilst I held tightly on with the other,
not daring to glance before me at the abyss below.
A strong rope was fastened to the back of the
vehicle, to which our stalwart brother lent all his
weight and strength in holding the carriage back ;
my maid meanwhile led his horse (much as Mr.
Winkle might have done), at the imminent peril of
her own toes ; and so, with infinite terror and no
disaster, we arrived safely at the bottom.   Many
times in the course of the journey we had recourse
to ropes held in the same manner on either side to
prevent an upset, for the " sideling " hills in the
bush roads not being cut or terraced to form levels,
the slope is often too great for a vehicle to traverse
without great risk of overbalancing.

During this memorable descent of the Sugarloaf, my attention was called to the beautiful view
which at one point appeared over the sombre forest
foreground.   This was a lovely glimpse of the Pacific Ocean, calm and sunny, with the bold precipitous cliffs of Maria Island rising grandly in
the distance, and the more varied outline of the
Schoutens stretching away to the north.   Beautiful
as it was, and long as I could, under other circumstances, have gazed upon it, I felt, and I fear

somewhat ungraciously declared, that the sight of
a single chimney of our father's residence—the so
desired haven whither we were bound—would have
seemed lovelier in my weary eyes at that moment
than the most exquisite scenery that mountains and
ocean ever composed.

Our day's progress, though occupying from eight
in the morning till five in the evening, did not exceed eighteen miles, and ended at a small public-
house at Little Swan Port, where a room, not
unlike a ship's cabin in size, served us perforce
as dining-parlour and dormitory, our brother and
the maid being accommodated for the night, one in
a loft, and the other on a settee in the landlady's
little kitchen.

The clever bed which Goldsmith celebrates as
contriving

> " A double debt to pay,
> A bed by night, a chest of drawers by day,"

had a perfect sinecure compared with the little
oblong table of our miniature apartment, which,
after officiating first in the menial capacity of a
wash-hand-stand, and then as a toilet, was enabled,
by the aid of a clean white cloth, to figure as a
remarkably compact dining-table for three—the

bed, in the character of a sideboard, sharing its
somewhat crowded honours; and, after well sus-
taining the dignity of a "festal board," this accommodating piece of furniture once more subsided into a toilet and wash-hand-stand, previously
to its being finally "made up" for the night with
cloaks and shawls as a bed for the baby!

The landlord of our inn had been many years
in the neighbourhood, and narrowly escaped being
one of the victims in the first murderous attack
made here by the aborigines on the settlers; but
more of this anon. Both he and his wife had long
known our family, and were most attentive and
obliging. The good woman persisted in loading
our little table with plate after plate, heaped up
with every description of eatable she could cook,
declaring, in spite of all my remonstrances, that
she _knew_ we must be famished:—toast, mutton-
chops, eggs, and fried ham followed each other in
quick succession, in company with a mighty tea-
pot steaming and fragrant, and a comely mountain
of home-baked bread, with English bottled ale and
other anti-teetotal beverages. Our repast was, as
usual on such occasions, a conglomeration of
dinner, tea, and supper, and in this instance com-

prised a display of enough food for at least three
sets of such meals.

On taking an out-of-doors survey of our quarters the following morning, I found that the cottage was built in a somewhat singular fashion, a
portion of it being continued over a sudden slope
in the bank, at the same level as the other parts,
and merely supported on thick, rough, upright
posts, giving the whole building the appearance
of leaning on its elbows to look into the river
below. It was also old enough to have acquired
a nice mellow colour, with patches of moss and
creeping plants about it; and some gay bits of
curtain, or an old gown, that fluttered at the
casement window, helped out the picturesque so
well, that the group of sturdy rosy children beside
it made up a sort of living " Gainsborough,"
quite refreshing to contemplate. A garden, not
very neatly kept, but apparently tolerably productive, lay between the cottage and the river,
or rather estuary, Little Swan Port being a considerable inlet of Oyster Bay.

Passing this by a wide but not very deep ford,
we commenced the last chapter of our pilgrimage,
which the execrable roads and the impossibility of

exceeding a very moderate pace with our baby-
traveller, had rendered very wearisome.

After we had gained the sea-coast, along which
our course now lay, the scenery became most beautiful and striking; and, after skirting the lower
portions of the seaward hills for some distance, we
gradually ascended a kind of terrace road, very
rudely formed along the side of the almost precipitous chain, correctly named " The Rocky Hills."
From this place we enjoyed a magnificent view;
behind and in front of us appeared the winding
mountain road—bad enough to traverse, Heaven
knows—but very charming to look at, just the
scene for a fine group of melodramatic bandits in
ambush behind a rock, or for a string of muleteers,
or a band of chamois hunters, or Alpine herds-
women, or any other figures appropriate to a wild
rocky mountain pass.   High overhead the common
forest trees grew in their wonted straggling and
fantastic forms; the rocks around us were adorned
by luxuriant bushes of a delicate and fragrant wild
geranium, with small finely-veined flowers of pale
lilac, and large downy leaves, contrasted here and
there with the broad-eyed white and yellow ever-
lastings, in their powdery woolly foliage.   Over

many of the flat rocks were spread large juicy-
green mats of the pretty fig-marigold (*Mesembry-
anthemum equilaterale*), and in some places long
pendent masses of the same plant hung down, cur-
taining the rugged cliffs in rich living draperies,
and shading many a cool little grotto-nook with
their heavy solid verdure, and its glorious broidery
of bright, glowing, purple, starry flowers, each with
its inner sun of pale gold.

Far below our narrow track the surf dashed
against the cliffs, its continuous roar reaching us
in a hollow murmur, and the bright waters of
Oyster Bay, blue as the sky above them, spread
forth in the most perfect bay-form I have ever
seen. The lofty Schouten promontory, with its
long range of craggy granite peaks, and the
Schouten Island, equally picturesque, stretching
away southwards from the point of the mainland,
form the limits of the bay opposite to the Rocky
Hills, whilst round the head of this silvery blue
dainty nook of ocean lies a fine tract of low land
(the estate of Cambria), with densely-wooded tiers
of hills rising behind. Southward of the Schoutens the small island called the White Rock, or
more generally in maps, " Isle des Phoques," rises

abruptly from the sea. It is not more than a mile
and a half in circumference, and was formerly the
resort of a great number of seals, which have been
almost wholly destroyed; and now the only residents there are the prodigious multitudes of sea-
fowl of all descriptions, which inhabit the crags
and clefts and strange intricate caverns of this wild
and almost inaccessible rock, which rises perpen-
dicularly from the water, and as the waves rise and
fall from twenty to thirty feet, the only mode of
access for persons visiting it is, to leap from the
boat when at the top of a swell, and, lighting bare-
footed on the slippery rocks, scramble up them—
a favourite amusement with my husband some few
years ago; and I delight now to hear his vivid
descriptions of the nights he has sometimes passed
there, watching the seals come in from the sea to
suckle their young, listening to the conversation of
the "old wigs," as the males are termed, or witnessing their fearful engagements—for they fight
tremendously, tearing each other in the most
savage manner, till the thick, fat, blubbery skin
hangs about them in absolute tatters. At sunset,
too, and all night long, the sea-birds come flock-
ing home, uttering their ceaseless cries, and seek-

ing their respective holes and nests with a noisy, bustling, fearless hurry-skurry, not heeding in the least the presence of strangers, but flying against them, or running under their legs. And through the night strange wild sounds are heard—the deep bark of the seals; the screams, cries, and soft musical tones of the birds; the moaning of the wind; and hollow booming and dashing of the sea against the rock, and in and through and all amongst its labyrinthine caves and grottoes, that nothing but a wave or a fish ever penetrated.

Farther to the south is Maria Island, chiefly composed of high cliffs and rocks, which rise at the northern extremity in a nearly perpendicular precipice, called the Bishop and Clerks, of about 1800 feet; the rock is a dark close limestone, and extremely rich in large fossil shells.

Long and weary was our progress over the terrible "Rocky Hills;" for, lovely as was the view around, it could not charm away my almost painful sensations of fatigue, as I stumbled along among the sharp stones and rocks and fallen trees, for to sit in the carriage was even worse, adding an agony of fright to the rough motion. I have often laughed since to think what a deplorable figure we must

have cut; but at the time it was a grave affair
enough. Mr. Meredith led the van, piloting the
carriage as he best might among the innumerable
obstacles that beset it; then came poor little baby
George, in the careful arms of his stout uncle,
whose horse I led the while; and the maid brought
up the rear. In about the worst part of the road
we met the wife of a neighbouring settler, calmly
seated on a fine old white horse, guiding it steadily
over the path, and carrying at the same time an
infant, about the age of my own, tucked snugly
under one arm, and a sturdy little fellow about a
year older on her lap, besides numerous bundles
hanging to the pommel. I gazed at her with almost
envious admiration and wonder as she rode quietly
on, quite composed and at ease, whilst I, with thrice
the apparent accommodation, was nigh fainting with
fatigue.

At one part of the road we found a gang of men
employed in its improvement; forming, in the
mean time, greater obstacles than they removed;
and so they have continued to be employed, aided
by frequent reinforcements of new arrivals, nearly
ever since; and still, after nearly nine years, the
comparatively trifling task remains unfinished, and

the station is deserted. The mismanagement of this gang was evident to the most casual observer; so notorious was their idleness, that it was a common thing to see them not even pretending to be employed, unless in making arbours of boughs to sit under in the sun! A more sleek-looking, stout, sturdy, lazy fraternity, I cannot conceive possible. This herding together of so many idle men under the pretence of "doing probation," as they call it, must be injurious to the well-disposed among them, and is no punishment to the worthless.

We continued to enjoy the same view of the fine bay, and the opposite mountains, only altered slightly by our change of position as we advanced, losing it occasionally as our road led over the inland ridges of the many jutting points, and regaining it as we returned towards the sea. On one fine sandy beach, where we rested awhile, quantities of huge whales' bones lay scattered about; they were as white as snow, from long exposure to the sun and air. The large joints of the vertebræ make very shapely rustic seats and footstools, when the greasy matter has all passed away from them. I rested on one during our halt, and, as I looked around, could not help fancying what treasures those despised bones would be in many a fantastic *Londonesque* garden, amidst its rock-work, vases, statues, and flower-pots.

We had now passed all the very bad portions of the road, and, after traversing in tolerable comfort a few more rugged hills, came in view of the little settlement of Swansea, more commonly known in the district as "Waterloo Point," that being the name originally given to it; the first stipendiary magistrate here, Captain Hibbert, 40th Regiment, having served at Waterloo.

The little rocky promontory jutting out into the sea, surmounted by the flagstaff and a few white-washed buildings, including the gaol, police office, and magistrate's cottage, looks at a distance like a small fort; and some mock embrasures, painted on the white walls, have also, when seen from a dis-tance, a right martial aspect. The church, originally built for a school-room, remained for some years a rough unfinished apartment, fitted up with benches, but within the last three years it has been raised in height and handsomely finished. The houses of three publicans and one or two stores were the only other edifices on the "Point" above the rank of huts; and as the soil around is too rocky and sandy to make gardens, and all the native trees have long since been cut down, these had but a bare and staring appearance.

Our poor horses seemed as well pleased as ourselves at the delightful change from the "Rocky Hills" to a good level road, and trotted gaily along, through the straggling township, and on through another interval of "bush," to the ford of the "Meredith River;" soon after passing which we turned aside from the road, and drove to the door of our father's hospitable mansion, where, in a long quiet sojourn among kind relations, I almost forgot the weary journey I had made to reach them.

CAMBRIA.

CHAPTER VI.

Cambria.—Hedges.—View.—Garden and Orchard.—Fruits.—Flowers. Rabbits.—Black Swans.—Christmas Day.—Pic-nic Parties.— Sponges.—Shrubs and Shells.

THE house at " Cambria" commands an extensive view of large tracts both of " bush" and cultivated land; and, across the Head of Oyster Bay, of the Schoutens, whose lofty picturesque outline, and the changing hues they assume in different periods of the day or states of the atmosphere, are noble adjuncts to the landscape. Below a deep precipitous

bank on the south side of the house flows a winding
creek, the outlet of the Meredith River, gleaming
and shining along its stony bed, and richly fringed
by native flowering shrubs, mingled with garden
flowers half-wild, poppies, stocks, wallflowers, and
bright-eyed marigolds looking merrily up, amidst
thickets of the golden wattle and snowy tea-tree;
whilst, on the higher ground, huge old gum-trees
stand majestically, spreading wide their white fantastic branches, and shiny yet sombre foliage. At
a short distance from the opposite bank of the
creek stands a thatched cottage, with its attendant
outhouses, partly concealed and shadowed by some
particularly fine gum-trees, such as would be deemed
highly ornamental even in an English park, for
trees of this kind growing singly or in groups on
rich land are scarcely recognisable as of the same
genus with the gaunt scraggy objects that swarm
together in the forests. The sight of this little
cottage removes, rather pleasantly, the feeling of
loneliness and isolation that generally pervades colonial country-houses, which are most commonly
built each in or near the centre of its own estate;
but in this instance the river, separating a large
farm from a little one, has attracted the owners of

both to place their houses near it. Large tracts of cleared, fenced, and cultivated land form a nearly level plain in front, and towards the north, in which direction the cottage, formerly the residence of our family, peeps from its grove of wattle-trees. Steep but not very lofty hills rise at the back of the Cambria plain, forming a small outpost of the rocky tier that wholly environs the Great Swan Port district on the land side, and, for want of comparatively little labour in road-making, renders either ingress or egress a matter of much fatigue and difficulty.

A large, well-built, cheerful-looking house, with its accompanying signs of substantial comfort in the shape of barns, stackyard, stabling, extensive gardens, and all other requisite appliances on a large scale, is most pleasant to look upon at all times and in all places, even when tens or twenties of such may be seen in a day's journey; but when our glimpses of country comfort are so few and far between as must be the case in a new country, and when one's very belief in civilization begins to be shaken by weary travelling day after day through such dreary tracts as we had traversed, it is most delightful to come once more among sights and

sounds that tell of the Old World and its good old
ways, and right heartily did I enjoy them.

The noble veranda into which the French
windows of the front rooms open, with its pillars
wreathed about with roses and jasmine, and its
lower trellises hidden in luxuriant geraniums, became the especial abiding-place of my idleness; as
I felt listless and inactive after my year's broiling
in New South Wales, and delighted in the pleasant
breezy climate of our new home.

Hawthorn hedges greeted me pleasantly again,
with their old remembered verdure and fragrant
blossoms; and those of gorse, the first I had seen
since leaving England, would rival the growth of
that sturdy mountaineer even on its native hills.
There were many of these live fences, although the
less pleasing ones of posts-and-rails, or paling,
logs, or brush were necessarily more prevalent; and
I found that the *un*accommodations of slip-rails
and gates of refractory temper were not wholly
peculiar to New South Wales.

Flocks of sheep, herds of cattle, and horses, gave
life and interest to my veranda-diorama, and the
distant road, half seen, half hidden by the undulating ground, sometimes displayed, in addition to

its common-place traffic of bullock and horse teams, a light cart or jaunting-car, or gig, with its living freight of " settlers " male and female, either journeying to or returning from the little settlement of Swansea, where there are one or two stores of very limited pretensions, and two or three public-houses, all the produce of the chief part of the district being shipped from this place.

A large garden and orchard, well stored with the flowers and fruits cultivated in England, were not among the least of the charms Cambria possessed in my eyes; and the growth of fruit trees is so much more rapid and precocious here than at home, that those only ten or twelve years old appear sometimes aged trees. Apples suffer severely here from the American blight, although some few among the best kinds are wholly exempt from its attacks; the orchard produces so great an abund-ance, as to afford a considerable quantity of cider every year, which is a very pleasant summer beverage.

Judging from the remarks on cider-making in " Loudon's Encyclopædia of Agriculture," I con-ceive that our Tasmanian cider is fermented too much, so as to deprive it of too great a proportion of the saccharine matter; as it is of a very pale colour, and much thinner and more acid than the English, and, except by persons long accustomed to its use, is not drunk without the addition of a large quantity of sugar, which, with a toast and a little nutmeg, makes an extremely pleasant "cider-cup."

Pears succeed excellently, usually bearing an abundance of fine fruit, as do also the medlar, quince, almond, cherry, and all the family of plums, from the portly magnum bonum, looking like the golden fruit of the Hesperides, and demanding to be preserved in syrup, to the luscious bloomy Orleans, delicate green and yellow gages, and the common damson. I have not yet seen the large prune damson in the colony. Seedling peach-trees, which sometimes bear the third year, usually produce an immense quantity of mediocre fruit, useful for tarts and preserves, but the better kinds of peach, together with the apricot and nectarine, are less plentiful. The summer frosts are the direst foes of the gardener and horticulturist in this island; often, when the trees are perfectly clothed with fine blossoms, one night will destroy almost the whole.

Of the smaller common fruits the gooseberry

produces the most certain crop, and bravely sustains its well-won fame in every pleasant shape of pies and " fool," and jam, and sparkling champagne, as in good old English homes. In moist situations raspberries also are fine and plentiful; currants usually bear less abundantly than in England; and strawberries are rarest of all; both these latter being luxuriant in foliage but with a scanty show of fruit. The Alpine strawberry seems to make itself more at home here, and bears well. The out-of-doors vines produce grapes scarcely equal to those grown in favourable situations without glass at home; but here the hothouse and greenhouse supply for so long a time a succession of the finest kinds in such beautiful luxuriance, that the vines on outer walls are but little valued.

The orchard, with its fine trees and shady grassy walks, some broad, and straight, and long, others turning off into sly quiet little nooks and corners, was a great delight to me. Shadowing a bowery path and rustic bench in one place, were fine tall trees of the beautiful English elder, rich in their noble creamy-white clusters of most fragrant blossoms, mingling with the bright yellow fringy flowers of the native wattle tree, which has a powerful

scent, like hawthorn, and tolerably well supplies
the place of the graceful laburnum—where that is
wanting; but here it grows nobly—large trees being
gaily clad in its elegant drooping flowers, the
" golden chains " of one's childhood; and not far
from these, their ancient friend and contemporary
in blossoming, the rich purple lilac, bearing as
heavy clusters as those I have so often robbed her
of in dear old England.   I do not think the white
variety has yet graced these our Antipodean climes,
at least I have not yet seen it.

On the cool grassy banks of a little pond under
the elder trees, and overshadowed also by a thicket
of filbert and hazel bushes—which bear plenty of
nuts in autumn—the New Zealand flax flourishes;
it is a noble-looking plant of the flag-kind, with
long broad leaves of prodigious toughness, and
which, torn in long strips, make excellent ties for
all garden purposes, such as binding grafts, tying
up carnations, or making up nosegays.

The cultivated flowers here are chiefly those familiar to us in English gardens, with some brilliant
natives of the Cape, and many pretty indigenous
flowering shrubs interspersed.   Most of these latter
are so hardy that I have no doubt the greater por-

tion of those now confined, by their English culti-
vators, in the greenhouse or conservatory, would
thrive better in the open air, provided they were
placed in a sheltered spot, and guarded from the
biting frosts of mid-winter—for to moderate frosts
they are well accustomed here—and, being ever-
greens, their varied foliage would be a valuable
acquisition in the autumn and early spring.

The gradual advance of the seasons is pleasantly
marked, in English gardens, by the progressive succession of flowers passing before us like a beautiful
procession, led in by the " Fair Maid of February"
and her attendant crocuses, and followed in unfailing order by the brilliant train of spring, summer,
and autumn flowers, till the last pale chrysanthe-
mums twine in the wreath of green old Christmas
himself: but here, even the gentle flowers rebel
against all Old World rules and customs, and so
crowd one on another in the year's pageant that we
can sometimes gather spring, summer, and autumn
flowers within three months, which I, loving the
old way best, greatly lament.   In favoured spots
near the sea, where the frosts are less keen than in
the more inland districts, the common red, scarlet,
and large purple geraniums grow many feet high,

and flower nearly all the year round; so do the crimson and pink China roses, and the common fuchsia; whilst the double violets push up such full bright flowers from amidst their clustering leaves, that, but for the exquisite perfume which vouches for their dear identity, one might fancy that a blue ranunculus had been invented.

Latterly, a few lovers of good flowers have introduced some of the better and newer kinds of geraniums, pansies, picotees, fuchsias, and other "florists' flowers," greatly to the enrichment of our Tasmanian collections, and every new arrival flourishes most satisfactorily in this fine climate.

A circular inclosure in the garden forms a small rabbit-warren, well stocked with the common kinds, many of which having long ago been turned loose, their abundance all over the district is now so great as sometimes to be troublesome and mischievous. The fence-banks overgrown with huge gorse-bushes form admirable retreats for the pretty little animals, and they increase so rapidly, and make such depredations among the young turnips and springing corn, that occasionally a proclamation of "war to the knife" goes forth, when a troop of sportsmen and spaniels take the field; at such times the golden-blossomed gorse-bushes do not wholly escape, many of the most effectual "covers" being burned down in order to dislodge the rabbits.

The most interesting ornaments of Cambria belonging to the animal kingdom were, in my estimation, a pair of beautiful tame black swans, the first of these birds that I had seen in their native land. They seemed to live very happily in the creek below the house, and always came at a call to be fed with bread or corn. I cannot in conscience pronounce them to be quite equal in majestic beauty to the white swan, but certainly few of the feathered tribe can exceed them when on the water. Their plumage of glossy raven-black, with a few snow-white feathers in the wings and tail, is as elegantly grave a dress as can be conceived, and the bright coral-red bill gives a gay air to the graceful and expressive head and eyes. In the long slender neck I at first missed the curve that looks so stately in the white swan, but soon got reconciled to it. Their note is very melodious and plaintive, with a kind of harp-tone in it, sounding very sweetly as they call to each other over the water, or fly high overhead at night, when it seems like an echo of music from the clouds.

Their nests are generally made in some low bank or islet, and formed of a rude heap of water-weeds. The hen lays five or six large long dingy-white eggs, and the cygnets are at first white, being clothed only in the soft thick white down which forms the inner garment of the swan at all ages, and to obtain which cruelty of the most brutal kind has been and is still practised towards the poor swans. The general custom was, to take the birds in large quantities in the moulting season, when they are most easily captured and extremely fat; they were then confined in pens, *without any food*, to linger miserably for a time, till ready to die of starvation, because, whilst they are fat, the down can neither be so well stripped off nor so effectually prepared. Troops of people make a trade in the eggs, taking these in immense quantities from all the known haunts of the swans, so as very nearly to exterminate them; and, in proof of this, I had been above two years at *Swan* Port before, in any of my numerous rides or drives, my desire to see a *wild* black swan was gratified, though, formerly, thousands frequented every lagoon. Even the tame pets at Cambria were not suffered to live in peace; during our stay there, "Jackey" was one day missing, and found shot dead, lying some short distance down the creek; poor Matey shared the same fate some time after, and lingered several days, after part of her bill had been shot away.

I shall not be deemed to have given a satisfactory sketch of my sable favourites, unless I add the result of my experience touching their quality when eaten.   A fine fat swan is by no means a contemptible dish on the dinner-table, as the worthies who shot at our tame favourites doubtless knew; dressed goose-fashion, they are thought to taste like that bird, but I consider them superior, being less coarsely fat, and of a more game-like flavour, especially if served without the customary strong "illustrations" of sage and onion bestowed upon goose.

My second Australian Christmas Day was passed at Cambria, and found me just as involuntarily sceptical of the time, as I had felt the year before in Sydney. To receive the good old-fashioned wishes of "A merry Christmas and a happy New Year," accompanied by bouquets of summer-flowers, from girls in white muslin frocks! and to hear such murmured sounds in pantry and larder as "Christmas Beef," "Christmas Turkeys," and "Mincepies," on a glorious Italian-skied, radiant, sunny, *hot* midsummer day! That the anomaly was believed in here, was, however, quite evident; for, before I was up that morning, busy hands had been at work dressing the house all over. Holly there was none; but the picture-frames and chimneys and sideboard were gaily and gracefully adorned with lovely native shrubs, and a wreathy crown or garland suspended from the drawing-room ceiling; whilst plentiful bouquets of garden-flowers made the house bright and fragrant; and a large family dinner party, music and dancing, and abundant mirth, all helped to do honour to the world-beloved day; so that, although not the real, proper, genuine *original* Christmas to me, it was a very bright and pleasant parody upon it.

Pic-nic parties were very popular with our summer circle at Cambria, and several pretty spots were successively selected as the scenes of our rural banquets. The calm, bright, settled summer weather of this delightful island is far better adapted for such expeditions than the fickle climate of England, whose wayward skies, like spoiled children, can never be found in the right humour, but will persist in weeping most vehemently when we expect them to smile their brightest. Here a fine morning might

generally be depended upon as heralding a fine day ;
indeed, weeks and months of fair weather succeeded
each other, until the farmers grew most impatient
for rain on their parching lands, and I found that
my admiration of this particular summer *as* a
summer, was by no means echoed by those interested
in the growth of crops, for it was unusually dry,
insomuch that I began to see visions of New South
Wales in the dusty road and yellow fields, that, when
I first came, lay like emeralds in the spring sunshine.

Our progresses to the appointed spots for our
sylvan banquets were performed in divers manners,
and the marshalling forth of the cavalcade often
made as motley and busy a scene as the " Going to
the Chase" or " Return from Hawking" of many a
fine old picture, though made up of matters less
essentially picturesque in themselves. One sketch
will suffice ; the first object on the canvas being a
capacious open cart, drawn slowly into the court-
yard by four fine oxen, the bed of the cart filled
with fresh straw. And now the bustle of preparation, which had hitherto been confined to kitchen,
pantry, and cellar, began to manifest itself outside,
as baskets and boxes packed with clean straw or

white cloths were busily carried forth; their envelopes not wholly concealing protruding rims of
plates, corks of bottles, or the handle of a sauce-
pan—for potatoes boiled out of doors are well known
to possess an unusually fine flavour, at least they
are always most relished; and the presence of a
gridiron or frying-pan is also essential, giving in its
use a kind of earnest reality to the preparations,
which the unfolding ready-prepared viands seems to
some deficient in. The baskets and boxes, safely
stowed, were followed by a heterogeneous collection
of parasols, cushions, shawls, and cloaks, and lastly
by some of the juvenile members of the party,
deeply shadowed in curtained poke-bonnets, who
being all comfortably packed, and little misunder-
standings between opposite parasols finally adjusted,
the bullock-driver thrashed the air violently with
his long ponderous whip, and the quiet docile team
moved slowly off. After a due time had been
allowed for these heavy troops to proceed in advance, the next division of the army prepared to
march, and the jaunting-car and phaeton drove up
to receive their living freight, who were usually
accompanied by some of the party on horseback;
and lastly, bringing up the rear, came our own

roomy nondescript before mentioned—and as our noble steed added to his more valuable qualities a habit of rearing and plunging the moment one's foot touched the step, my cleverness was tasked to the utmost to get safely on board and make a desperate snatch at the baby, held up at arm's length; which perilous feat accomplished, and the nursemaid packed in the excrescence behind, away we dashed after the rest.

A bold rocky point on the west side of the bay, one of the many we had traversed on our last day's journey, was our destination on one occasion; the cliffs were full of strange fantastic caves and hollows, where the sea chafed and roared very grandly, and sent jets of foam flying high through the narrow clefts, beneath which it surged and swelled. Some of the upper and drier caves were strewn thickly over with innumerable kinds of sponges, blown in from the sea; some, great masses one or two feet thick—others, delicate little web-work on the stems of kelp and corallines; some branching into five or six finger-shaped portions, like a hand with swollen joints. One smooth close kind I often found, exactly the shape of a French roll; others were like pears or strings of sausages. And the various colours and texture of these strange zoophytic creations seemed infinite: many of them were so coarse as to seem like quantities of bristles stuck together in a rough irregular net-work, and from these were gradations to those so fine that they required a microscope to detect any fibres in them. These last had almost always smooth tubular openings passing through them from end to end.

By the time I had made a collection of "particularly curious" specimens, enough to fill a small boat had I carried them away, we were summoned to assist at the banquet "al fresco," beneath some trees at a little distance from my interesting sponge-museums among the caves and cliffs, to which, after our repast, I and my scramble-loving better-half returned, and continued our explorations till the time for our re-embarkation and departure arrived.

One of our expeditions was to the mouth of Swan Port, our way lying along the broad smooth beach at the head of Oyster Bay, which extends for nine miles in an unbroken sweep, and is so pleasant to ride upon that only one vehicle, the roomy jaunting-car, was required to carry some of the juveniles, the provisions, my maid, and the baby; most of the party preferring to ride on horseback. After our

merry canter along the fine sands, we dispersed
about the beach, gathering shrubs or picking up
shells : among the former were some very handsome
bushes, some—a species of *Leucopogon*—bearing a
very small white berry, and others a pink and white
fruit called native currants, not remarkable for fine
flavour, but very ornamental and pretty; and many
of the shells at this end of the beach were larger
or altogether different from those nearer home.
The view up the winding estuary of Swan Port,
with its low islands and the dark wooded hills rising
behind, made a pleasant picture, and the ever-beau-
tiful Schoutens rose grandly before us.

These days always passed so rapidly that it was
generally nearly dark when we arrived at home,
and the evenings closed with music, dancing, and
pleasant saunters in the veranda, where the bright
moonlight put to shame the artificial gleam from
the open windows, and showed my favourite view of
the bay and Schoutens almost as clearly as by day.

The almost daring feeling of security, as it at
first seemed to me, which is general here, would
assuredly astonish any one who should witness it
whilst remembering the fearful stories they tell now
in England of our awful condition, social degrada-

tion, and so forth.   What family in England would
think of living in a large lone country-house, with
French windows to the lower rooms unsecured by a
single bar, shutter, or bell, if their own and their
neighbours' servants, and, with rare exceptions, all
the rural population around them, were, or had
recently been, prisoners convicted of all varieties of
crime ?   No one in his senses would dream of such
"rash absurdity," as it would be considered, and
perhaps correctly; each house would be a garrison,
and its indwellers captives to their own terrors.   Yet
such is the common custom here, in this "den of
thieves," this "gaol of the empire;" and the rarity
here of burglary or robbery of any description, as
compared with their constant occurrence at Home,
proves the smallness of the risk.

CHAPTER VII.

Bush Fires.—Their Use.—Diamond Bird.—Robin.—Blue-Cap.—Cormorant.—Gulls.—Islands in Bass's Straits.—Pied and Black Red-Bills.—Blue Crane.

DURING the hot dry weather of the Christmas time, very extensive bush fires spread about the country, and were sometimes extremely mischievous in their destruction of fences, which are very liable to be thus burned, unless care be taken, previously to the dry season, to clear away all fallen wood and rubbish, and to burn the high grass and ferns for a breadth of three or four yards on either side. The fences of sheep-runs, which extend in lines of many miles in length, over the uncleared hills and forests, are those which most frequently suffer; but growing crops, stacks, farm-buildings, and dwellings are likewise sometimes swept away by the rapidly-advancing fire.

By day, the effect of these great conflagrations

was far from pleasant, causing an increase of heat in the air, and a thick haze over the landscape generally; whilst from the various points where the fires were raging, huge columns and clouds of dense smoke were seen rising, as if from volcanoes: but at night, the scene was often very grand; sometimes the fire might be watched, on any rising ground, spreading onwards and upwards, swifter and brighter as it continually gained strength, till the whole mountain side was blazing together; and after the first fierce general flame had passed away, and the great trunks of trees alone remained burning, the effect resembled that of the scattered lights seen on approaching a distant city at night. The rocky Schoutens glittered with partial lines and trains of fire, that marked their rugged and lofty outline like burnished gold amidst the darkness. Each night showed some new change in the great illumination, until a heavy fall of rain extinguished it altogether, much to the satisfaction of all who feared its nearer approach.

A recent scientific writer (the Count Strzelecki), in treating of this colony, condemns the practice of burning, as seriously injurious to the pasturage, and seems to suppose that the custom originated with the colonists; whereas the aborigines practised it constantly, knowing the advantages of destroying the dense growth of shrubs and coarse plants which cover the country in many parts, and spring up again after the fire with young and fresh shoots, which many of the wild animals then gladly feed on. The grass also grows again immediately after the fires, and is greatly preferred by all animals to the old growth; whilst, from the destruction of tall ferns and scrub, it is rendered more accessible to them. Sheep-owners know how serviceable occasional bush fires are, and generally arrange to burn portions of their sheep-runs at different times, so as to have a new growth about every three years. Where this is neglected for a length of time, the rank luxuriance of the great brake fern and other uneatable plants, and the accumulated masses of dead wood, bark, and leaves, form such a body of fuel, that when a fire does reach it, the conflagration is thrice as mischievous in the destruction of fences as it otherwise would have been.

Although every one else perpetually complained of the heat during this glorious summer, to me it was perfectly delightful, so lasting an impression had the scorching weather of New South Wales left behind it. Sea-bathing was a great luxury, too, and a snug bath, built near the house, over a nook of the salt-water creek, sufficiently deep to afford a good plunge, enabled me to enjoy and benefit from its invigorating effects without tasking my indolence by taking a morning walk to the more distant sea-beach.

In the trees and bushes near the creek, I frequently made new acquaintances of the bird kind, but only know a few of them by name. Among these was that tiny flitting fairy called the Diamond bird: it truly is a dainty little jewel; all gold and shaded amber, with silver spots. Not less beautiful, and far more common, was my old darling the robin, as exquisite a beau as ever, with his back of blackest black, and his breast a living flame of scarlet; a warm brave little heart there beats within it too, or his sparkling eye tells no true story! With him came another of Nature's marvels of beauty and brightness, dressed also partly in black, black *bird-velvet*, off the same piece as robin's coat, but with a cap and mantle of blue:—such blue! The deepest summer sky is mere dull gray to it! This wondrous little bird is called the "superb warbler" (*Malurus superbus*),

and superb in truth he is. So bright, so swift, so
merry, so musical as these little beings are, sure
nothing else ever was ! The bluecap has a domestic
contrast, too, in his quiet-coloured little wife, who,
like her Old-World namesake, Jenny Wren,

> " Will still put on her brown gown,
>   And never go too fine."

But though not dressed in as gay hues, she is as
merry and sprightly as her mate; a perfect little
" dot" of a bird, (I wish Dickens could see her!)
quite round, like a ball set on two fine black pins,
with a sweet little head at one side, and at the
other, or more truly on the top, the drollest little
long straight upright tail that ever was seen. The
robin and Mr. Bluecap and Jenny, are all much
alike in shape, and the way in which their indescribably funny little tails are cocked up over
their backs, sometimes almost touching their heads,
as they hop and pop about, up and down, and in
and out, cannot be imagined—it must be seen. Mr.
Meredith says they seem to him to spend their
whole lives in trying to prove an *"alibi,"* con-
vincing you they are in one place, yet showing
themselves in another at the same instant; whilst I,
in attempting to follow with my eyes their almost

invisible transits from spray to paling, and from
the paling on to the rose-bush, and then back again
to the cherry tree, always feel as if I were witnessing
some exhibition of legerdemain or conjuring, and
am prepared for surprises and mystifications without limit.

"Extremes meet," it is often said; but never can
the axiom be more perfectly illustrated than when a
great, heavy, ugly, stupid, gross-looking monster of
a cormorant comes sousing down amongst a party
of these dainty little fairy birds, as I have sometimes seen one, when attracted by the shoals of fish
glancing in the bright pebbly shallows of the creek.
Settling himself, after much preliminary bobbing
and flapping, on a stout limb of a dead gum-tree,
he sits like a wooden effigy of a bird, watching his
prey.

Very different are many other of the sea birds
that sometimes visit the creek, but are more commonly seen on the beach and rocks. All the gulls
are beautiful, whether pied, gray, or white, the
latter especially; they are *so* white, and skim
over the blue sea in the distant sunlight like
snow-flakes, only transformed to bright-eyed birds
as they near the shore; when their sweet mellow

cry comes floating with them, soft as the tone of
a far-away bell.

Although gulls are not generally very tempting as
articles of food, I have heard Mr. Meredith recount
his great delight at having once, some years ago,
killed nine at one shot, when he had been ship-
wrecked on an island in Bass's Straits, and had
lived for some days on a miserable sort of porridge
or burgoo, made of flour recovered from the wreck,
and so damaged by salt water that it would not
bake, mixed with water so strongly impregnated
with alum that it could scarcely be drunk. After
this diet, meat, even though that of a sea-bird,
became valuable, and the nine gulls were a most
precious acquisition; but, being shot at dusk, they
were put aside until dawn, to be prepared for breakfast; and then, woful to relate, all that remained of
them were two legs, the rest having been devoured
during the night by rats. A species of native rat
abounds on many of these islands, and snakes are
numerous on all, however widely separated by the
boisterous sea and strong currents that flow between
them. Mr. Meredith was told by an old "Straits-
man," who had for years been wandering all about
them, hunting seals and mutton birds, that he never

was on one, though only containing a few acres, on which he did not observe snakes; and my husband gives the same account, so far as his knowledge of them extends. On one occasion, during the sojourn on "Prime Seal Island" before mentioned, he had observed a fine "Cape Barren goose"* alight, and, taking his gun, was stealing warily towards it, keeping a rock between himself and the goose, when a rustling amongst the scrub caused him to look down, and he saw part of an enormous snake, which was rapidly moving across, close beneath his feet; fortunately, the loss of the goose, which he alarmed by his precipitate retreat from the snake, was the only harm done.

Among the sea-birds, the "red-bills" are great favourites of ours; they are so very sprightly and handsome in their clear brilliant black and white plumage, gaily set off by their bills and legs of the brightest coral. They run along the sands with exceeding swiftness, always running into the water to take wing, when alarmed by the approach of such terrific things as ourselves. They scarcely make

---

* The "Cape Barren Goose" frequents the island from which it takes its name, and others in the Straits. It is about the same size as a common goose, the plumage a handsome mottled brown and gray, somewhat owl-like in character.

anything fit to be called a nest, but lay about two
eggs on the beach or sandbank, and the young
ones, until able to escape danger by flight, lie close
and motionless, and thus often evade detection; but
if by chance any one approaches the defenceless
little ones, the old birds are extremely bold and indefatigable in their endeavours to divert his attention ; flying or running close round him, and then
circling away a short distance to entice pursuit;
sometimes they flutter lamely along, as if hurt and
incapable of flight, until they have succeeded in
removing the threatened peril from the precious
little babes in the sand, when, with a backward
glance and a saucy cry of triumph, away they fly,
as sound and swift as ever.

Besides the pied red-bills, there are some rather
larger, whose plumage is wholly black; but these,
although handsome, are less so than the others.
Both species are sometimes eaten, but I rejoice to
say their flavour is too "fishy" to be generally
liked; for I love them so well whilst alive, that I
grieve to have them destroyed. The wide extent of
the sea beaches here requires the presence of all the
birds that belong to, or are wont to visit them, to
add their small items of joyous animal life to the

great and grand attributes of ocean, and to people with their busy activity the otherwise lonely strand.

The figures of my favourite red-bills, under the name of "oyster-catchers," in Gould's "Birds of Australia," are less faithful than most of his admirable plates; they are too heavy-looking, and represent the bills and feet as orange-coloured, instead of their real hue of pure brilliant coral-red.

A beautiful blue crane often came and sat in a bare tree over the creek, watching the fish : I had amused myself for some mornings in watching him with equal attention, and admiring his long elegant neck, slender legs, large bright eyes, and lovely delicate silvery-blue plumage, and I vainly hoped that we might still go on quietly together; but, alas! despite my extreme discretion in not attracting attention to my feathered companion, he was one morning seen, doomed, shot without mercy, and a day or two after appeared as a second-course roast, which was much praised. I did not taste my unlucky friend; I should, however, imagine, from what I had observed of his way of living, that the *post mortem* examination would reveal to the palates of those who did, rather strong evidence of his ichthyological researches.

CHAPTER VIII.

Excursion to the Schoutens.—Scenery.—Kelp Forests.—Fishing.—
White Beach.—Rivulet.—Gully.—Lace Lichen.—Ferns.—Echoes.
—View.—Dinner on the Beach.—Return.

I OFTEN call to mind with great pleasure one excursion in particular, which we made (during our
sojourn at Cambria) to the Schoutens. It was in
April, when the pleasant autumn weather was
growing cool, and frequent frosty mornings denoted
the approach of the mild winter of this delightful
climate, that our expedition was planned, and as the
days were " drawing in," as old ladies say, it was
advisable to make the utmost use of the daylight.
Accordingly, we rose and breakfasted before sunrise,
and the crisp grass, silvered over with hoar-frost,
crunched under the horses' feet as we drove off;
our small party being arranged in the roomy jaunting-car, drawn by a pair of horses driven tandem-
wise. A box and basket, well stored with materials

for luncheon, accompanied us, and also a servant
to take care of the horses. Away we went, first
through grass and turnip fields, and then bumping
over the tussocks on the sandbank, until we made
a descent on the glorious beach, where, on the broad
hard sands, our gallant steeds might put forth their
energies without a chorus of cries, deprecating the
bone-breaking jolts of an uneven road; and the
fine " nine-mile beach" was merrily and quickly
traversed.

The grand view before us, of the Schouten range,
grew more and more distinct and beautiful as we
advanced, and the sun rose higher. The moun-
tainous chain or group of the Schoutens is most
picturesquely composed; the mainland portion commences, next the mouth of Swan Port, in three
chief eminences, running nearly parallel east and
west; these are connected by a narrow isthmus of
low land running from their western side, with
another group of sublime bare granitic peaks,
trending to the south, and between which and the
triple mount, the bright blue waves of the Pacific
flow into " Wineglass Bay" ("Thouin's Bay" of
the published maps). A strait, called the " Schouten
Passage," separates these kindred crags from the

Schouten Island, which stretches away still farther south, its swelling heights and almost inaccessible rocky ranges crowned by a lofty dome-shaped mount, and its southern extremity ending in an abrupt precipitous bluff.

Beyond all these, we saw Maria Island, rising high and shadowy in the morning light, and the " White Rock " (" Isle des Phoques ") gleaming like the sail of a ship, as it caught the first sunbeams on its steep fort-like sides.

Behind us, the lower view had dwindled almost to insignificance; Swansea and the neighbouring little bays and points being almost lost; but above them were now seen ranges of the lofty mountain-tiers in the interior, clothed in the usual sombre hues of the forest, with the morning vapours still hanging round them in gauzy mists, or rolling upward, brightened by the early sunbeams.

On arriving at the mouth of Swan Port, we found a boat awaiting us, and quickly deserted our jaunting-car, leaving the groom to take care of the horses, whose comfort had also been cared for, and a good feed of corn carried with us for them to discuss in our absence. The cloaks and boxes being transferred to our new conveyance, we em-

barked to cross over to the " Old Fishery Bay,"
where one of Mr. G. Meredith's whaling stations
was formerly situated. The view up Swan Port
was now added to the grand mountain landscape I
have attempted to sketch, and most entirely I enjoyed the new and beautiful scene.

The sea here was so perfectly translucent, and
the white granite sand at the bottom so bright, that
on looking down, a whole world of strange and
exquisite things were clearly visible. We gazed
upon forests of broad-leaved trees of sea-weed,
their strong roots clasping the rocks some fathoms
below, and their thick round stems ascending
through the clear water to within a foot or two of
the surface, spreading forth their broad, long, grace-
fully-curved, slowly-waving leaves in perpetual un-
dulations, as if each were instinct with individual
life, and all blended together in a grave and gentle
dance. Among the leaves of these marine forests
glided bright, silver-glancing, filmy-finned fish, and
when we sailed past these, and came over portions
of the sand where no kelp grew, we saw gigantic
sea-stars, spreading their long arms out, purple and
red; and shells, and more fish, glancing and darting to and fro so temptingly that our party proposed

catching some; and in a moment three or four
hooks and lines were over the side, the boatmen
being well provided with such sea-stores. Before I
had watched one of them sink near the bottom, two
or three others were pulled up, with fine fish, of a
kind called here "Flat-heads," a name tolerably
descriptive of their form. The head is broad and
flat, the eyes prominent, and placed on the top; the
body narrows from thence to the tail, and is armed
with several strong sharp spines. So eagerly did
these poor flat-heads take the bait, that a dozen
might be seen hurrying to each hook as it was
lowered, and all the fishers had to do was, to drop
their lines and pull them up again. About ten
minutes thus employed served to furnish such an
abundant supply, that it was decided we should
not bestow any more time on the sport, and we
proceeded on our way.

The huge granite-cragged peaks seemed to rise
higher and higher as we neared them, and soon
entering a lovely little bay, sheltered on all sides
save the opening by wooded crags and glittering
granite rocks, the boat's keel grated along the snow-
white gravelly beach, and we landed at the " Old
Fishery." The beach was dazzlingly white. I sat

down on it, and, gathering up a handful of the shining gravel, found that it is pure white quartz, apparently the remaining portion of decomposed granite, the mica and felspar being washed away, and the disintegrated quartz thrown up on the smooth beach, like sand. The effect was most beautiful, and to me, strange; and the clear blue water rippling in gentle waves, and singing its soft murmuring music amongst the tiny pebbles, was so pleasant to eye and ear, that I had half forgotten the long scramble we had planned, when, all preliminary arrangements being made, I was aroused from my sea-dreams.

An old hut, the remains of a bread-oven, and other tokens of former habitants, would have given an air of desolation, as I think deserted human dwellings always do, to any place less beautiful; but all of nature was so bright and joyous, that I had not a shadow of the sentimental, even for the cold hearth of the crazy old hut. Numbers of whales' bones lay all around, both on the white beach—they rivalling it in whiteness—and among the grass and low shrubs above. A rivulet of pure fresh water gurgled down from the mountain at the back of the station, and its little still pools lay cool

and tempting, shaded over with acacias and other
lovely shrubs. We walked for awhile beside the
rivulet, crossing it from time to time to gain the
best path. Numbers of flowers were still in blossom,
the bright crimson *Epacris* being the most conspicuous, and my hands were soon full of them.

We now began to climb a rather steep ascent, our
purpose being to mount up between the western
and middle peaks of the Triad, and, from the top of
the gully, look over into Wineglass Bay and the
Pacific Ocean; so on we went, with high resolves
for the execution of the project. The gully varied
considerably in width, and often in the narrowest
places we found huge blocks of granite had tumbled
pell-mell into the gorge, some being as large as a
house, and from that size downwards; and when
the sides of the ravine were perpendicular cliffs, it
became a matter of some puzzle, considerable
difficulty, and still more amusement, to surmount
the barrier. Sometimes I could crawl beneath the
rocks, if they happened to tilt conveniently up at
one side, and then what stores of exquisite mosses
and lichens, and dainty delicate ferns, I detected in
their dim and cool bowers! Once or twice (whether
so inspired by the genius of the place that I began

to fancy myself something less material than I really am, I know not), in squeezing between two rocks that just left a tempting crevice, and so offered a chance of escaping a scramble over their tops, I became firmly jammed, and had begun to speculate on the pleasant prospect of starvation and death, and the matter for contemplation which my bones would furnish to some future discoverer, when by timely assistance, or the summing up of my whole remaining strength in one last struggle, I was extricated, and went toiling on.   The first few hundred yards so completely tired me that I felt as if I must give up the idea of reaching the top of the gully, and sat down, weary, breathless, and dispirited, on a log; but after resting for a few minutes, I seemed to gain new strength, and went on resolutely, clambering over rocks, logs, bushes, and briars, diving under huge boulders of granite all damp and mossy, and often shrinking in terror lest my foot should disturb some horrible venomous snake hidden amidst the thick beds of mingled living and decayed vegetation that filled up the lesser gullies and hollows.

I found that most singular and beautiful lichen, the *Cenomyce retispora*, spreading in large white

masses over the red granite rocks, adorning the
rough coarse stone with its elegant garb of fine and
delicate lace.   It is white and thin, and perforated
all over with small regular apertures, like plain
Valenciennes lace, gathered and plaited and puckered
up in all conceivable diversity of turns and twists,
so as to form a pretty close mass, like an assemblage
of baby's cap-borders all pressed together, and
growing about as high from the rock as the width
of those same little trimmings.   There is a kind of
coral found on the Tasmanian beaches so like this
lichen, that I must suppose the sea-nymphs and
fairies have modelled them both in some trial of
skill; but I am quite unable to decide which party
must have been deemed victorious, both specimens
of Nature's fancy-work are so exquisitely wrought.

The ferns, too—the green and graceful ferns—
how beautiful they were!   Besides the common
brake, and a kind of hart's-tongue, very similar
to those of England, I gathered one or two kinds
of maiden-hair, one like the *Adiantum capillus
Veneris,* but much larger than the English species,
the stem taller, and the pinnules larger, but their
slender hair-like foot-stalks as delicate as my
fragile little favourite at home.   Other ferns had

broad fronds like the hart's-tongue of England, with
similar fructification, and one species was quite new
to me, nor can I find any botanical description
answering to it in Loudon's " Encyclopædia of
Plants," that invaluable and rarely-failing lexicon.
The stem of my new fern is thin, smooth, and
erect, from ten to fifteen inches high, with two
forked stalks branching off from its top.   The
pinnæ which proceed from them on each side are
long, very narrow, and of a very dark green.   The
sori extend in two rows of small round spots down
the under side of the pinnules; and the upper side,
which is only the width of the impression raised by
the sori, has the appearance of being formed of two
rows of very small green beads, which diminish to
points at the narrow end.   This is but a clumsy
portrait, yet I cannot sketch it better in words; and
although I gathered many specimens, they withered
and dried up before I reached home, my tin box
not forming a part of our preparations.

The perfect distinctness of the echoes here was a
source of much amusement to us; our names,
called loudly, seemed to be taken up by choruses of
airy voices shouting back the words.   I never
before heard my Christian name arranged with so

many variations. A hearty laugh roused a most unearthly supernatural peal of repetitions; each mossy stone of the cliffs and peaks above us appeared to give out its own independent voice, and then they all echoed each other, till the very air seemed vibrating with mirth; and then, after we had again and again repeated our laughing chorus, I suggested how grand it would be to have a cannon fired in this enchanted glen!—and Mr. Meredith tried his fowling-piece as the best substitute at hand. The report was taken up and prolonged into a peal of thunder, and when the loud near echoes ceased, the far-off crags and caves rolled forth upon the air continued reverberations, sometimes pausing for a moment, and then swelling out again, as though the mountain genii were too deeply outraged by our presumption to forget or forgive it; and as each told the angry tale, others carried it away to repeat it again and again.

Our rough scramble up this wild gully was amply rewarded when we reached the top, and, resting on a fantastic perch of rocks and roots of trees, I had time to look calmly about me and enjoy the splendid view.

On either side of the ravine rose the towering summits of the mountain, bare masses of granite heaped up on high like giant altars, or rising abruptly from belts of shrubs and trees, like ancient fortress walls and turrets. But the downward and onward view was like enchantment! Far below my giddy perch (from which to the sea-level the steep craggy side of the mountain was fringed with a various growth of forest trees and shrubs) lay, calmly slumbering in the bright sunshine, that blue and beautiful nook of the Pacific named Wineglass Bay. We could see the silvery circles of the tide break on the white beach, but only a most attentive ear could at that height detect the low whispering sound they made. Beyond the beach, a green grassy slope ran back to the foot of the mountains, which rose majestically to an altitude of many hundred feet, their lower and less steep portions clothed with forests, and their bare lofty conical peaks pointing to the clouds; countless points and promontories stretched out into the bay, some crowned with fantastic rocks that looked like forts and castles ; these continued one beyond another, into the clear blue distance, where one little island stood alone, as if to mark the union of the fairy bay with the broad, bright, blue Pacific.

I could scarcely draw at all for looking at the glorious scene, and the few minutes that could be allowed for my attempt were gone all too soon, and we began our downward progress, wherein the stumbling and scrambling of the ascent were repeated with liberal interest; and heated, tired, and thirsty, we again looked lovingly into the rivulet's shady pools, and scooped up the water to drink.

On reaching the beach where we had landed, we found that the boatmen had made for us a nice dining-pavilion in a shady nook, among some myrtle and honeysuckle trees, the boat-sail being cleverly converted into a tent, open at one side, and the cloth laid on the grass beneath, whilst joints of whale's vertebræ, white and smooth and clean, were placed round for seats;—what could be more appropriate at the " Old Fishery?"—and our chickens and ham, rabbit-pie, tarts, fruit, cider, and wine, rendered doubly good by our well-earned appetites, received the ample justice they deserved.

After our pleasant repast, I wandered round the nearest point to another beach, seeking shells, but found very few, the pebbly gravel apparently grinding them in pieces as they are thrown up.

The day was fast closing when we sailed back to the mouth of Swan Port, and very soon after the jaunting-car had again taken in its passengers, the sun set, but the horses cantered gaily along; the " song-voiced " of our little party occasionally " rousing the night-owl with a catch," as we rolled over the smooth hard sands. We were compelled to walk over the sandbank for safety, it being impossible for the driver to avoid the holes and great tussocks at night; and so dark was it, that I had some difficulty in groping my way after my more active companions. The lights gleaming from the windows at home proved a welcome beacon to the weary party, and our pleasant day's wandering closed without the most trivial drawback to our enjoyment; indeed, for a long time I marked the day of our Schouten expedition as the whitest day in my calendar since leaving England; and my good husband, to whom the glorious mountains have been familiar from boyhood, made a charming plan for taking us the next summer in a boat, with proper appliances and means for a sojourn, such as a tent, mattress, blankets, kettle, tin plates and pannicans,

tea, sugar, bread, and shooting, fishing, and sketching tackle, and so go coasting round about the
picturesque Schoutens, landing wherever fancy led
us, and leading a week or two of gipsy-life;
but I am sorry to say this pleasant castle in
the air never advanced beyond the ground plan,
although for several succeeding summers we promised ourselves that the *next* should certainly see
our project realized.

CHAPTER IX.

Swan Port Conchology.—Peculiarly-formed Arca.—Banks of Oyster-
Shells.—Living Oysters.—Sea-Hares.—Land Shells.—Mutton Fish.
—Beauty-Snails.—A Volute.—Corallines.—Star-Fish.—Sponges.

THE fine broad sandy beach near Cambria was a
constant source of delight to me, for although our
wanderings had led us over the sea and near the
sea perpetually, yet I had not until now enjoyed a
sea-side ramble for years, and many a long morning
I idled pleasantly away in sauntering on the "Long
Beach," which stretches from the Meredith River to
the mouth of Swan Port: this was my favourite
haunt, and a most deceptive one too, for often when
I thought we had only rambled a very moderate
distance, and turned to retrace our steps, it seemed
as if those smooth tantalizing sands were interminable; and the few landmarks telling us the
whereabouts of our goal, the "creek," beside which
lay our path from the beach to the house, appeared
to recede as we approached them. The grand range

of the Schoutens, the distant Maria Island, and the
little fort-like promontory of Swansea in the foreground, often enlivened by the arrival or departure
of small coasting vessels in the beautiful bay, made
a picture that no one could very quickly weary of,
and to me it was always charming, and always
wearing some new phase of beauty.

Many of the shells we found were familiar to me,
my kind relatives here having years ago supplied my
cabinet at home with specimens of the greater portion; but the pleasure of picking them up myself in
this nook of the world which I had formerly so little
dreamed of visiting in person, was by no means a
contemptible gratification, and as one day after
another brought some new representative of my old
treasures before me, I became tenfold more interested in the quest. I found that both live and
dead shells of some two or three kinds would be
thrown up in considerable numbers for some days,
or even weeks, and then perhaps months would
elapse without the same species being seen at all,
or but very rarely; but by this nice distribution we
had always some kinds in season.

As the collections of shells I made at Swan Port
contained a tolerable variety, perhaps an enumera-

tion of them may be interesting, although my knowledge of conchology is too limited to enable me to
determine often more than the genera.

Serpula, one species, very commonly found in
small masses of multitudes of little intertwisted
white-ribbed tubes, but not containing the living
worms.

Spirorbis, on leaves of algæ.

Pholas papyracea, and, I believe, *P. dactylus*,
but only dead shells.

Solen ensis, fresh and perfect shells, not alive.

Panopœa, Glycimeris, dead shells.

*Anatina rostrata; Tellina radiata; Tellinides.
Donax*, a small species.

Astarte Danmoniensis, and others; one species
of Astarte being a large white, heavy, orbicular shell,
with the ridges fine as hair, smooth and close.

Cyprina, Cytherea, and *Venus*, many species;
one of the latter very beautiful, from one to two
inches broad, and with four or five broad up-turned
projecting ridges, fringed beneath like the fur of a
mushroom, and lengthening posteriorly into curved
spines, from a quarter to three quarters of an inch
in length. These were the most beautiful bivalve
shells I found, and they were very rare; their colour

was usually white, with the fringe-linings of the ridges a delicate blush pink. I used to compare them to a lady's "drawn" silk bonnet, but we very seldom indeed found them perfect, the long spines and fragile edges of the shell being generally worn and eroded even whilst living.

At one time patches of the sand were nearly covered with quantities of the fine milk-white *Cardium*, which I used to prize so much in my collection, that I was almost involuntarily careful so to tread as not to crush the gracefully heart-shaped shells.

In this same collection I had also many single valves of a small *Arca* of peculiar form, one end being rounded, and the other elongated to a point (something like *Pandora rostrata*), the hinge consisting of numerous fine teeth. We constantly found single valves on the beach, but sought in vain for a live or entire shell, until one day, whilst idly picking to pieces a lump of zoophytic sea-stuff that had been washed up amidst kelp and sponges, I found some of the oft-sought little shells imbedded in it alive; but only a few rewarded my subsequent searches for them, although I pursued the quest most industriously.

I sometimes have found old water-worn valves of a larger Arca (*Bysso-arca Noæ*, I think), and valves of a *Pectunculus* occur in like manner.

A large chestnut-brown *Modiola*, of a peculiar form, and from three to four inches long, was among our most prized shells, not being often found entire. I think it is nearly the same shell as the largest of those figured as Date Muscles, from Brazil, in Murray's "Encyclopædia of Geography."

Multitudinous colonies of the small dark blue muscle covered the rocks left exposed at low water, and clusters of a larger common kind were continually washed up.

Quantities of a small, transparent, and most fragile species of *Avicula* were repeatedly strewn over the sands; these were most delicate pellucid little shells, like the thinnest glass, or *crisp* goldbeater's skin, tinged with nicely-pencilled shades of green, brown, olive, and red; but I never found one with a fish in it, and delicate indeed must be the denizens of such dainty domiciles; pill-boxes fitted up with cotton, wool, and cambric paper, were all too coarse to preserve them.

A few small live *Pectens* (the common scallop shell), with the upper valve flat, and the lower one

concave, most beautifully and variously marked
with fine colours, were the chief objects of our
search for a week or two, and then came such shoals
of them, both large and small, that a whole nation
of scallops must have been suddenly up-turned on
the beach, nearly all alive; and, as a natural consequence of their abundance, they greatly diminished in value. The fish within was firm, white,
and well-flavoured, when boiled, but the quantity of
sand which had washed into them could not wholly
be got rid of, and prevented the otherwise nice fish
from being palatable.

Oysters, at Oyster Bay, may well be supposed
abundant, although they are not often obtained for
the table. Enormous quantities of dead shells are
found, forming large banks, forty feet high, on two
low isthmuses, one of which unites the two groups
of the Schouten Mountains, and the other joins the
northernmost of these with the mainland. Similar
banks are also found at Little Swan Port. These
prodigious accumulations of oyster-shells appear
inexhaustible, and are very useful as lime; the
coasting vessels often bring cargoes of them across
to Swansea, where they are sold to the settlers at
sixpence a bushel. Large oyster-beds still exist

in the bay, exactly opposite to the shell-banks, and
after high winds, both live and dead shells are
thrown up on the two former of the shell-banks,
but not on any other beach in the vicinity. This
having doubtless been the case for centuries, the
aboriginal inhabitants would be accustomed to resort
thither for the oysters, and very probably added to
the shells thus naturally collected, by procuring the
oysters also from the beds themselves, which they
could easily do, having rude bark-rafts or cata-
marans, and being, like most savages, expert divers.
They would naturally convey the oysters to the
nearest shore for the purpose of eating them, and
this being in both cases the adjacent shelly beach,
the banks there would gain perpetual additions from
their ample repasts. This process, continuing perhaps for ages, is too obvious an assisting cause to
be entirely passed over, although the still-continued
increase of the banks, from shells now continually
thrown up, furnishes ample reason for the surprising
accumulation. In dredging for oysters upon the
sea-beds, the proportion of dead to live shells
brought up was as ten to one, leaving the profit a
very inadequate return for the labour bestowed.

The rafts used by the aborigines of this island

must be placed in the lowest class of such fabrics, even as the people themselves were the lowest of the human species. They were formed of many little bundles of gum-tree bark, tied with grass, first separately, and then bound together in the required form, thick and flat, without any attempt at the shape of a boat or canoe, and not keeping the passenger above water when used, but just serving to float him on the surface. In, or rather *on*, these, the natives sat and paddled about with long sticks, or drifted before the wind and tide; and in calm weather frequently crossed over from the mainland to Maria Island; but on such occasions they provided a little raised platform on the raft, on which they carried some lighted fuel to kindle their fire when they arrived there.

In Little Swan Port beds of living oysters now exist, and on the adjacent shore are high banks of shells, similar to those I have mentioned; but there is no surf or "wash" in the still waters of this estuary, to cast up shells, so that unless the one kind of "natives" consumed the other to such an extent as to account for the accumulation, the banks must have been up-raised from the sea.

In Prosser's River, another estuary, farther south,

are beds of live oysters, but in this instance they are unaccompanied by the usual shore banks of dead shells.

At " East Bay Neck," a low isthmus between Tasman's Peninsula and the mainland, large banks of cockle-shells occur, in the same manner as those of oysters at Swan Port, at about four or five yards above high-water mark, and are now overgrown with grass and rushes.

At " Piccaninny Point," a small rocky promontory on the east coast, immense quantities of dead cockle-shells are constantly thrown up after a gale; ship-loads might sometimes be collected, but no accumulation can take place, as they are quickly broken by the action of the waves among the rocks.

In Port Sorell, on the north coast, wide tracts of sand laid bare at low water are full of dead shells, chiefly a small species of cockle (*Venus* ——), which furnish the only kind of lime used in the district, the shells being partially cleared from the sand previously to burning them.

I am not aware if these little facts are worth recording for aught beyond the evidence they afford of considerable and geologically recent changes having occurred in many parts of the

Tasmanian coast; the shells in all the banks named being recent species, identical with the live ones near them. Now, to return to the Swan Port shells, from which I have rambled too far.

Several kinds of *Patella* were very common, one large species having rich lustre-like rays, when held in a particular light; and a very delicate *Infundibulum* I sometimes found perfect, but much more frequently broken, being exceedingly fragile and thin. An *Emarginula*, and a small species of *Fissurella*, I also found, but these rarely.

Several of those strange-looking slugs called sea hares (*Aplysia?*) were at one time thrown on the beach, and I obtained the internal shells of two; these were very thin and horny, and, when dried, shrank to half their original size, which was about an inch and a half long by an inch broad, thickened at one side. The slugs themselves were four or five inches long, nearly black, and marked somewhat like a leech, very thick and solid; but too little life remained in them, when found, to revive in the water, though I immediately carried them to a little pool in the rocks, hoping to see them perfectly recover.

The only land shells I have seen in this colony

are two species of *Achatina*, or possibly old and young specimens of the same shell; the largest about an inch and a quarter long, brown, with two bands of white; the others very similar, but much less.

Mr. Meredith one day brought me a piece of peat-like earth, from a drain that was being dug, not far from the sea, which was full of small fresh-water shells of various species. Many of them, such as *Planorbis, Lymnæa, Paludina,* and *Cyclas,* were identical with those of English brooks and pools, and with living specimens now inhabiting those of Tasmania, but so minute, that out of a little boxful of earth (a " percussion-cap" box) I could have picked some hundreds of perfect shells, and the ground whence it came was equally full for a great distance; it seemed one mass of these fragile little shells nicely packed, with the finest and smallest vegetable fibres all amongst them, holding the whole together. As fresh-water lagoons formerly occupied a large space in the immediate vicinity of this shelly peat, the only puzzle I find in the matter is the absence of all larger shells.

I have found individuals of a kind of *Sigaretus*, which I cannot identify by any description I have, although they may very probably not be new species.

The *Haliotis* is much better known here. Dead, but very perfect shells of *H. rubra* were frequently thrown up on the beach; some, five or six inches across, and from that size, in various gradations, down to the delicate little young ones, not larger than a small bean, all splendidly irridescent within, unless injured by a marine worm, which seems particularly partial to shells of a pearly substance. It must have been one of these delicate little pearly ones which first suggested their common name of "Venus's ear," so nicely curled over, so thin and transparent; but the colonists, sad matter-of-fact people that they are! who utilitarianize everything, and attach some vulgar work-day sort of association to all of the sublime or beautiful that they approach, have bestowed on the creature of the rainbow-tinted pearly mansion, the equivocal appellation of "Mutton-fish," and this with as little reason or propriety as they have shown in most other instances of the kind, for the animal of the *Haliotis* is scarcely eatable under any circumstances; at least it possesses about as much claim to be ranked among things cookable or edible as did the old boots which we are told some of our gallant explorers have been fain to attack in the extremity of their Polar starvation. Such was the quality of one I tried to taste, that, whilst a leather glove or a piece of India rubber remains to me, *I* will not ask for a mutton fish! They are found alive on the rocks in from one to five fathoms water, and adhere so strongly that it requires some dexterity, and a very strong knife, inserted in a peculiar manner, to detach the fish from the rock.

A handsome *Trochus*, of a light-brown colour, and slightly rough with many small tubercles, was occasionally found; and various species of *Turbo* abounded. Some of these, rejoicing in the ancient name of Periwinkles, were, when boiled, pronounced very nice by some of our party; but they looked too green and caterpillarish, and had too strong a fishy sea-weedy sort of flavour, to find favour with my palate.

The lovely *Phasianellæ*, or Beauty - Snails, abounded on these beaches, and by the infinitely varying patterns of their markings and colours almost baffled my endeavours to find two alike. Some were white, spirally circled round by delicate but well-defined bands, ribands rather, of pale red, diminishing to microscopic smallness of touch as they reached the apex of the shell: but the more general colours were all kinds of brown, red, and olive, blended together in beautiful patterns, some being, it would seem, a careful imitation of Scotch plaids and ginghams, so accurately and regularly is the design painted by the poor little short-lived architect; the same pattern being continued and repeated in the same shell, from the apex to the mouth, gradually expanding in size. I am not acquainted with any other shell which displays such great diversity of markings as this. The outer lip is so thin, that even in live shells it is scarcely ever found quite perfect. Their size varies from one to two and a half inches in length, the largest being by far the most rare.

A shell, similar in form to the *Phasianella*, but rather more slender, and never occurring so large as the former, is still unknown to me by name. The exterior is smooth, usually brown, and highly polished, with fine wavy or diagonal lines of white; but within, it is grooved, pearly, and highly irridescent; more richly tinged with the exquisite blue and green of the prismatic colours, than any other shell I am acquainted with. Possibly it is a *Turbo;* but it seems almost too long and slender to belong to that round, portly, corpulent family.

A large *Fasciolaria*, a *Fusus*, *Triton cutaceus*, and a common kind of *Murex*, we also found, and two species of *Cassis:* one somewhat similar to *C. erinaceus*, but more inflated, and the recurving outer lip marbled with touches of deep brown on the buff ground colour of the shell. Some of these are two inches long, and nearly as much broad. The other species of *Cassis* is considerably less, and thicker, with a smooth thickened outer lip, and small puckers or tubercles on the upper part of the larger whorl. The colour of these shells is various; some being a pale buff, others a shaded chestnut brown, and some nearly black.

A pretty little white *Columbella*, common here, used to be much collected by the female aborigines, for making necklaces; some of which were several yards long, formed of these little shells neatly bored, and strung closely on kangaroo sinews, and were worn by their sable owners twisted many times round the neck, and hanging low over the breast.

The shell which used to be hailed with the cry
of greatest triumph at its capture, was a *Volute;* a
fine, smooth, heavy, important-looking shell, which
made the smaller fry in our baskets comparatively
insignificant.   Its usual size was about three inches
or more in length, by about one and a half in
breadth ; its colour a pale buff or nankin colour,
and this softly clouded with dim purple, and
marked most singularly with fine brown zig-zag
lines forming deep points and angles ; the sym-
metry and connection of these delicate, yet bold
and distinct pencillings being most curious.   The
inner part of the shell, which has three plaits on
the columella, is of a deeper shade of buff, and
the whole shell is finely polished and very ornamental.   I have in England seen a figure of it,
or one very similar, in the coloured plates of
a conchological work ; but the artist evidently
had not enjoyed my good fortune in seeing perfect and live shells, for it was a very sorry portrait of my favourite.   The animal itself bears the
same colours and marking as its shell, but even
brighter.

Cypræa castanea was not unfrequently found ;
and a pretty buff-coloured *Ancillaria* was one of

H 2

the commonest shells in the collections I used to receive from this place years ago, although when rambling on the beaches myself, I did not frequently find it.

One species of Cone was all we had to represent that splendid family; nor was this one a very brilliant specimen, being usually small, from one to two inches long, of a dull ash colour, irregularly clouded with reddish brown.

I think I have now enumerated all the shells, or very nearly so, which are found at Swan Port. In addition to shells, several beautiful kinds of corallines were frequently thrown up in great quantities; but, after becoming dry, my "treasures of the deep" in this department always fell to pieces, from, as I imagined, the drying-up of the slender animal threads which passed through and connected the joints during life. Some of these corallines were snow-white, others tinged with pink or green, and all most delicate and beautiful; one might fancy that the tricksy sea-sprites had been trying to model some of our upper-world moss and joint grasses with the sculpturesque materials of their ocean caves.

Several species of *Echinus*, too, visited us occa-

sionally, the commonest being brown and nearly
globular, with short thin spines. Another kind, less
often found, was of a flatter shape, from one and
a half to three inches across, greenish or purple in
colour, and covered with strong pointed quill-like
spines half an inch long. The third and rarest
species closely resembled the *Echinus mammillatus*
(fossil) of the English chalk formation in the
general form and the large tubercles on the shell;
the spines were large shelly tubes, the size of a
wheat straw, sometimes an inch long, and the same
thickness from end to end, moving upon the
tubercles as on a pivot.

Some of the Star-fish here were gigantic, many
measuring above a foot across; great, thick, solid,
slimy, long-armed creatures, that I found most
difficult to preserve (from the quantity of moist
animal matter they contained), unless when they
had been thoroughly sun-dried on the warm sands.
These had eight or ten arms each; other smaller
species had only five, and one kind had no arms at
all, but was in form a pentagon or hexagon, with
the points protruding but very slightly; the whole
covered on both sides with shelly plates and
tubercles, and, when freshly caught, of brilliant

colours, orange, scarlet, and purple, and varying in size from one inch across to two or three.

The sponges too, which I frequently found, were very singular; sometimes a great mass of porous, prickly, slimy stuff lay upon the beach, glowing in the most vivid scarlet hue that can be imagined; and when I first saw these fiery appearances, I used to hasten towards them, wondering what new prize awaited me. One day, having carried a thick rolled pudding-shaped mass home, in hopes of preserving it in its brilliant colour, I took it to the fresh water to wash and squeeze out the slimy matter, and whilst so employed a severe sensation of prickly tingling and stinging attacked my hands, which became red and inflamed, and the symptoms rapidly extended up my arms. A young relative who was helping me suffered in a similar manner, and we felt rather apprehensive as to the consequences of our experiment; but fortunately the discomfort of feeling for a day or two as if we had been stung by nettles, was the only ill result we experienced; and I have never since attempted to take such liberties with the red rolled pudding sponges. Indeed, my adventure with this individual sponge reminded me very forcibly of Miss Edgeworth's story of Rosamond and the blue jar; for the splendid colour that had so dazzled me seemed to reside wholly in that very slimy stuff I had taken such pains to squeeze out, and when that was gone, and my sponge dry, it was merely a dull brown!

CHAPTER X.

Our New Home of "Riversdale."—Colonial Housewifery.—Female
Servants.—Progress at Spring Vale.—A Dead-wood Fence.—
Buildings. — Site and Plans. — Materials. — Timber. — Lightwood
Tree.—Stone.—Clearing Fields.—Green Marshes.—Honeysuckle
Tree.—Wattle Tree.—Brushy Pine.

FOR some time our own future destination remained
uncertain, until it was at length arranged that Mr.
Meredith should purchase a small estate of about
1200 acres, situated seven miles inland, north of
Cambria, and adjoining, or rather forming, one
corner of the Meredith estate.   The situation of
"Spring Vale" had won our admiration, although
as yet the land remained in a state of nature, and
required a great outlay of money and labour to
render it habitable or profitable.

In May, 1841, we temporarily set up our vagrant
household gods in a house then vacant at Riversdale, which, being within three miles of Spring Vale,
formed a convenient abode for us during the erection

of our own cottage.   Once again I was busily and pleasantly occupied in making a new place look as much like an old home as possible.   The favourite pictures of dear old faces soon peopled the strange walls with loved familiar looks.   The rooms were large and good, and though at first not too amply furnished, had a cheerful and cosy aspect.   Our little pet soon after our removal began to trot about, and the sweet little voice, as musical as a bird's, that went humming and carolling from room to room, was, to parental ears, a sound that would make any spot charming.

And now began my real experience of colonial housewifery and its attendant troubles, although these did not prove very distressing, and nearly all originated in servants; but, as I dislike hearing my neighbours' long narratives of their domestics' delinquencies, I shall not inflict a very minute detail of my individual sufferings upon my own kind friends.   Prisoner women servants are generally of a far lower grade than the men, and at the time of which I now write, Mrs. Bowden had not begun her admirable reformatory work among them.   My first prisoner nurse-girl was taken at random by our agent in Hobarton, from among the herd of incor-

rigibles in the female house of correction, or
"Factory," as it is termed; and was indeed a
notable example:—*dirty*, beyond all imagining!
she drank rum, smoked tobacco, swore awfully, and
was in all respects the lowest specimen of woman-
kind I ever had the sorrow to behold. Before I
had time to procure another, she drank herself into
violent fits, so that four men could not hold her
from knocking herself against the walls and floor,
then went to the hospital, and, finally, got married!

Various fortune attended me after this memorable
beginning, but I never had such signal ill-luck
again, and we have usually kept our female servants
longer than most other families; and when they
have left us, marriage has been the usual cause.
One, a Highland girl, I, in my too charitable innocence, believed to be really good, virtuous, and
honest, and truly repentant of her former misdeeds:
she was a kind nurse to our little boy, and a cheerful obliging servant; she remained with us six
months, professing the most devoted gratitude for
our kindness to her, when, during an illness which
confined me to my bed, she took from beneath my
pillow the key of the store, and, with the assistance
of the groom, drank and otherwise disposed of some

six or eight dozens of wine and spirits. The effects
of such extensive libations being soon evident, the
worthy pair were dismissed, the maid being sen-
tenced to six months' hard labour at the "wash-
tubs" in the Factory, and the man to a "chain-
gang" on the roads for two years. My housemaid
was at the time in the "cells," suffering fourteen
days' solitary imprisonment (or, as they term it,
"*doing solitary*"), for striking her fellow-servant,
the nurse. She returned afterwards much improved,
and remained with us until she married. The successor of my hopeful Highland protégé was a
short, clever, brisk, good-tempered Yorkshire
woman, who stayed with us a year and a half, and
then married comfortably. With such chances and
changes progressed my new household; but I have
never since detected any act of dishonesty in one of
our servants, though all have been prisoners. The
offices of "cook" and "kitchen-maid" are here
generally filled by men, as cutting wood and carrying water we considered to be too laborious for
women.

Mr. Meredith meanwhile was indefatigably industrious in the improvement and civilization of
our new place, "Spring Vale"—so named from the

bright springs of pure water rising in the low lands. Early after breakfast every morning, often in winter while the stars were yet shining in the sky, my husband rode or walked up from Riversdale to direct and assist in the work going on, nor returned to dinner until late in the evening; so that my days would have been very lonely, had I not had my dear little boy to cheer them. Still, these were days full of pleasant hopefulness, and we looked forward with great delight to the completion of our plans, and our final removal to our own snug home—the home in which we purposed to live quietly through the remaining years of our sojourn on this side of the globe.

But much had to be done even before the house could be begun. Wheat was still ten shillings the bushel (the price during the famine in New South Wales had been twenty-six shillings the bushel), and we needed to have some of our own for the next year's consumption and seed; May was nearly gone, and the next February must see our first little crop ready for the sickle, on land which as yet plough had never broken, and which was heavily timbered with large gum-trees. To clear the ground was the first thing to be done: oxen and implements were purchased, and men hired to fell the trees, grub up the roots, and cut the ponderous trunks and branches into lengths to form a "dead-wood fence," that is, a mass of timber four or five feet thick, and five or six high, the lower part being formed of the enormous trunks of trees, cut into logs six or eight feet long, laid side by side, and the upper portion consisting of the smaller branches skilfully laid over, or stuck down and intertwisted.

A very old ruinous shepherd's hut served, when patched up, for some of the labourers to live in, until the new stone one could be built, and when this was finished, the old stonemason was to commence our cottage. I believe that a large proportion of the stone and brick buildings both in and around Swan Port are the work of the same man—one of those thin, wiry, withered, erect old people who look just the same for forty years together, never were known to look young, and never seem to grow a month older; at all events, I can see no difference in our old friend of the trowel since he first began chipping the ironstone and dabbing the mortar about in our service, nine years ago, although, when he began working for us,

I well remember feeling some misgivings as to his living long enough to finish even the first building.

We had often visited and carefully noted the relative advantages of several sites for our cottage, before making our final selection, as we wished it to be sheltered from the prevailing high winds, near the fresh water, and at no great distance from the public road, which passed through our land, the shape of which was triangular. A rocky range of high hills, or " the Tier," as it is generally termed, forms the northern boundary; the " Swan," or " Big River," the eastern; and the " Cygnet," or " Brushy" River, the western; these two uniting at the south point. We finally decided on placing our house on a rocky bank facing the south-east, at the foot of which we purposed having our garden, whilst the stabling and outhouses would occupy the higher level ground behind the house.

I made innumerable plans, each seeming to me in its turn perfectly unexceptionable, until my husband, with his awful precision of compasses and calculation of "ways and means," ranged in array against me, proved one after another their impracticability. At last a partnership plan was concocted, to our mutual satisfaction, combining comfort and economy with a sufficient regard for appearance; and materials requisite for its completion were carefully calculated and ordered. Some of these consisted of what is here technically termed " sawed stuff" and " split stuff," by which is meant timber which is *sawn* into regular forms and thicknesses, as flooring boards, joists, battens, &c., and that which is *split* into " posts and rails," slabs, or paling. Some of the species of *Eucalyptus*, or gum-trees, are peculiarly adapted for splitting. The peppermint-tree (*Eucalyptus piperita*) and the " Stringy Bark" are remarkable for the perfectly straight grain which they often exhibit, and are split with surprising evenness and regularity into paling and boards for " weather-boarding" houses and other purposes, in lengths of six or eight feet by one foot wide, and half or one-third of an inch thick. The great height to which the trees grow before the branches begin, leaves a large space free from knots or twists of any kind; any curve in a tree renders it unfit for splitting, but the crooked-grained wood is best for sawing, being less liable to split whilst being worked or nailed. All houses in the colony, with few exceptions, are roofed with split shingles. The species of gum-trees called

"iron-bark" and "stringy-bark" are extremely
hard, and, when well planed and polished, bear
some resemblance to oak, and are much and
successfully used in colonial shipbuilding; but the
cedar of New South Wales, and the "Lightwood"
or "Blackwood" (*Acacia melanoxylon*) are used
here for all the ornamental parts of house-fittings,
and, when nicely finished and polished, are equal in
appearance to mahogany, giving a far neater aspect
to a room than the painted doors, wainscots, and
window-frames used in middle-class houses in
England. The lightwood is a harder and more
closely grained wood than the cedar; it is also
more finely marked, and is capable of a more perfect polish. When growing, it is generally a very
handsome tree, and the dense foliage affords a better
shade than most other Tasmanian forest trees.
It commonly attains the height of thirty or forty
feet, but in moist sheltered mountain gullies very
far exceeds that size. I have seen some upwards
of a hundred feet high. The leaves are a long
oval in shape, of a dry dim texture, alike on both
sides, longitudinally veined, without any distinct
midrib, and are of a yellow green colour, which,
with the round, compact, lumpish form of the tree,

gives it a slightly oak-like character in the distant
landscape, to the beauty of which a group, or a few
single lightwood trees, are a valuable addition.
The bark, too, is rough and compact, more like the
trees of the Old World than the riband-stripping
smooth white trunks of the gum-trees. The little
round blossoms of palest yellow, which in spring
come out all over the tree, give a soft fresh bloomy
aspect to its evergreen garb, and perfume the air
with their hawthorn scent; when near an apiary,
they are ever "musical with bees," and seem to
yield the busy little creatures an ample store both
of wax and honey. One singularly handsome tree
of this kind we marked for preservation, amidst the
doomed throng of less eligible residents on the piece
of scrub and forest destined to become our garden.

The walls of our cottage were to be built of the
common "iron-stone" of the country, quarried from
the bank where it was to stand, the cleavage of
which very conveniently separates it into flat slabs
of all sizes and thicknesses, suitable for rough
stone buildings; and, when well fitted and cemented
together, and neatly faced with cut freestone at
all the corners, door and window cases, &c., it
makes a most substantial fabric. Our outer

walls were twenty inches thick, and the inner ones eighteen.

The grove of wattle-trees speedily disappeared from the bank, around the growing cottage, except ing a few handsome groups or single trees reserved for ornament; and the various details of quarrying, burning shells into lime, sawing, and carting, all went briskly on.

The first field being once cleared, fenced, ploughed, and sown, other land underwent the same trans- formation. I often vainly interceded for the life of some noble tree, which, as its tall kindred fell all around it, looked so grand and ornamental, and so pleasing an object in the general clearance, that I would gladly have preserved it; but the harbour which trees in the middle of fields afford to the opossums, and the destructive, but most beautiful, little parrots which abound here, was always urged against me, and the death-doom was rarely averted, even by my most eloquent pleading: still, both our lovely rivers being skirted by forest land and fine belts of trees, besides the numbers which adorned the unploughed marsh and sheep-run, amply re- deemed our pretty spot from the charge of bareness, usually so well merited by colonial farms.

Each time that I rode or walked up from Riversdale, some evident improvement was visible, in
clearing, fencing, draining, or building; and, as
spring advanced, the sheep and cattle feeding in the
deep, long, green grass of the marshes, and the
pretty little soft white lambs skipping about, looked
like a bit of England. How beautiful were our
broad deep drains, with bright cold water bubbling
up in them from countless springs, and flowing
generously along in a never-failing stream! And
how often we used to stand in our green meadows,
looking into them, and talking of the dry and
parched ground of our homes at Homebush and
Bathurst, as a kind of additional zest to our keen
enjoyment of the inestimable blessings of a temperate climate and abundance of pure water!

Perhaps my use of the common colonial term
" marsh " may be misunderstood at home, as I
remember that I myself associated it at first with
the idea of a swamp; but a " marsh" here is what
would in England be called a meadow, with this
difference, that in our marshes, until partially
drained, a growth of tea-trees (*Leptospermum*) and
rushes in some measure encumbers them; but, after
a short time, these die off, and are trampled down,

and a thick sward of verdant grass covers the
whole extent: such is our "marsh"—a fine meadow
of 180 or 200 acres, and green in the driest season.
The open forest land skirts it on all sides, except
where fenced corn-fields intervene, so that the horses
and cattle live most luxuriously, in sunshine or
shade, as they like best, as in many parts of the
"scrub" are groups of honeysuckle-trees, so dense
that even rain can scarcely penetrate them.

The honeysuckle-tree (*Banksia latifolia*) is so
unreasonably named, that I must not pass it by
without a remark; nor have I quite forgiven it for
disappointing me by being so *very* unlike any sort or
species of the sweet old flower whose name it so un-
fittingly bears.   I cannot remember any Old-World
tree to which I can in any way compare it: it might
be pretty well represented by one of the tall muff-
like grenadier's caps, set on a stick; the latter being
the short trunk, and the cap the dark; thick, solid-
looking foliage of the tree. The leaves are rather
small, and generally of a dull rusty olive-green,
except when the young spring shoots cast a gleam
of fresher colour over the sombre mass. The
blossoms form cones, which, when in full bloom, are
much the size and shape of a large English teazel,

and are of a greenish yellow; they are scentless, until the pollen is shed, when a faint odour, not particularly pleasant, is just perceptible; but birds and insects seem to discover honey in them. The honeysuckle trees grow to about thirty feet in height, and often form fine groups in the open landscape, as, when several grow together, their formal outline is not preserved, and in hot weather they are valuable, from the dense shade they afford. The wood is of a singularly fibrous texture, and is used to make "knees" in boat-building and some other purposes, but is not very much prized for fire-wood; for the latter purpose, wattle (*Acacia*) and shroak (*Casuarina*) are most valued, and many of the gum-tree woods burn well and brightly.

I have never seen the lovely common wattles grow so luxuriantly, or form such ornamental trees and groves, as at Spring Vale; and I often thought, if I could give a sly rub to Aladdin's glorious old lamp, and order the obedient Genii to transport some of the graceful golden-fringed trees into certain pretty gardens and shrubberies at home, how enraptured the beholders would be! Nothing can be more beautiful than some of them; tall and elegant, from twenty to forty feet high, thick with their

delicate "sensitive plant" foliage, feathery and
pendulous; and covered, from the very summit to
the branches that bend and sweep the ground, with
the bright canary-coloured blossoms. Canopies and
roofs of gold and jewels, such as dazzled our fancy
in old fairy-tales, are no longer fables, when, pushing
aside some heavy down-bending bough, we creep
beneath, and stand within the natural bower of one
of these exquisite trees in full bloom.

A very beautiful species of pine, or rather, I
imagine, a cypress, grows in and near the river-beds
here, in great abundance and luxuriance, varying
from nine to twenty-five feet in height; I know not
its proper name, but here it is called "the brushy
pine." It forms a perfect cone of verdure, narrow-
ing to a point at the top, the deep rich green being
sometimes tinged with a bluish shade, almost like
the bloom on a grape. Not a portion of the stem
is visible in a well-grown tree of this kind; but the
whole is a compact mass of foliage, more perfect in
form than the most accurately-clipped box or yew
of an antique garden, and necessarily far more
beautiful, from such being the natural shape, with
the slender terminal sprays all uninjured. The
cones are small, and clustered together in brown

knobs or bunches close to the branches. Plants are entirely raised from seed, which grow well in moist and shady situations. Our river banks are in many places absolute groves of these very handsome trees, of all ages and heights; but most beautiful when, as is frequently the case, they form nice family groups of one, two, or more tall middle-aged trees, with a rising generation of symmetrical young cones clustered around them.

WEEPING GUM-TREES AND OLD FORGE.

CHAPTER XI.

Home Occupations.—The "Weeping Gum" Tree.—Household Duties.
—Society. — Snakes. — Quail. — Wattle-Birds. — Walks. —Wild
Flowers.—Acacias.—"Wattling."—Parasite Creepers.—Native
Mistletoe.—Clematis.—Comesperma.—A "Dry Path."—The First
Stack.—Melancholy Accident.—Losses.

THE spring and summer of 1841-2 wore away,
and our home was progressing, but much too slowly
for our wishes; for it may well be believed how
eager we were to remove thither, and put an end to
the weary daily travel to and fro, and my long
lonely days away from all that interested me, save
my children, for we had now two.

Sometimes I added to my little collection of portraits of the pretty native flowers, or improved myself in sketching gum-trees, which I found demanded far greater care in their delineation, even in my slight pencil sketches, than I had at first been disposed to accord them: a gaunt straggling tree, that will persist in showing all its twisted elbows, and bare Briarean arms, with only tufts of leaves at the fingers' ends, is quite a different affair from a round compact oak or elm, decently apparelled in a proper quantity of foliage. A kind of *Eucalyptus*, with long drooping leaves, called the "Weeping Gum," is the most elegant of the family, and is generally very well dressed. A group of these, which gracefully drooped over and beside a blacksmith's forge, near us, always won my admiration as I passed them on my way to Spring Vale, where some of the *Eucalyptus* trees growing on the rich lowlands are really very beautiful, and would be deemed so even amidst the magnificent patriarchal oaks of an English park; large, lofty, with dense glossy foliage, and finely grown, they have more the character of a Portugal laurel grown into a forest tree, than anything else I remember at Home.

Sometimes, but very rarely, we were so fortunate as to obtain the loan of a new book, and great was the delight of such an acquisition, for our reading was usually limited to the old familiar volumes of our own small library, and the English newspapers, with which the kindness of our home friends supplied us. The regular transmission of the wise and witty "Examiner" has been a source of great enjoyment to us in our exile, and serves to keep us comparatively acquainted with the doings of the civilized world. Reviews of charming books that one cannot procure, and notices of glorious pictures that one will never see, are truly often provoking enough; but yet it is pleasant to receive such renewed proofs that the great and good of the Old World are still labouring in their vocation for the delight of millions who, more fortunate than ourselves in this particular, can and do enjoy in reality what we now but dimly imagine.

Sometimes in the summer we joined the pic-nic parties from Cambria; and sometimes, after exhausting my small store of the simple airs and merry old tunes—my husband's favourites—that I could play from memory, I resolutely dived among my old music books, loaded the piano-desk, and filled up an evening with somewhat lame revivals of the strains of other, although not happier, days; but all these were indulgences in my usual sewing, nursing, housekeeping life.

At first I found the business of the store-room the most novel of my household duties, and the weekly or semi-weekly distribution of rations the least pleasant of them, as, besides our own hired farm-servants—who of course received their supplies from us—there were the sawyers, stonemasons, carpenters, drainers, and fencers, all of whom we had to supply with flower, meat, tea, sugar, salt, soap, tobacco and "slops" (*i. e.*, shirts, trowsers, jackets, &c.); so that accurate accounts must be kept, and I confess I did not much admire this indispensable huckster's shop affair, the business of which also included the giving out materials for the building and articles for farm use, such as nails of all kinds, rope, files, glass, glue, oil, paint, whiting, turpentine, blankets, bed-tick, rugs, wine, and other commodities; but all this is (or rather was at the time in question) a matter of course in a settler's establishment.

Several small coasting vessels find continual employment in the trade between Swan Port and

Hobarton, in conveying the settler's produce to the town, and bringing back the supplies they require. The land transit being all but impracticable for a cart, no goods are conveyed by it, except when some adventurous hawker succeeds in forcing his weary horses across the mountain barrier; and everything we require, from a cask of wine or ton of sugar, down to a sheet of pins or a pair of gloves, must be brought by water to Swansea, and thence home in our carts*.

Our circle of society at Swan Port was limited to two or three individuals beyond our own family, although the population of the district is numerically large, and comprises many industrious and thriving settlers, who were our very good and respected neighbours, and whose neat well-conducted farms are examples to most other rural districts in the island. We had no inducement to go from our home, except to our father's; and of course family visitings to and fro formed a regular and very pleasant part of our weekly duties.

* Since the above was written, the little settlement of Swansea has so far increased in importance, that two good stores of the "general" class are now established there, and appear to carry on a considerable trade in grocery, drapery, ironmongery, haberdashery, confectionary, crockery, glass, timber,. slop clothing, ale, porter, salt beef and other provisions, flour, and *et ceteras* infinite.

The quantity of snakes which were destroyed at Spring Vale during this summer was truly alarming ; scarcely a day passed without Mr. Meredith's telling me on his return home that one, two, or more had been killed by himself or the men. One day he had gone out rabbit-shooting there with Dr. Alexander (28th Regiment), then visiting us, accompanied by our old pointer and a favourite spaniel. The latter, whilst hunting busily about, suddenly uttered a short yelp, as if slightly hurt, and the next moment Dr. A. shot a large black snake, which it was found had bitten her in the nose; so that excision of the part was impossible. The poor little creature went on hunting for a few minutes, when she seemed to grow dizzy, and reeled about ; then lay down, trying several times to get up and hunt, but very soon she became violently convulsed and sick, then foamed at the mouth, and died in less than twenty-five minutes from the time she was bitten.

A short time previously to this, Mr. Meredith was on the jury at an inquest held on a poor shepherd, servant to a settler in the neighbourhood, who, whilst out one day with some of his employer's family, saw a large black snake raising itself to

attack him, and made a blow at it with a rotten
stick, which broke off short, and the snake, enraged
but not hurt, bit his wrist.   No remedies were
attempted, but the poor fellow continued his occupation, till, feeling too ill to proceed, he went to a
hut in the neighbourhood, where one of his fellow-
servants lived, who was married.   These good
people did all that their kind feeling suggested, or
their means allowed, for his comfort; they laid him
in their only bed, and set up tending him all night,
but he became rapidly worse and insensible, and
early in the morning died.

Such terrible evidence of the black snake's
mortal venom was not calculated to diminish my
horror of the whole fearful tribe, and often in walking through long tussock grass or low scrub I
have shrunk aghast, as my foot fell on some round
stick, or a rustling in the dead leaves came with a
boding sound upon my ear.

One day as I sat at home sewing, with my eldest
child playing about on the floor, our favourite cat
jumped in through an open window, and began
pawing and tossing something under a chair.
Little George immediately went towards her, and
seemed highly diverted, crawling nearer and nearer,

and trying with his baby-talk to attract my attention to his playfellow: looking down, I saw what I supposed to be a lizard, and being vexed with the cat for hurting the harmless little thing, drove her away, when, to my horror, there lay a snake, writhing and curling most actively; so, holding the child and the cat both away, I ordered the unwelcome guest to be very summarily despatched.

So many "narrow escapes" from snakes are related here, that the comparative rarity of serious accidents is perhaps the most remarkable. Whilst at Cambria, my nursemaid, a free girl from London, who had never seen a snake, was one day crossing the court-yard with the child in her arms, when she saw what she fancied was a large eel gliding along; and, calling to the cook that one of his fish had got away, was on the point of seizing it in her hand, when the man screamed out to her that it was a snake, and so indeed it was, a very large one. They are apparently fond of lurking in quiet sly corners near the house, perhaps for the purpose of catching mice; and, to their other unpleasant propensities, I must add a *penchant* for quail. Mr. Meredith, in walking to Spring Vale one day, was passing quickly through some

long tussock grass, and saw a large black snake
swiftly and silently gliding along, with its glittering
eyes fixed on some low object which it seemed
eagerly pursuing, without heeding his approach.
The next moment he saw a brace of quail run out
from the spot and take wing, but the snake had
vanished before he could pick up a stick to destroy
it. I heard the other day, from good authority, of
a snake which was killed having four parrots
quite entire, and scarcely ruffled in plumage, taken
from its stomach; the parrots in question being,
it should be added, each about the size of a thrush.

The quail, the sole representative here, save the
rarely-coming migratory snipe, of the delicious
game of the Old World, is a delicate little bird
about half the size of the partridge, with somewhat
similar beautiful brown plumage, but they are not
generally numerous.

The wattle birds (*Anthochœra* —— ?) are a
less rare delicacy, and I now think them very nice,
although their flavour is too peculiar to be wholly
liked at first. They are extremely pretty; about
the size of a blackbird; the back plumage is dark
gray, tipped with white, with a long tail of the
same colours; the under part is lighter, with a

bright shade of amber on the breast, and a tinge of the same colour blending in other parts with the gray. The graceful head is adorned with a pair of long pendant ear-drops or "wattles," formed of a bright orange-coloured bag like membrane, about an inch and a half long, and a quarter of an inch, or rather more, in width, pale in colour next the head, but deepening at the end to the hue of the *Ecremocarpus* blossoms. These, as the active merry birds dance about the branches, and twist their heads in all kinds of elegant arch coquettish attitudes, remind me of the long gold earrings of some pretty, vain, fine lady. Their common note seems to be four or five syllables of some unknown, rather guttural, language, which I have in vain tried to pronounce, so cannot be expected to spell, but it sounds something like "cockaty-rucki! cockaty-rucki!" Their tongue is very long, and, being divided at the end like a thin hair pencil, is well adapted for extracting the honey from the *Eucalyptus* blossoms which forms their chief food, and their flavour partakes very strongly of the powerful aromatic property of the trees. The wattle-birds are not always equally plentiful, but about one year in three they positively abound.

Mr. Meredith used sometimes to go out before breakfast, and in a few minutes shoot a dozen within fifty yards of the house. When plucked, they are found, if in proper condition, to be enveloped in a thick layer of yellow fat, and in roasting amply "baste" themselves. They are dressed entire, the same as woodcocks, and form a valuable addition to the country bill of fare, which cannot generally be accused of having too much variety.

The house of Riversdale, which we now occupied, being, with the adjacent water-mill and other buildings, the centre of a large agricultural farm, I had not many nice wild-wood walks near home. The road leading to Spring Vale, which for the first mile passed over a sandy forest tract, was my favourite, as the "Bush" on either side afforded abundance of wild flowers. In spring several kinds of white *Epacris* came out in bloom, and the shrubs, bearing different sorts of yellow pea-blossoms, abounded: some richly tinged and veined with scarlet or brown, their foliage, consisting of little more than bare green spines, as difficult to gather as gorse itself; others had leaves spined at each point, whilst many more were rather less repulsive in their manners, yet without being very inviting.

A more amiable family were the Acacias, or, as
called here, "wattles," so named originally, I
conceive, from several of the genus being much
used for "wattling" fences or huts. A "wattle and
dab" hut is formed, in a somewhat Robinson
Crusoe style, of stout stakes driven well into the
ground, and thickly interlaced with the tough lithe
wattle-branches, so as to make a strong basket-
work, which is then dabbed and plastered over on
both sides with tenacious clay, mortar, and, finally,
thatched. I have also heard of a refractory wife
being occasionally subjected by her liege lord to a
process of "wattling," but this I imagine implies
an application of the acacia boughs of a totally
different nature to that above described, although, as
I have been assured, it proves, in some cases,
singularly efficacious. All the acacias bear pretty,
soft, yellow fringe-blossoms; but it were needless to
describe them minutely, as, long even ere I left
England, the species most common here were to be
found in every greenhouse or conservatory.

One almost microscopic white flower (*Leucopogon* ——), growing on a low shrub, was very
beautiful when closely examined, each tiny petal,
scarcely the size of a small pin's head, being

exquisitely fringed with short white filaments. The bright geranium-coloured *Kennedia prostrata* crept along the ground, its rusty olive-green trifid leaves being seldom noticed until, on stooping to pick up the glowing little pea-flower, we found out the far-spread net-work of stems and leaves belonging to it.

The gay clustering wattle blossoms were, whilst they lasted, my usual substitute for the dear buttercups and daisies that fill little hands at Home. There was, certainly, a thin, lanky-looking, white Aster, which I tried to call a daisy, and the *Richea glauca*, with its round yellow ball of florets, I often gathered for my little boy, completing his small handful with the really pretty Australian hare-bell, as blue as his own sunny eyes, and the gay wild pink convolvulus, not brighter than his cheeks; but even these seemed sorry substitutes for the dear old cowslips and primroses, buttercups and daisies, woodbines and foxgloves, and the thousand and one sweet and lovely flowers that English country children revel in.

The low bushes of a small species of *Casuarina*, that grew beside my oft-traversed path to Spring Vale, were tenanted by a curious kind of parasitic plant; and I bestowed upon it sundry minute investigations, in the vain hope of discovering its name and family connections. Its multitudinous, slender, thread-like stems, ravelled, and twisted, and woven together in hopeless entanglement, spreading over, and round, and through the casuarina bushes, were always traceable to one small disc or foot, fastened to a branch, smaller discs being attached at intervals, to other limbs of the victim, until the devouring little climber reached the summit of the bush, and spread abroad its slight tendril arms to lay hold of some loftier support. The stems were seldom thicker than sewing cotton, and destitute of leaves, but very minute white starry flowers, less than small pins' heads, made microscopic constellations all amongst the mazy coil, and were duly succeeded by little, long, oval-shaped berries, about one-fifth of an inch long. I have seen several species of this kind of native parasite since, but all are of a much larger description, covering trees of moderate height so entirely as to hide and destroy them, and causing them to present a most strange and often grotesque appearance; these creepers have stems like thick cord or rope, twisted and knotted strongly together, and so tough as with some difficulty to be cut or broken. They are nearly, if not quite, destitute of foliage, and bear round berries, like those of the bryony at Home, sometimes as large as good grapes. Some persons, with more approach to reason than most of the colonial terms can boast, have named these plants "native mistletoe."

One of the loveliest climbing plants of this, or indeed of any other country, is the native Clematis (*C. blanda*), which joins to a luxuriant growth of handsome foliage the most abundant and graceful display of blossoms that I have seen in any of the beautiful tribe. The flowers are large and quite white, growing in full handsome clusters, thickly placed, and making the most exquisite garlands imaginable, when a single stem can be culled by itself; but in its lavish and luxuriant wild growth, it spreads over the near bushes, trees, or ferns, in such a rich close mass of clustering flowers and intertwisted leaves, that I have often found it easier to gather a mat large enough for a mantle than to disentangle a wreath for George's little straw hat. The scent, too, is very delicious, and the starry heads of feathery seeds in autumn are only less beautiful than the summer flowers.

A dwarf species of clematis (*C. gentianoides*) grew plentifully on a stony hill between Riversdale and Spring Vale, reminding me pleasantly of the pretty little white wood anemone of England. The single white flowers, on stems five or six inches high, appear on small roots with bright green leaves; they are very delicate and fragrant, and would probably improve or become double by culture.

Once, as we were driving to Cambria, I saw at a short distance from the road what seemed to me a bright blue silk handkerchief spread over a tall shrub, and, on alighting to investigate the mystery, discovered, for the first time, my now familiar friend, the most beautiful Comesperma (*C. volubilis*), whose exquisite gleaming blossoms formed a perfect cover to the bush they had climbed over. The small winged flowers are produced in such abundance, that the green stems scarcely show at all, merely forming an intertwisted and netted groundwork for the dainty broidery of living sapphires which they support. Often, when I have gathered chaplets of this most exquisite creeper, I have wished I could transfer them to the glossy hair of some of my dear young countrywomen, and displace their mimic coronals of cambric and wire with my bright flowers of the wild wood. The chief use I have put them to has been to adorn my baby's caps; and between the lace-borders, one or two slender tendrils of comesperma, covered with blossoms, excelled all the ribbon that ever was woven.

The summer of this year was particularly dry, and most of the watercourses were empty, save here and there where deep pools occurred in their stony beds. One day a slight shower had fallen, and I was hesitating whether it were wise for us to go for our usual walk, as the long reedy leaves of the cutting grass, and other plants, hold the moisture, and might wet our feet; when a young relative, then visiting us, earnestly exclaimed—" Oh ! but *I* know where we can have a delightful walk, if we go down the lane, and then turn and go up the bed of the river; it is sure to be nice and dry there ! "

Truly, thought I, we *are* at the Antipodes !

Sheep-shearing in November, hot midsummer weather at Christmas, the bed of a river the driest walk, and corn harvest in February, were things strangely at variance with my Old-World notions. The result of our first harvest from thirteen acres was highly satisfactory, and I went up to see the little wheat-stack, and surveyed it on all sides with more real genuine pleasure than those twenty times its size have given me since.

The satisfaction with which we urged on our works of improvement at Spring Vale was at this time sadly checked by the distressing and sudden death of a worthy man, formerly a prisoner, who had for many years been a good industrious servant in the family, and was now employed with others in "grubbing" a piece of new land which was heavily timbered. One of the ponderous trees, of eight or nine feet girth was, in the usual way, severed from its main supports by a great trench being dug round the foot of the tree, and the roots chopped through; the huge trunk was just ready to fall, and Mr. Meredith, who was there observing the work, saw it giving way, and called to the men to jump out of the trench, which they did, and were all perfectly safe; but this one poor fellow, although an "old hand" at such labour, in some strange confusion of mind, stepped back again, exactly under the falling tree, which, gaining rapid impetus as it came, fell, before there was a chance of snatching him from destruction, and the whole ponderous mass

crushed him to death instantaneously. The tree
was sawn through on either side as quickly as possible, and the unfortunate man's body extricated, but
life must have become extinct in the very moment
of the frightful accident.

The comparative rarity of such terrible calamities
in new countries where "clearing" is perpetually
going on, is even more remarkable than their occasional occurrence; but the imprudence of persons
who pursue these needful but certainly dangerous
tasks, alone, is a wilful risk of life. Not long ago
we heard of a horrible instance of this. A poor industrious man went from home one morning, as
usual, to the piece of ground he was clearing at
some distance; but, on his not returning at night,
his wife supposed he had gone on some business he
had to attend to a few miles off, and no alarm was
felt about him until the lapse of several days, when,
on a search being made, his dead body was found
on his own clearing, with one leg broken by a heavy
tree which had fallen on it. The poor creature had
evidently made the most desperate efforts to extri-
cate himself; his hands and face were torn and
lacerated, and the broken leg almost dragged off in
his attempts to get free, but all had been in vain:

he must have died in a state of agony, starvation, and despair, absolutely frightful to imagine; whilst if a fellow labourer had been near to saw the tree through, all, save the fracture of the leg, would have been avoided.

Many disheartening reports of the disastrous state of affairs in New South Wales had reached us since we came to Van Diemen's Land, and the non-appearance of various sums of money in rents, bills, &c., which were falling due to us, supplied unpleasing corroboration of the rumours; but we were totally unprepared for the discovery which now overwhelmed us—that some of the insolvencies in Sydney involved the loss of all we owned in that colony. Until now the thought of returning to England in the course of ten or twelve years had abode with us like a pleasant, although rather distant, prospect, which Hope's telescopic vision ever brought nearer and more distinctly before us; but at this cruel blow the fairy-picture shrank and faded away into the smallest and dimmest shadow of its former self, and ever since Hope seems to show it to us only through the wrong end of the telescope!

CHAPTER XII.

The Aborigines of Van Diemen's Land.—Their First Murders of the Settlers.—" Mosquito."—Murders at Swan Port.—The Murderers chased.—A Native Shot dead.—Warning by Native Women.— Murder of Robert Gay.—Native Woman wounded.—John Raynor.—Attack on Buxton's Cottage.—Burning and Murders near Jericho.—Murder of the Hooper Family.—Murders at St. Paul's Plains.—Erroneous Impressions.—Aborigines Removed.

EVEN in so slight a description of a new country as mine is, some notice of the aboriginal inhabitants may naturally be expected; and although from personal observations I know nothing respecting them, Mr. Meredith's long and disastrous experience of their character and habits enables me to give some particulars, which may possibly tend to a more correct estimate being entertained at Home of the strife so long existing between them and the colonists.

Seven or eight years before my arrival in this colony, the aborigines had been removed to Flinder's Island in Bass Straits, where large and comfortable dwellings were erected for them, and they were well clothed, fed, and instructed at the expense of the Colonial Government, under the care of a resident medical superintendent, until the year 1847, when his Excellency Sir W. T. Denison, our present lieutenant-governor, imagining that they might be rendered more happy, and be more efficiently superintended here, caused those remaining to be brought again to the colony, and a new establishment has been accordingly formed on the west shore of D'Entrecasteaux' channel, where they now are. Of the charitable and humane feelings which actuated Sir W. Denison, but one opinion can be entertained. How far he was justified in gratifying them by making this change is a separate question, as the colonists, especially those who had formerly suffered such fearful experience of the aboriginal ferocity and cruelty, were strenuously opposed to the measure—on the grounds that every adult man among the natives had been actively engaged in many, some of them in hundreds, of most brutal and unprovoked murders, and that in all probability a return to their old haunts would lead to a renewal of the horrors which, since their removal, have been unknown, but which in former years rendered a residence in the colony one long series of alarms, suffering, and loss, with the daily imminent peril of a frightful death.

Mr. Meredith's experience of the habits and deeds of the aborigines extends over many years, and from the notes he has made for me, and our frequent conversations on the subject, I shall compile this chapter as nearly as possible in his own words. Many a time, contrary to our usual primitive country hours, has midnight found us still seated by our glowing hearth; I intent on hearing, and he relating the horrors, and terrors, and hairbreadth escapes of his younger days in the colony, when every bush within spear-throw of the house was a source of danger, and to stir beyond the door-sill unarmed was nothing short of *felo de se*. The plain relation of easily-proved matters of fact may perhaps tend to dissipate erroneous ideas as to the original enmity between the settlers and the aborigines, who for some years after the colonization of the island lived peaceably together, the natives visiting the houses and stations of the colonists in the same amicable manner as the blacks in New South Wales do now—coming and going as it pleased them—" camping " near to the homes of the white people, with the free consent of the latter—receiving presents of food and other things, and not manifesting any jealous or angry feelings.

In considering this subject it should also be borne in mind who and what the early " settlers " were. They were neither pirates nor robbers, as were many of the early dwellers in and usurpers of new countries in days of yore; but British farmers and country gentlemen, not usually considered a desperately ferocious and blood-thirsty class, nor by any means disposed to commence hostilities against quiet unoffending people, such as the Tasmanian aborigines originally appeared; but purposing to till their ground and feed their sheep without injury or molestation to the natives, both parties being at that time so few in number, that the quantity of land occupied by the English, and partially thinned of the wild animals useful to the blacks, was comparatively speaking so small, as not to be felt by them as a deprivation, even had they not gained rather than lost by the change, in the food given them by the settlers. No murderous propensities displayed themselves until the arrival amongst them of a notable leader in crime and cruelty, under whose guidance they committed their first open murder; and ever after they seemed to hunger and thirst after the lives of the colonists, whom they persecuted and killed with relentless and unquenchable ferocity, as the few instances I shall cite, out of many more that I could enumerate, will sufficiently prove. The following passages I quote either from Mr. Meredith's own notes, written at my request, or from my own transcriptions of his narratives as related to me.

" Considerable error prevails with respect to the cause of the hostility between the aborigines of this island and the white population, the general impression being that it arose in consequence of unprovoked acts of aggression and violence on the part of the whites, than which nothing can be further from the truth. The deadly enmity exhibited by the natives, through a series of years, towards the colonists and their servants was, in the first instance, unprovoked by the white population. I remember distinctly the first act of violence of that long and fearful tragedy—it was perpetrated by the natives, under the direction of ' Mosquito,' a native of Sydney, who had been tried there for the cruel murder of a white woman. By an act of mistaken humanity on the part of the Sydney Government, Mosquito was reprieved from the gallows, and sent to this island, where he was set at liberty, and suffered to roam about unmolested. At first the natives here showed some jealousy towards him, but they ultimately became friendly, and gave him a gin, or wife, named ' Gooseberry.' Mosquito generally divided his time between them and the white people, roaming the bush with them in the summer, and living during the winter in Hobarton, usually called ' the camp,' in those days. Constant friendly intercourse took place between the two races until November, 1823, when the Oyster Bay tribe, having Mosquito at their head, committed a cool and unprovoked murder at the stock station of Mr. Sylas Gatehouse, at Grindstone Bay, on the east coast.

" Three men were at the station at the time, John Radford, and Mormer (a native of Otaheite), Mr. Gatehouse's servants, and Holyoake, a servant of my father's, who had been for some time in the colonial hospital in Hobarton, and, being pronounced convalescent, was on his way to his master's house; but having travelled about sixty miles, and being still in a weak state of health, he was staying at this hut a few days to rest, being still thirty miles from home. A short time ago, whilst on my way to town, I passed the night at the public-house which is kept by Radford, at Little Swan Port. I then took down from his lips the following account of the whole affair:—

" 'In November, 1823, I was in charge of stock for Mr. Gatehouse. One Thursday morning a party of blacks came to the hut, with Mosquito as chief. He brought me a tin pot from a deserted hut in my charge, as he said, *lest any of the black fellows should steal it*. They encamped at Grindstone Bay, and remained quiet until the Saturday after. In the mean time, Mosquito came into our hut, and got Holyoake to shave him. The tribe consisted of about seventy-five, and until Saturday morning they all employed themselves as usual, in hunting, fishing, &c. On Saturday morning they were having a corrobbory, dancing and singing. Holyoake, Mormer, and I went to the sheep-yards to part some sheep; whilst there, Mosquito called to Mormer to join him on the opposite side of the creek, and Mormer went over to him. When we were thus divided, the natives

that were on the same side of the creek as we were
picked up their spears*, and moved towards the
hut; those on the other side doing the same.
During this movement, Holyoake and myself stood
between the natives and the hut, to which we
hastened, and arrived first, when, missing our guns,
I called to Mormer to ask if he had removed the
guns, as they were not there. He said " No," and
hurried towards the hut, being then about fifty
yards from it, the natives following him. These
movements brought us all together at the hut, on
one side of which was a deep creek; on another
side was a brush fence; and on the third stood the
natives, with a space of ten yards left clear, through
which was our only chance of escape, as it was
now plain to us that they meant mischief, and were
trying to close in the open space. We had some
valuable kangaroo dogs, and seeing Mosquito
loosing them, I called out to him, " Don't take our
dogs away!" His reply was, " I shall do as I like,
now." We all then made a run; as I was passing

---

* The aborigines, when they wished to appear unarmed, had a
habit of walking without any weapon in their hands, but very
adroitly trailing their spears, which they held fast by their toes,
along the ground after them, to be picked up at any moment they
were required.

K 2

the corner of the fence, Black Jack speared me in the side. After the start I never saw Mormer again; he must have been killed at once. I continued running for seven or eight hundred yards, when I stopped to pull my boots off; I then saw Holyoake within fifty yards of me: he called to me to " pull a spear out of him." I returned and pulled out the spear, but whilst doing so, received another in my thigh, which I pulled out, and we ran together; I often waiting for Holyoake. We ran thus for some six hundred yards, when the blacks overtook Holyoake, and some passed him, running after me. The last I saw of Holyoake, he was standing throwing sticks and stones to try to keep the natives off. Seeing I could be of no service to him, I used my speed to save my own life, and succeeded in escaping. It was the first time I ever knew of an encounter between the blacks and whites, and I had been living amongst them then for three years. I believe their sole motive for the attack was the plunder of the hut. A man named John Kemp had been killed at Grindstone Bay previously to our occupying the station, which was in 1821. This man lived by himself, in charge of the provisions and stores of a sealing party, who, on their return, found him dead, with spear-wounds in his body, and the stores all stolen.'

" Radford was chased about three miles by the natives, and made his way to another stock station at Prosser's Plains, distant about twenty-five miles from the scene of the murder.   Thence the intelligence was conveyed to Mr. Gatehouse, who lived at Pittwater, and he at once proceeded with a body of armed men in chase of the natives, to avenge the murder of his servant.

" The natives in the mean time moved on towards the north, and reached my father's residence, where, as the late murder was unknown, their appearance created no alarm.   Mosquito, who spoke tolerable English, came to our house and said he understood the governor had given Mr. Meredith the land thereabouts, and requested permission to encamp on it, promising that neither he nor any of his tribe would frighten the cattle or commit any damage.   Permission was given, and the tribe remained encamped within two hundred yards of my father's house for six or seven days, when they departed, and went about two miles farther, to the house of Mr. Talbot, who then lived at Oyster Bay, where the like favour was sought by Mosquito, and permission to encamp was given by Mr. Talbot's overseer.

" On the same evening, Mr. Gatehouse and his armed party arrived in pursuit, but so eager was he to take vengeance for the death of his servant, that he gave orders to ' fire ' before he was within gun-shot of the blacks, and although all the guns were loaded with buck-shot, not a single native was killed, nor do I believe one was wounded. On the first discharge of the guns, the natives plunged into a lagoon, on the banks of which they were en-camped, and by diving and swimming alternately, reached the opposite bank, and escaped, with only the loss of their weapons (consisting of spears and waddies) and the chief of their dogs. After this the tribe separated into two parties, one of which attacked Mosquito and wounded him severely, after which he came alone to the house of a settler near us; and, although the murder was then well known, he was suffered to go away unmolested.

" I have been somewhat minute in the detail of this transaction, because it was in fact the com-mencement and the cause of that deadly feud that ever after existed between the natives and the white people on this side of the island; the former murdering numbers of the latter, both old and young, male and female, with indiscriminate fury, and, owing to their extreme cunning, activity, and stealthy cat-like nature, retaliation was all but impossible. I know of only *one* instance, in which a native lost his life by the hands of a white man; the occasion was this:—my father had lost three horses, and two men were dispatched to look for them. During their search, they fell in with a tribe of natives, who instantly gave chase; one of our servants was armed with a pistol, and the other with a gun. The natives ran in two lines, one on either side of the men, with the view of surrounding them, and when parallel with them, began throwing their spears. The man who had the pistol then cocked it, and pulled the trigger, but it missed fire; on this the natives yelled, and ran with increased energy, calling to each other to close the lines, and surround their victims; at this juncture the man who had the gun fired at the foremost native, and shot him dead; the others ran to their fallen companion, and our men escaped, being then within 600 yards of a farm-house, where they were reinforced by the farmer's sons.

and returned to the place where the black was shot. The other natives had dragged his body into a hollow tree, and covered it with dead wood, but none of them were then to be seen. To complete my story, I should add, that the horses were all found, but two of them were dead, one having thirteen spears in its body, and the other only one; but that one had penetrated the heart.

" I do not dwell on the above solitary instance of the death of a native by the hands of white men, with the view of inducing any one to believe that the colonists would not have retaliated more frequently if they could. The natives, under the guidance of Mosquito, commenced and carried on what they intended should prove a war of extermination, both of man and beast. They spared neither age nor sex; the aged woman and the helpless child alike fell victims to their ferocity; and the feelings of the whites towards them in consequence may easily be imagined. For a space of some months, during which time I noted down their proceedings, the number of murders of white people which came to my knowledge *averaged eight a week;* and many doubtless occurred which I never heard of.

" In several instances, the lives of white people were saved by the native women, who would often steal away from the tribe, and give notice of an intended attack.   On one occasion one of our boat's crews had landed for the night on the shore of Great Swan Port, made their preparations for supper, and lighted a fire, when two native women came stealthily to them, warning them to hurry away, as the tribe was hidden behind the nearest bank, only waiting till the moon rose to make a descent upon them.   Accordingly, the men hastily gathered up their paraphernalia, and decamped to their boat, but had scarcely pushed out into deep water before they saw the enemy come stealing down, one black figure after another gliding past their fire, evidently with the intention of surrounding them.

" The disappearance of all the young children among the natives compels us to the inference that they were destroyed; doubtless on account of the difficulty of conveying them about in the rapid flights from place to place which the blacks now practised in the perpetration of their murders.   No white people ever found or killed any children that I am aware of, and few after this time were seen with the tribes; the dreadful conclusion seems therefore unavoidable.

" Colonel, now Sir George, Arthur, arrived here as lieutenant-governor in 1824, shortly after the first murders, and my father immediately proposed to him plans for the conciliation and temporary coercion of the natives, warning him that unless some effectual means were at once adopted, the murderous habits of the latter would for a time be fearfully destructive to the colonists, and eventually cause their own extermination. The advice was disregarded, but the result verified its wisdom.

" It will suffice to mention here two or three from among the many fatal outrages committed by the blacks in our immediate neighbourhood. After the murder at Grindstone Bay, the natives remained quiet for some months, and people had begun to recover from their suspicions and dread of them, when they murdered another of our servants. Two of my father's stock-keepers, Robert Gay and David Raynor, lived together in a hut near the head of Moulting Bay*, in Swan Port, Gay being

* Moulting Bay, so named from the number of black swans which formerly frequented it in the *moulting* season, is amusingly enough marked on some modern maps as " *Port Moultan*."

in charge of the place.   One morning, in the winter
of 1824, Raynor rode out after cattle, purposing
to remain out all night, but from some cause he
changed his plans, and returned home in the
evening.   On approaching the hut, he was surprised that the dogs did not come out barking as
usual, and, thinking that his mate had very imprudently left home and gone hunting in his absence, rode up to the door somewhat angrily, when
he found some kangaroo-skins, which were always
kept inside, scattered about.   On entering, he
found the hut in great disorder, and the stores
of food, &c., all gone.   Then, looking round, he
saw numbers of prints of naked feet, showing
that many persons, male and female, had been
trampling about, and being by this time convinced that the natives had been there, he grew
alarmed, and rode off again to the next station,
reporting the circumstance.   This was near the
farm of Mr. John Amos, who, with a party of
armed men, went with Raynor to his hut the
following morning.   Poor Gay's foot-prints were
soon distinguished, as he had worn boots, whilst
the blacks' feet (traces of which there were many,
evidently in pursuit of him) were naked.   About

four hundred yards from the hut was a creek, in which the body of Gay was found, covered over with sticks; on being drawn out, many spear-wounds were discovered, and one spear remained in one of the feet, having been driven through his thick boot-sole into the foot; but for this one spear he might probably have escaped, being a very swift runner, and this fatal weapon must have struck him when flying at full speed from his murderers. All his finger-joints were broken, and the body brutally mutilated, according to the usual custom of the blacks, when not hurried or disturbed in their deeds of horror. Everything, of any value, that the hut had contained was stolen—stores, dogs, all were gone, and not a native was to be seen or heard of in the neighbourhood.

"This same David Raynor had another narrow escape some years after. He was coming home on horseback, driving wild cattle near the Apsley River, and not a native was in sight, when two spears, thrown at him, gave the first intimation of their vicinity; one struck into the thick padding of the saddle behind his leg, and the other carried off the red woollen sailor's cap he wore, and pinned it to the side of a bullock in the herd at some distance beyond. Raynor then rode for his life, and the terrified cattle flew in all directions; but some short time after the bullock, which he had described as being speared, was found with a deep spear-wound in the side, then nearly healed.

" Within a fortnight from the time of Gay's murder, the same tribe went to my father's whaling-station at the mouth of Swan Port; they hailed the boats, and the men took them in, and, thinking they would gain some reward for capturing the murderous savages, pulled across the bay homewards, and then kept the native party, consisting of six men and four or five women, for two or three days, intending to send them by a vessel to the governor; but, whilst arrangements were being made for conveying them safely and unharmed on board, they effected an escape—some ran one way, some another, and pursuit was vain; but one of the women was slightly hurt in the confusion, and rushed into the sea, where she swam and dived for some time, before she could be induced to come ashore. Her wound was carefully dressed by a surgeon who chanced to have arrived, and considerable anxiety was entertained lest it should prove worse than it then seemed; a bed was made up for her in a warm hut, and she was finally left for the night. Early in the morning the hut was visited, to see how the patient fared; but, though the door had been closed and fastened, the chimney had not, and up it the dark lady had gone.

" John Raynor, another of three brothers, all in my father's service, was one morning out hunting, and, about nine o'clock, sat busily skinning a kangaroo which his dogs had just caught, when suddenly the animals yelled, as they always did whenever they saw or scented the blacks, and, on looking round, he perceived some of them near him. He jumped up and ran, but instantly received two spears, one in his breast, which he pulled out readily, and another in his back, which he wrenched at, and broke off short. He still ran as fast as he could, until, coming to a large log, he tripped, and fell over it in such a manner as to conceal him, for he knew nothing more, until, coming to himself at night, he by degrees recalled the circumstances, and with some difficulty made his way home. He remained ill for some time from the wounds he had received, but ultimately recovered, and went to Hobarton. On his return

thence, when within four miles of Grindstone Bay
(the scene of the first murder), he was passing
through a thick close scrub of wattle-trees, when
a number of the natives, who were hidden among
them, rushed out and knocked him down, completely stunning him with blows from their waddies.

" Stock-keepers were then living at the Grindstone Bay station, and, three days after the attack
upon Raynor, these men saw something approaching their hut, which at last they discerned to be a
man, but, from his reeling staggering gait, they
believed him to be drunk. He advanced slowly
along the path, sometimes creeping on all fours, and
sometimes walking, with a rolling unsteady pace.
With great effort and difficulty he climbed over the
fence near the hut, and then they found it was
poor Raynor, cruelly maimed and wounded, with
one eye knocked out, and the other quite blind,
his frightful sores all festering, and alive with
maggots! The poor fellow had awakened from his
long stupor, and, on recovering his recollection, had
crawled along the path, which was fortunately tolerably well beaten; and so, after unimaginable agony
and toil, he had contrived to reach the hut. Every

kind attention was paid to him, and he was afterwards carefully conveyed to the Hobarton Hospital, but he died there.

" About the year 1827 the natives made a most determined attack upon the cottage-home of a settler at Great Swan Port, named Buxton, who was himself absent at the time; but his wife, four daughters, and two sons (one aged fifteen, the other a child), were at home, the only other inmates being a servant man, and a person travelling on the east coast, who was resting on his journey. The cottage was, like those usually inhabited by the early settlers, built of turf, with a thatched roof. Early in the morning of a summer's day, the family was alarmed by the peculiar yelling of the dogs, denoting the near approach of the natives. On looking out, the place was discovered to be wholly surrounded by a large body of them, and as, unhappily, they were not then accustomed to approach the white people with any but hostile purposes, their appearance produced no small amount of terror and dismay, especially as, from some inadvertence or neglect, the besieged family had no means of defence, being wholly deficient either of arms or ammunition (I forget

which).   Still, the natives durst not rush into
the hut, and the inmates remained prisoners within
from the early morning until four in the afternoon,
when the blacks, being resolved to dislodge them
by some means, set fire to a brush fence which
ran close beside the hut, and could not fail, if it
continued burning, to ignite the thatch.   As the
fire approached, some of the party were obliged to
go out and extinguish it, when the traveller received a spear in his back, and the servant one
in his stomach, from the wound of which he died.
This success greatly emboldened the blacks, who
immediately came nearer, and got into the trees
close to the cottage, whence they began throwing
fire-sticks on to the thatch, and set fire to it; but
Mr. Buxton's eldest son succeeded in putting it
out, and regained the hut without being wounded.
A party of the natives below now made a fire on
the ground, and carefully burned the ends of
spears, so as to carry fire with certainty, and
these they began to hand up to the others in the
trees.   The wretched group in the cottage now
believed themselves inevitably doomed; death in
its most horrible shape seemed awaiting them at
a few seconds' distance, and all hope of escape

had departed, for the two dwellings nearest to them, whence alone they could expect succour, were severally fifteen and twenty-seven miles off. Yet was a rescue at hand, even at the doors! A party of twelve or fourteen soldiers, in search of bushrangers, then very numerous, came up at this fearful juncture; and the instant they were seen, the whole besieging army of natives *vanished* —rapidly and silently as the shadows of a hideous dream, and in a few seconds not one was to be found near the place. The traveller who had been speared was a sufferer for some time, but he eventually recovered.

"Some time after this event, a terrible tragedy was perpetrated at Jericho, where my father had a quantity of cattle in the care of a stock-keeper named Gough, who lived in a hut with his wife and his two little girls; and a mile distant from him, an old couple named Mortimer occupied another small hut. One morning about eleven o'clock, Gough and his servant, being at home, saw old "Mother Mortimer" coming towards them as fast as she could run, and calling out to beg and beseech them to go quickly to her hut, for that the blacks had set it on fire, and she wanted Gough to

save some of her little property, her husband being
away from home. Gough and the man took their
guns and ran off on their charitable errand, whilst
the old woman stayed with Mrs. Gough. They
found Mortimer's hut totally burned to the ground,
and everything destroyed, but not a single native
was visible. Gough immediately feared that they
had gone, or certainly would go, to his own home,
and ran back again at the top of his speed; but
too late to save his unhappy family from the brutal
blacks. The first object that met his sight was the
body of his young wife, pierced with many spears,
and her brains knocked out. A little beyond lay
the old woman Mortimer, her head cloven in two
with an axe. Near the hut he found his eldest
girl, her head beaten to pieces; and near her the
youngest, stunned with blows on the head, and
otherwise dreadfully hurt, but still alive and moaning. As usual, the natives had vanished.

"The poor little girl who recovered said that her
father was only just out of sight when the natives
came, proving the truth of Gough's suspicions
that the attack on Mortimer's hut was a mere ruse
to secure his absence from his own, which they
could then plunder at their ease, and probably the

main body was concealed round his hut, only awaiting his departure to begin the attack. The terrified women had shut themselves and the children in the hut, and the blacks threw spears at them through the windows (the panes of glass in which were pierced with round holes, as if balls had been fired through them). The natives then came down the chimney, and old Nancy Mortimer struck at their legs with the axe, whilst Mrs. Gough tried to escape by the door, but they were then directly murdered. The hut was stripped of all the stores.

" Not far from this last place, in the pretty valley near the present 'London Inn,' a small farmer named Hooper, with his wife and either seven or eight young children, lived in a hut placed between two rocky hills, near a stream of fresh water. One day, some persons went to see Hooper, and were surprised at not finding him or any of the children about, or at work as usual, and proceeded towards the cottage, where, lying all round, frightfully mangled and full of spears, were the dead bodies of Hooper, his wife, and *all* their children. As usual with the savages, when not disturbed in their work of fiendish butchery, they had cruelly muti-

lated their helpless victims, hammered their bones
in pieces, broken their fingers, &c., &c.

" A black woman some time after told the whole
of their plans and schemes to achieve this terrible
murder; she said that a party of them had for
three days kept watch unseen on one of the rocky
hills close to the cottage, intending to wait there
until Hooper went out to work without his gun,
which he usually carried, as was the general and
necessary custom in those days of terror. One
unhappy day he *did* go out without it, and instantly
the descent was made and the massacre effected
with the terrible success they anticipated.

" At a hut in St. Paul's Plains six or eight men
were living together, being shepherds and other servants of a neighbouring settler; one morning they
found their hut surrounded by forty or fifty natives.
The men had several guns, but only a few rounds
of ammunition; still, with only common presence
of mind and courage, they would have been in
no immediate danger; but, in the extremity of their
terror, they lost all prudence, and began firing
whilst the blacks were still beyond the range of the
guns, so that before they could do any execution
their powder was all spent. Even then, had they

remained in the hut, the natives could not have
known their want of powder, and would probably
have kept off; but, panic-stricken at the bare idea
of the natives—so intensely had their atrocities excited the terror of the white people—the frightened
men agreed to 'make a run for it,' and putting this
hopeless expedient into practice, they all started
from the hut together. The blacks, soon perceiving
that they made no attempt to shoot, instantly closed
round and knocked them down, and killed them all
except one, who escaped into the tier of mountains
near the station, running so far that he totally
lost himself, and could not find his way back for
three days. Within two hours after the murder
I passed the station, walking slowly, and leading
my horse, which had fallen lame; and as I went
by at a short distance, I wondered why none of
the men usually there were then to be seen about.
I left my lame horse at the farm of a settler near,
and walked on homewards. The following day I
came upon the freshly-deserted camp-place of the
tribe, some miles nearer to Swan Port, in which
direction they, like myself, were hastening; but
fortunately we did not meet. A dray was sent to
the St. Paul's station the day after the murder,

with provisions and stores, when the dead bodies were discovered."

But enough of these harrowing details! Surely I need transcribe no more; nor would I have particularised even these, but in the hope of making known something of the real state of affairs as formerly existing between the aborigines and the colonists, which is so greatly misunderstood in England; where, as I well know, the white people are most erroneously believed to have been the aggressors. I verily begin to think there is some peculiarity in the atmosphere around Van Diemen's Land, which is adverse to the transmission of truth, for somehow or other all accounts carried home partake of the same distorted or wholly imaginative character. Nor can I marvel at wrong impressions concerning the treatment of the blacks being received in England, when even in the colony some persons of education and supposed common sense were, some years ago, actually cheated or quizzed into the belief that the settlers made a regular practice of catching the natives, and boiling them down to feed pigs! I shall close this most unpleasant chapter with Mr. Meredith's brief account of the final capture of the blacks.

" The outrages committed by the natives continued without any attempt on the part of the Government to suppress them, *beyond the formal publication, in the Government Gazette, of a proclamation, commanding the natives not to pass from the west to the east of a certain imaginary line drawn through the island in a north and south direction!* The use of such a medium as a printed proclamation in a Gazette to address a horde of savages, who could not speak the English language, far less read it, would not have occurred to any governor less gifted with sagacity than Col. Arthur; and with that notable experiment he contented himself until the year 1829, when the whole male population of the colony, capable of bearing arms, was called out for the purpose of driving the natives on to Tasman's Peninsula. Many, whose better sense informed them of the impossibility of such a scheme succeeding, joined in the ' Black War,' as it was called, from the fear of being deprived of their assigned servants, and cut off from all chance of receiving additional grants of land; such being the manner in which Lieut.-Governor Colonel Arthur, now Sir George Arthur, exhibited his displeasure towards those settlers who differed with him as to the policy of his local acts. As was foretold from its commencement, the 'Black war' proved an utter failure, and cost the colony 27,000*l.*! Except in the transfer of large sums of money to the contractors favoured by Government, matters remained as before the expedition was undertaken, until a person named Robinson, a bricklayer by trade, but an active and intelligent man, undertook and performed the singular service of bringing every aboriginal man, woman, and child, quietly, peaceably, and willingly into Hobarton, whence they were shipped to Flinder's Island, which is between forty and fifty miles in length, twelve to eighteen in width, and abounding with the smaller species of kangaroo, &c.; the coasts are plentifully supplied with fish, and in addition to this abundance of their natural food, the natives were provided at the expense of the colony with dwellings, ample rations of flour and meat, bedding, clothes, garden implements, seeds, fishing-tackle, and all things which could be necessary for their present or improved condition; besides medical attendance, and the means of careful and judicious instruction in all things fitting or possible for them to learn.

" From the time of Mr. Robinson's extraordinary

capture, or rather persuasion of the natives to follow
him, a complete change took place in the island;
the remote stock stations were again resorted to,
and guns were no longer carried between the
handles of the plough. The means of persuasion
employed by Mr. Robinson to induce the natives to
submit to his guidance have ever been a mystery to
me. He went into the bush unarmed, and, accompanied by an aboriginal woman, his sole companion,
met the different tribes, and used such' arguments
with them as sufficed at length to achieve his
object, after having occupied many months in its
pursuit. He received some reward from the local
Government, although not nearly adequate to the
merits of his service. He alone, unassisted in
any way, accomplished what Colonel Arthur, with
the aid of the military, and all the male population of the island, and an expenditure of 27,000*l.*,
had failed to do. The debt of gratitude the colony
owes to Mr. Robinson can never be overpaid; by
his capture of the natives, he saved the lives of
thousands of defenceless persons, and was the means
of restoring that prosperity to the colony which
the accumulating number of murders was fast un-
dermining."

SPRING VALE COTTAGE.

CHAPTER XIII.

Joyful Removal to Spring Vale.—Improvements.—Clearing and Burning.—Great Flood.—The Half-drowned Man.—Two to be Extricated.—The Rescue.—The "Big Pool."—The Sweet Bay.—Black
Cockatoos.—Pied Magpies.—Black Magpies.

By the end of August, 1842, our cottage had advanced so far towards completion, that we could
live in it; and, without waiting for anything further,
we began the welcome business of removal thither.
Never, perhaps, did the unpleasant process of
changing one's house appear so delightful. The
very carts and drays as they started off, loaded with

the heterogeneous contents of our abode, had, in my eyes, quite a cheerful and jaunty air, as they went nodding along; and the promiscuous arrangement of chair and table legs looked as if scarcely restrained from a dance on the spot. My piano, carefully replaced in its English case, and laid upon a dray well padded with bags full of straw, and drawn by six oxen, moved away with a grave and solemn demeanour, as if conscious how important a part it played in the procession, and would probably be much scandalized at the riotous and unmusical conduct of certain small pigs, who, with their portly maternal parent, occupied another vehicle in the train.

On the following morning, after breakfast, our horse-cart came to the door, and received its precious freight, consisting of the children, the mamma, the nurse, and the cat, the latter safely tied up in a bag, greatly to dear little George's amusement and mystification. Portfolios, desks, workboxes, books, toys, and such " small deer," completed the load, and so we arrived at last at our new home. How busy everybody immediately became, what sounds of brooms and scrubbing-brushes, of mops and pails; what hammering and unpacking went noisily

on, may well be imagined; but so merrily and
rapidly went on the work, that even on the first
night we were tolerably snug, and in another day
or two were truly " at home."

Our walls were still damp, from their own great
thickness, and the fresh plaster, one coat only of
which we waited to have put on before removing,
purposing to finish the interior in summer. Certainly the scores and crossings of the plasterer's
trowel were not ornamental, and the dark colour of
the walls might seem somewhat gloomy; but as
soon as they dried sufficiently, I had a remedy at
hand for all their unsightliness; I hung up the old
pictures once again, and heartily welcomed them to,
as I then believed, their last Australian home.

Too many useful and necessary things had
hitherto demanded attention and labour, to allow
of any merely ornamental work being done; and I
dare say any one else (especially if unaccustomed
to the transformations of a new country), who
looked at our lonely dwelling, and the scrubby
thickets and dead wood all around it, and the high
heavy log-fence which then stood just in front,
would bless himself that it was not his fate to inhabit such a wilderness; but to us—seeing it as we

did through the decorative medium of our own
plans and projects—all was bright and hopeful. In
looking *at* the house, we knew exactly where the
veranda would " come in," and where the climbing
roses, and vines, and clematis, would be trained
over it; and when we surveyed the view from the
windows, the coarse reality of scrub and log-fence
was nicely softened by the " mind's eye " view of the
green sloping lawn, and neat well-laid out garden
beyond, which formed part of our arrangements, and
which was already well stocked with choice fruit-
trees from the Cambria orchard.

The work of clearing away the scrubby trees and
wood in front furnished Mr. Meredith with occupation for many an afternoon, and, with strong gloves
on, I enjoyed lending a helping hand to the task;
whilst even little George was delighted to carry
sticks to the heaps, and earn scratched knees and
torn pinafores in the service. Our piles of wood
and leaves made grand bonfires at night, and the
streams of bright flames and sparks, rising amidst
the masses of dark honeysuckle trees, illuminated
the whole scene with a wild and most picturesque
glare of light.

We had not been located at Spring Vale more

than a fortnight or three weeks, when an unusually
heavy fall of rain set in, and continued for some
days. The rivers on either side of us rose very
rapidly, as they both descend from steep mountains,
whose narrow rocky gorges pour down an enormous
accumulation of water. Our low lands were soon
entirely flooded, forming a great lake, and the chief
of the cattle and sheep were with difficulty saved,
and driven to the dry ground.; but some calves and
sheep were drowned, despite the utmost care, as the
rivers, breaking forth at different points, formed temporary islands, where the poor frightened creatures
retreated for safety, until swept away by the increasing and rapid overflow of the water.

About two o' clock on the first day of the flood,
we heard a great noise of " Coo-ee-ring," in the
direction of the ford over the Swan River, and our
servants, on going down, found that a man, in
attempting to cross on horseback, had been so
frightened by the breadth and roaring of the water,
that he had slipped off the horse, and, with some
difficulty, scrambled into a tree, then in the middle
of the stream. Mr. Meredith hurried down to see
what could be done for him, and at this time he
might, with common presence of mind and the

assistance offered him, have walked on shore, as, although broad and rapid, the water was not yet deep; but nothing could induce him to make the attempt, although he entreated that the horse, which had safely swam out, might be " turned in again towards him;" for what purpose, it were difficult to say, as when he was on its back before he could not keep his seat. The river was now rising and spreading with terrific rapidity; each moment the chances of escape grew less, and the cowardly fellow's situation more dreadful. All aid was soon impracticable, as the huge masses of timber that came rushing along, and the hidden boughs and stakes in the scrub that now formed part of the river's bed, would have instantly disabled the stoutest swimmer, and no boat could be obtained.

The rain still poured down in torrents, with a cold southerly * wind, and the dim gray twilight fast darkened into night, over as dreary a scene as can well be imagined. The tree in which the unfortunate man had taken refuge was, just at nightfall, swept away by the torrent; and, half-drowned for the second time, he luckily contrived to lay

---

* The cold rain is of course from the south in this hemisphere, although it still seems strange, even to me, to speak of it as such.

hold of another tree, as he was washed along. which, although slender, and shaking under him with the force of the water, served him better, having a forked branch in it, on which he could rest one foot at a time; and so the poor wretch clung to it, wet to the skin, and nearly frozen in the cold night wind. Our servants, who would willingly have risked their own lives for his had there been a chance of success, made up a fire against a great gum-tree on the nearest bank, and three or four of them determined to remain there the whole night to keep up the fire, and shout to him, "to cheer him up a bit," as they kindly said; and another party did the same on the other side the river.

It was late before we could think of going comfortably to bed, whilst a fellow-creature remained near us in such a wretched and awful condition; for it seemed scarcely possible that he could "hold on" till morning. And at intervals, all through the dreary night, amidst the gusts of wind, the pelting rain, and the deep loud roaring of the flood, which now encompassed our little hill on three sides, I could hear the shouts of our people, as they hailed the poor wretch, both to comfort him, and to assure themselves by his replies that he had not dropped

L 3

into the river. At length morning came, and showed him still clinging to the tree, in the midst of the vast, broad, turbulent, rushing torrent. The man's master, and several other settlers from the neighbourhood, came to see what could be done, but all shrunk from the idea of perilling their own lives in so hopeless a risk. Mr. Meredith, who had also been down to the river, had returned to the house, and we were at breakfast, when a hasty footstep came along the hall, then a loud sob was heard, and the nursemaid burst into the room, crying bitterly.

" If you please, sir——"

" Well ! what's the matter ? "

" Oh, sir ! if you please, sir, *Bill's up a tree too!*"
And on inquiry, we found that one of our good old servants had foolishly suffered himself to be flattered and persuaded that " he was the man to fetch the poor fellow out, if any man could," and had, with thorough kindness, but most insane folly, attempted to swim out to him : the eddying current had swept him away, dashed him against some hidden logs so as to hurt him severely, and left him barely strength to grasp a tree a little nearer our bank than the other, and clamber into it; so that now there were two, instead of one, to be extricated.

Devices innumerable were discussed and dismissed
in turn; the day wore away, and our poor fellow
said he could not "hold on" much longer.   Long
lines had been prepared, but none could be thrown
far enough to reach the trees; and after gathering
together and sending down every cord and twine
and fishing-line in the house, for another trial, I
could not rest at home, for I knew that Mr. Meredith would not allow a faithful old servant to perish
in the cause of humanity, even if he risked his own
life to save him.   The rain had abated, and I ran
down to a bank on the water's edge, whence I could
see both the unfortunates clinging to their trees,
their clothes saturated with wet, and their frightful
position more than realizing my belief of its
horrors.   The river roared and boiled along beneath
them, carrying down with it huge trees, whole lines
of fencing, blocks of wood, and branches of all
sizes, which, as they dashed against the slender
trees, made them shake as though they were giving
way too.

At last a man on the opposite bank, after innumerable failures, succeeded in shooting from a gun
a stick, to which a long fine line was attached, and
to the end of this a strong rope.   After many

trials, the stick fell in the tree where the first man was hanging, and he hauled in the twine until he caught the rope, which he tied round his body, and, after some hesitation, obeyed the command to throw himself into the river. The people on the bank hauled away manfully at their end of the rope, but the current was so strong, that the man was carried down some distance, and kept so long under water, that I thought he must be drowned; but he re-appeared, and was dragged through a thick half-submerged scrub, safe to land, where the good people had prepared hot tea, and fire, and dry garments, and I soon lost sight of him among the bustling group that closed round him.

Mr. Meredith having now completed his plan for rescuing "Bill," took a tall pole, and, carrying with him a long line coiled up, waded off towards him, swimming being impracticable, from the quantities of submerged and driving logs and sticks; three of the men followed him, with similar poles to hold themselves up by against the current, whilst our friend Mr. Jukes, of the "Fly,"* took the command

* Who, in the narrative of his wanderings, has not condescended to immortalize our pleasant island of Tasmania, and tells me that no one will read what any one may write about it. _I_ hope to find his prophecy not _quite_ true.

of the coil of rope, more in-shore.   Having gained
a great heap of wreck collected round a tree some
distance from the bank, Mr. Meredith climbed into
this tree, and from it managed to throw the line on
to the tree where our servant was, who hauled it in,
till he got hold of the rope, which he tied round
him, and then dropped into the water. He was soon
drawn through the broad deep channel to the heap
of wreck, and from thence the men held him up
and guided him ashore.   I waited no longer, but
ran quickly home to prepare dry clothes, warm
blankets, and the wherewithal to comfort the "inner
man" of the dripping party, who soon followed me,
thankful that our poor servitor's thoughtless expedition had not had a more serious result than the
joking advice of his companions, "not to go a
bird's nesting that way again."

Some days elapsed before the rivers retired sufficiently within their usual bounds, for persons to cross
them safely.   Another flood, but of less magnitude
than this, occurred in the following November; but,
beyond the annoyance such visitations always occasion, by cutting off communication and destroying
fences, its consequences were not very important.

These rivers of ours, so terrible when swollen

with winter rains, on the melting of the mountain snows (snow being unknown in nearly all the lower parts of this delightful island), dwindle to mere brooks during the summer months, and are often wholly lost sight of, except in a few deep shady pools. One of these, in the Cygnet River, was called the "Big Pool," though, as in every river in almost every district, there are some half-dozen bearing the same not very definite or descriptive name. I proposed to distinguish this by some more characteristic one, such as Lake Cygnet, or the Dryad's Mirror. It is very deep, the banks appear nearly perpendicular, and the water has a deep blue colour as you gaze down into it, but is so clear and still, that the forest which encircles it may see each knotted and twisted gum-tree, and each tall and thickly-verdant lightwood and wattle, reflected as in a mirror; and indeed I can only account for the singular arching-over of the fine old trees, by the fancy that they had for ages so loved to bend down and gaze on themselves in the calm deep water, that they had at last grown into their present position.

The wild unspoiled beauty of the place made it a great favourite with us, and I rarely went there without seeing some new bird or insect, or finding

a shrub or flower which I did not know before.
Several beautiful species of ferns grew here luxuriantly, in the dark moist nooks; and the trunks
and twisting roots of the old trees were clad in
mosses and lichens of various form, and infinitely
varying colour.

That beautiful shrub, the "Sweet Bay" of the
colonists (*Prostanthera lasianthos*), grew here to
the height of fifteen or even twenty feet, with its
handsome sprays and clusters of white purple-
pencilled flowers, thrown into fine relief and contrast by the deep rich green of the elegant foliage;
and the starry clematis wove its bower of emerald
and silver among the branches, in many a quiet
shadowy nook, where the noon-day sun might only
find tiny loopholes in the high leafy screen above,
to peer down into our sylvan haunts.

The beautiful black cockatoos seemed to share in
our admiration of this spot, for we often found a
large party of them in the tall trees near the pool,
and sometimes in the dead boughs of fallen ones
which formed a sort of barrier at either end of it,
and seemed to furnish the cockatoos with good store
of grubs and insects, to judge by the pleasant and
congratulatory tone of their conversation.   These

are like the black cockatoos of New South Wales,
except that the top-knots and tails of the latter
are trimmed with crimson, whilst my more intimate
and familiar friends of Spring Vale had their jetty
garb more delicately varied by a pale and lovely
shade of canary-yellow, or rather pure primrose
colour. Their cry is much more pleasing than that
of the white cockatoo, and instead of being, like
that bird, a great pest to the farmer, they are quite
harmless, never molesting the richest crops of grain,
but only visiting old dead or dying trees, and picking out of them the large white grubs, which form
their chief food. These grubs are often three or
four inches long, and proportionably thick; perfectly white, smooth, and rather glossy; more like
models of grubs in white wax, than living things;
the aborigines eat them greedily, and I have heard
that some English people do so, and say they taste
like nuts or almonds! They change to gigantic
moths, of most exquisite plumage, their principal
colours being those of the owl and hawk tribe,
among birds, but charmingly varied and shaded;
the *feathers* are of extraordinary length, so that
the insect's legs and head have the appearance
of being clothed in long rich fur garments, and

their wings, some of which have beautiful large pink eyes or spots in them, look as if Titania's busy sprites might comb and dress them like hair.

The cockatoos search for these dainty morsels with great avidity; the strength of their beaks is enormous; I have often watched them at work in a tree, tearing away first the bark in great strips, and then large pieces of the wood; and on going afterwards to examine the chips they have left, have truly marvelled at their dexterity and perseverance, for the grub is often deep in the wood, and a great thickness must be torn away before it can be dislodged. They are right merry craftsmen, too, and call out cheerfully and kindly to one another, as they ply their work, discoursing, doubtless, on the quality and obstinate resistance of their prize. They are usually seen in parties of from five to ten or fifteen, and always give me the idea of most friendly, clever, good-humoured birds; and, accordingly, we took them under our especial protection, never suffering them to be molested near us, so that they grew comparatively tame, and would sit pecking in trees quite close to the house, and let us approach them tolerably near, to observe their polite bowings and curtseyings, as they gravely moved about, with their elegant golden crests alternately raised or depressed; but if we still lessened what they deemed a prudent distance, the whole party took wing. The cockatoos appeared to roam about during the day to considerable distances, but we generally saw them flying home at night in the same direction. I have often wished to procure a young bird to rear tame, yet allowing it perfect liberty, but have never heard of any one who had found or seen a nest. One of our servants offered to procure me one very readily, but, on inquiring how he meant to achieve the capture, I found his notable expedient was to fire at one very near to him, and "wing it," which not being exactly the treatment I contemplated for my tame pet, I declined the proposal.

My conscience half reproaches me for suffering even the beautiful black cockatoos to take precedence, in this gossiping chronicle, of our yet more prized and beloved friends, the common magpies, the merriest, handsomest, most harmless and entertaining birds that can be conceived. As every one on our land was prohibited from destroying them, or, indeed, any birds, save parrots, hawks, and cows, we had generally a large assemblage near the house; and their sweet songs, warbled forth at in-

tervals during the whole day and night, reminded
me pleasantly of the note of the English blackbird.
Many of the full, rich, deep tones are exactly
similar, although the magpie's song has less variety
of cadence : still, it is, alone, an ample refutation
of the assertion made by some unobservant person,
and echoed by many thoughtless ones, that " the
Australian birds have no song," than which nothing
can be more untrue, for many of them have very
sweet notes; and any one who would do as I have
often done—sit quietly down in a woody retired spot,
and, without noise or motion, listen to the countless
voices warbling all around him, in every variety of
tone and key, would soon become convinced that
the Australian, or at all events the Tasmanian,
birds, not only sing, but sing very pleasingly; and,
of all the choir, the magpies take the highest rank.

They are very beautiful birds, too, with a good
deal of the form and air of the English magpie,
but with a shorter tail.   The plumage, of the
glossiest black and most brilliant silvery white, is
elegantly contrasted and arranged, and their bright
intelligent eyes, and graceful demeanour, seem to
denote a degree of refinement rather above their
neighbours.   In the summer, and when the nights.

are moonlight, at whatever hour I have chanced to awake, I have heard them carolling away as if it were just sunrise, and often, with a sleepy wonder, marvelled when, or if ever, they tucked their busy heads beneath their wings, and went to sleep like other birds.

Our servants used to complain that my handsome friends would persist in pecking the meat, when the oxen or sheep were freshly killed, and were hanging outside, and I have myself observed them examining it with most minute attention; but on two of them being shot for the offence, I was so much grieved, and gave such peremptory orders that so unwonted an outrage should never again be perpetrated, that they have peeped into our beef and mutton ever since with impunity.

Sad and melancholy creatures are the tame magpies so often seen here, cooped up in wretched cages made of an old tea-chest or soap-box, with a few bars on one side, and hung up against a hut, where they forget their own "wood-notes wild," and learn to swear, or to whistle "Jim Crow;" their dim, soiled, ragged feathers, and lack-lustre expression, scarcely suffering one to believe them of the same race as the bright merry wild magpies.

The black magpie has very much the aspect of a crow, being jet-black all over, saving only a small bar of white on the wings and tail; it is a far less agreeable guest than its pied namesake, being very destructive in corn-fields. Just as the blade is springing well up, these mischievous birds descend in flocks, and, with their long powerful bills, dig up and devour the rooted grain, so that they sometimes cause great loss to the farmer, and our firelocks had a full share of their unwelcome patronage. They have several notes or cries, but none are very musical. They usually associate in large parties, although their slovenly stick-nests are solitary. Some persons like these birds when cooked; but, after exhausting all my culinary skill upon them in roasts, stews, curries, and pies, I have finally given them up as not cookable, or rather as not relishable when cooked. Whether it be the *crowish* look they have which gives us unpleasant fancies about them, or that the flesh really possesses the flavour we attribute to it, I am not quite decided, but our prejudice against them is too strong to be overcome. No one would think of eating one of the other magpies, as they are known to devour neat, besides their usual food of worms, grubs, &c.

PORCUPINES (ECHIDNA).

CHAPTER XIV.

Garden-making.—Walks and Rides.—Native Raspberry.—Old Don and the Kangaroo.—Tasmanian Quadrupeds.—Forest Kangaroo. — Brush Kangaroo. —Joey and Beppo.—Wolloby. — Kangaroo-rat. —Bandicoot.—Porcupine.—Wombat.—Its Haunts.

DURING the summer and autumn of this year, (1842-3), we effected many of our purposed improvements: the veranda was built, the log-fence in the front was removed, and a more distant paling supplied its place sloping down the hill, so as to include some nice wattle-trees in our "lawn," so called; although I much question if its smoothly-shaven namesakes at home would own kindred with the piece of long-bearded, wild, uneven grass and weeds, which we affectionately so designated. The cottage being placed on a rocky bank, the soil close around it was not adapted for a garden (our principal one was at the foot of the slope, in a rich flat), and my indispensable flower-borders were consequently formed with some labour. Many cartloads of stones and rocks had to be carried away, and a quantity of rich earth and manure carted in: the borders were then laid out on a very simple plan, and edged with thyme, almost the only substitute here for the bright, clean, neat box-edging used in England. Roses of various kinds, geraniums, and a host of other good old flowers, were soon planted, and another pleasant source of interest and occupation opened to me. Of the latter I had, indeed, no lack, between the care of my household and our dear children; and besides these there were chickens, and ducks, and turkeys to rear; butter, cream, cheeses, and other country comforts to make; calves to pet; mushrooms to seek, and convert into ketchup (these being frequently very abundant and fine); and a whole catalogue of pleasant busy little idlenesses to indulge in, that carried one week after another with reproachful celerity.

Then our long rambling rides or walks often occupied the longest half of the day, especially if Master George were of the party, trotting along on foot, with occasional interludes of " pick-a-back," on papa's shoulders. Sometimes our corn-fields had to be visited, the wheat and oats growing most luxuriantly. Sometimes we went to look at the turnips, wherein lay our hopes of fat beef for winter; or to see the potatoes, which we were told were certain not to succeed, many farmers here having ceased to grow them, the summer frosts being destructive; ours, however, promised well, and we gladly anticipated the luxury of having an abundance of them, after having been compelled to do wholly without them, and to adopt all kinds of unsatisfactory substitutes. The terrible potato disease had not at this time been heard of; nor do I think it has yet really appeared in this colony.

Quantities of the pretty downy-leaved wild Geranium grew in this same potato field, which was part of a large inclosure on the bank of the Swan River; and beneath the broad belt of majestic trees which skirted it, forming a continuous grove beside the water, I used to find store of lovely shrubs and

flowers, and tangles of the wild native raspberry,
the only thing I have yet seen really like an eatable
fruit that these strange unfinished countries produce. One might fancifully believe that the Australian colonies were discovered too soon, and that
Nature—that familiar term which we so often use
to spare the light or irreverent mention of the Great
Divine mover and guide of all—had not completed
her design; and that the dry seedy trees and juice-
less herbs of Australia would, in a few more ages,
have changed into kindlier and better things; and the
great impenetrable reedy desert, which spreads over
thousands of miles in New Holland, would, perhaps,
then have been uplifted into hills and mountains,
whose fresh streams and grassy valleys might have
supported a population commensurate with the
immense extent of territory: but the charm is
broken! Art and invention, and busy, gold-digging,
mammon-worshipping men have intruded ere the
great task was accomplished.

But the raspberry seems to have been brought
nearer to completion than most things here, and were
the fruit more abundant, it would be of great value;
but when we found what we called " a quantity" of
raspberries, there were never so many as I should

have wished to gather for George alone, so that they are scarcely worth mentioning, except for their great beauty. The leaf and stem resemble those of the blackberry, but are smaller and slighter, never shooting up great thick stalks covered with spines like sharks' teeth, such as I remember among my blackberry haunts at home, but slender and weak; the blossoms small, with the bright, pinkish, lilac petals turning inwards to the centre; and the berries of a bright clear transparent scarlet, like the berries of the woody nightshade. Their flavour is pleasant, but not comparable to that of the garden raspberry.

Our old pointer, Don, always accompanied us in our rides and walks, and sometimes started a brush kangaroo, giving chase most gallantly, though without the remotest chance of catching his hopping game, which went bounding off, over tussocks and logs, through scrub, and under or over everything in its way, in a half-flying style, most marvellous and incomprehensible to our good old English dog, who, after a long chase, used to come panting back to us, wagging his tail, and *looking* his apologies for the failure, as plainly as if he said, " I really beg your pardon, master, but the hares I used to hunt at home have not the ugly trick of hopping which these practise, and, positively, I don't understand it!"

My beautiful spaniel, "Dick Swiveller," generally shared the chase and the disappointment, but, being a Tasmanian by birth, perhaps the puzzle was less to him.

English sporting dogs point the kangaroo as they do any other game, and Don always chased the creatures most determinedly, but in vain; until one day, when, in hunting a rabbit, he jumped over a great old fallen tree, and hit upon a poor kangaroo that was asleep under its shelter. Don, although quite as much astonished as the kangaroo, killed it on the spot, and when his master carried home the prize, followed it closely, smelling and gently licking it, and then looking up at me, telling me with his expressive, honest, old face, how great a triumph had at last thrust itself upon him. Poor fellow! he hunted more than ever after this glorious affair, and several times disturbed a fine brush kangaroo very near our house, chasing it often across our path, and once as we stood still in a shady part of the public road, listening to the *thud, thud, thud,* of its measured jumps as it approached us : the beautiful gentle-looking deer-faced creature leaped almost against us, and then instantly turning short round, hopped over a log, and away into the thick scrub, but at no violent speed; he had been pursued by old Don too often to deem that necessary, and, as usual, away went Don and Dick after him, and with the same result. The dogs used here to hunt the kangaroo have the shape and general character of the greyhound, but are very much larger in size, and coarser altogether, uniting great strength with speed.

As I have mentioned the kangaroo, perhaps my most systematic method will be to give a short description of the indigenous animals of Tasmania, rather than introduce stray sketches of them in the accidental manner in which I have made their acquaintance.

I commence with the largest, the Great or Forest Kangaroo (*Macropus giganteus*), the "Forester" of the colonists, which I have not yet seen in its wild state. Many years ago they were very numerous, and might constantly be observed feeding in the day-time on the open country in groups of from five to twenty. The oldest and heaviest male of the herd was called a "Boomer," probably a native

term.　When chased, these patriarchs of the forest,
being large and heavy, were always the least swift,
and consequently most frequently taken, until at
length the great boomer kangaroo has become in all
the inhabited districts an extinct animal.　The
females, and younger males, or " bucks," are much
less, the elderly gentlemen alone attaining the great
size described by the early settlers.　So many idle
vagabonds have been in the constant habit of roaming about with packs of twenty or thirty huge dogs
each, to procure kangaroo skins for sale, that the
forest species is now very rarely seen.　An excellent
Act of Council was introduced by Sir Eardley Wilmot, and passed into law, tending to the partial
protection of the kangaroos, preventing persons
from hunting on Crown lands without licences,
which are granted by the police magistrates.　If
the latter always took the proper means to ascertain
the characters of those who apply for licences, and
conscientiously refused to grant them to men of
known bad character, the benefit conferred by this
Act would be very great.　But as many of the so-
called " kangarooers " are notorious cattle and sheep-
stealers, the want of proper discrimination in the
magistrates is productive of infinite evil, and in

some instances not only neutralizes the effect of the Act, but adds to the mischievous power of the vagabond "kangarooers," by permitting their location on any of the Crown lands, however close to private property, thus enabling them to carry on their nefarious transactions with success and impunity.

Formerly, the size attained by the old "boomers" was enormous; the hind quarters frequently weighed (when skinned and dressed) from 70 to 90 lbs., and the whole animal from 120 to 160 lbs. These were large powerful creatures, measuring in their common position about five feet in height; but when they rise on their toes, with the strong thick tail serving as a prop and support, they stand above six feet high. When brought to bay, the old boomers fight very resolutely, and if one can take up his favourite position, in water about three feet deep, so that the dogs must swim to reach him, he can keep off a whole pack. As each dog swims up, the kangaroo lays him under water with his hand-like fore paws, holding him down until another claims his attention, and so disposes of one after another until the dogs are exhausted; and sometimes he tears them dreadfully with the long sharp solid claws of his fore feet, which he uses most adroitly, ripping and cutting in any direction with sure effect. It is, I believe, generally supposed that they inflict the most severe wounds with the hind feet, but this is not the case until they are overcome and thrown down; as, when fighting erect, they always raise themselves on their hind toes. Their general colour is dark gray, or ash colour, lighter beneath. Mr. Meredith, on one occasion, long ago, saw a pure white kangaroo, and more recently we heard of another white one having been seen : these, I imagine, are albinos, which seem to occur occasionally among all animals.

The ordinary jump of the large kangaroo is about sixteen feet; and they can clear a four-rail fence, about five feet high, in their course, without any visible alteration or exertion.

All the species of kangaroo are easily tamed, and become as familiar as any other domestic animal ; but as all dogs here are accustomed and trained to hunt and kill them, pets of this kind are certain, sooner or later, to come to an untimely end. One which was reared here some time back at last stood higher than the woman it belonged to, and used to accompany her whenever she left home, just as a dog would do, hopping along by her side in a most friendly and companionable manner; but one day, meeting some strange dogs, it was unfortunately hunted and killed. The young of all species of kangaroo are commonly called Joeys, without regard to sex, but I am not aware if this is a corruption of some native name, or one bestowed by the early colonists.

The Brush Kangaroo (*Macropus Bennettii*) stands three feet high in its usual position, with the hind elbow or heels bent up. Its colour is dark iron-gray, lighter beneath. The doe, like that of the forest species, has one young one at a time, which she carries and shelters in the pouch, until the baby so much outgrows its cradle, that the long legs and tail poke out.

The sweet gentle expression of face peculiar to the kangaroo tribe is most beautiful and winning; their eyes are full, dark, and soft, and the erect, animated, widely-open ears, in perpetual motion, give at the same time a keen and yet timid expression to the head. I never had so good an opportunity of observing the different species of kangaroo, as in the collection which Sir Eardley Wilmot kept as pets in a wooded and bushy paddock close to Government House, Hobarton, where, within the paling fence, they enjoyed their liberty, and being tolerably accustomed to visitors, allowed themselves to be looked at very composedly; but in their perfectly wild state, a passing glance is all that can be obtained. The habits of the brush kangaroo are different from those of the forester; they are never seen feeding in herds by day, and if two or three chance to be started from the same vicinity, they all set off in different directions. Usually they are not seen until roused from the bush log or tussocks they have been crouching in, like a hare in her form: their common average jump is about twelve feet.

I have now (1850) two young brush kangaroos, Joey and Beppo, living in a grassy inclosure close to the house, and associating with my poultry very amicably; though they sometimes slily creep after the peacock, as if with the intention of biting his long gorgeous train, when it looks green in the sunshine, supposing it perhaps to be some new vegetable. They are fed with green food, bread, or corn, and are fond of new milk. They hold grass or leaves in their hands, and eat very daintily and elegantly, never seeming in any hurry, but helping

themselves with a degree of refinement and deliberation that might offer a salutary example to some
nobler animals. For a year I had only "Joey,"
and an old hen turkey annoyed him exceedingly at
one time, in her stupid terror lest he should hurt
her chickens, and chased him round the inclosure
at a furious pace; but by putting the old lady under
a coop, I restored poor "Joey's" peace and tran-
quillity. Both he and little Beppo (which we have
reared this year in the house like a pet kitten)
sleep some hours during the day, under the bower
of boughs over their kennel, and hop about and
feed chiefly in the night-time.

The Wolloby is the species next in size to the
Brush Kangaroo in this colony; the name is usually
spelled Wallaby, but the full native pronunciation
can only be correctly represented by using the *o*
instead of the *a*. In the aboriginal languages of
these colonies, the vowels are sounded peculiarly
full and round.

The wolloby, in its common position, stands
about two feet high; the fur is gray, mingled with
a brown tan colour, and is much softer than the
larger kangaroo's, being more like that of the
opossum. These animals frequent thickets and

the dense close scrubs near rivers and watercourses,
where they baffle the most active dogs by winding
and popping in and out, like a rabbit in a furze-
brake. In chasing kangaroos, or, as it is technically termed, "kangarooing," large powerful dogs
are used; but in thickly-wooded and scrubby
places, a sharp clever *little* dog is also required,
to put the game out of the thickets, where the
great dogs could not penetrate. The wolloby and
brush kangaroo often visit gardens and fields at
night, to banquet on the dainties they find there;
and by far the greatest portion of those destroyed
are caught in snares set for the purpose, in the
tracks or "runs" they frequent. There is, it
would seem, about the same difference in the
habits of the forest, brush, and wolloby kangaroos,
as that existing between those of the deer, the
hare, and the rabbit.

The Kangaroo-Rat (*Hypsiprymnus murinus*) is a
pretty little animal about thirteen inches in height,
with grayish fur, harsher than that of the kangaroo,
and the face has more of a *rattish* expression;
nevertheless it is certainly a pretty animal, and so
easily tamed as to be frequently made a pet,
gambolling and frisking about the house, and

following those who caress it, like a favourite dog or cat. In their natural state they eat grass, and also scratch and burrow at night for roots, and have unluckily a very clever trick of digging their own potatoes, or rather those of the settlers, which they appropriate without scruple. They form warm nests of dry grass on the ground, well-sheltered, and open at one side only. A prejudice exists against eating their flesh, which is well-flavoured and whiter than that of the true kangaroos, the latter being dark-coloured, lean, tender, and more similar to hare than any other meat I am acquainted with, and is undoubtedly excellent, when hung for a sufficient length of time, and properly dressed. A very rich gravy soup is often made from it, and a colonial dish called a " steamer," consisting of the meat and some good bacon finely minced, and stewed in rich gravy, is also good; but the hind-quarters roasted, with hare-stuffing and currant jelly, form a dish that Dr. Kitchener himself would have applauded, and which now is generally considered a dainty even here, especially by our town-friends. Yet I have had servants who looked upon our eating kangaroo as something absolutely monstrous, and turned away in horror

at the thought of partaking of what they express-
ively designated as "*just a wild beast!*" A
haunch of tiger or a wolf-chop would, in their estimation, be quite as reasonable and proper food;
but fortunately they could always find an abundance
of tame mutton in our kitchen to console their
outraged sensibility.

The kangaroo-rat is not by many persons considered fit to be eaten, nor have I ever had one
cooked, for we partake the common prejudice—
whether caused by the name, and the unpleasant
association of ideas inseparable from it, I know
not; but as it is a prejudice which serves to save
the lives of the poor little animals, I have not the
slightest desire to have it removed.

Of the Bandicoot, two species are found here:
one (*Perameles Gunnii*) is of a light brownish
ash-colour, half as large again as a full-sized rat,
and somewhat broader in proportion; the other
(*Perameles obescula*) is rather less, and its colour
an ashy fawn, striped with light gray.

One of our servants lately found two young
striped bandicoots, pretty little soft creatures like
great mice, and brought them to the children for
pets. We kept them for some weeks, feeding them

on bread, milk, and raw potatoes; one was accidentally hurt, and died; the other I turned out into the
garden, thinking to bestow rather a luxurious life
upon him, amidst potatoes, fruit, and other good
things: but I could not prevail on him to accept
his liberty; he took up his abode in the parlour,
and soon found a warm snug bed among the multifarious contents of a deep work-basket, where he lay
coiled up all day, and grumbled and bit at any one
who disturbed him until his usual time of rising,
about dusk, when he regularly bounced out of the
basket, ran to the corner where his saucer of fresh
milk was always placed, nibbled his bread or potato,
and scampered about all the evening like a great
tame mouse, running under our chairs and over our
feet and dresses, and up the folds of them, with
confiding boldness, but not allowing any one to lay
hold of him. His end, poor little fellow, was, I
fear, a violent one, for I strongly suspect my demure
tabby cat must have evaded our wonted vigilance
and gained access to the parlour during the time
poor Cooty was awake; for one morning, to the
children's great regret, his bed was cold and empty,
and he was no more seen amongst us.

The Porcupine (*Echidna*) is fully four times the

size of an English hedgehog, covered on the back
with spines three or four inches long, which
protrude from a coat of thick grayish fur; its feet
have long toes, with long strong claws, and, instead
of a mouth and teeth, a long narrow round bill
appears to complete its extraordinary visage. It
usually weighs five or six pounds, being exceedingly
fat. Persons who are partial to sucking pig like
the flesh of the porcupine, which somewhat resembles it, but is too rich for most palates. These
creatures are found in wet springy ground, where
they probably feed on tadpoles, worms, and ants.
They burrow in the earth, and often frequent
hollows in moist rocks, and if pursued or hemmed
in, make their escape by scratching a hole and
sinking into it. Mr. Meredith once brought one
from the Schoutens to Swan Port, and on landing
put it down on the broad open beach, where, being
left for a few moments, it burrowed down into the
sand and vanished in an incredibly short space of
time, scarcely leaving a trace behind.

On another occasion one was found by the dogs
on one of the rocky hills of the tier, and was safely
carried down to me in a covered tin boiler. Knowing the mysterious subterranean habits of my new

friend, I was not a little puzzled how to accommodate him without losing him; and, as a temporary arrangement, he was deposited at the bottom of a wooden churn, which I thought sufficiently deep to prevent his absconding. Shortly after, on going to look at my captive, I found him, as is shown in my sketch, clinging by his long claws to the top of the churn, with his conical head peeping over. The duck-like bill is nearly as thin and round as a tobacco-pipe, and about two inches long, and gave an indescribably droll kind of pursed-up whistling expression to the strange creature's face, as his bright little eyes peered about him from out their furry nooks; the short broad tail, thickly beset with spines, like the back and sides, being spread out in a fan shape, not unlike that of a lobster. I was very curious to watch the ways of this anomalous little animal for a while, and to keep it confined for that purpose; but there was something so pitiful, though absurd, in the pleading, helpless, puzzled look of its queer face, as it seemed prying into mine, that was to me quite irresistible, knowing, as I well did, the difficulty, not to say impossibility, of keeping it alive, far less making it happy; so I at once carried it to my garden, let it crawl away, and saw it immediately commence a sidling kind of motion, casting up a circular ridge of earth, beneath which in a few seconds it had effectually screwed itself out of sight. I hoped it would have taken up its abode there, but we never could find a sign or vestige of it afterwards.

The Wombat (*Phascolomys* ——), like the porcupine, is eaten and relished by some persons, but is fatter and coarser, with a strong rank flavour. It is a most harmless, helpless, inoffensive animal, by no means agile, and falling an easy prey to its pursuers, if cut off from its retreat to the rocky hollows and crevices in which it lives, and which it squeezes into, through a smaller opening than would be supposed capable of admitting its fat squab body. Its head resembles that of the badger, but with a rounder snout. It has very small eyes, strong bristly whiskers, very short ears, short legs, short tail, and long coarse gray hair. Its body is broad and flat, and weighs from 30 lbs. to 50 lbs., and the creature's whole aspect betokens slowness and inactivity.

The children of a settler at the river Mersey had a pet wombat, which lived with them for some time, and used to play with them, and follow them about with great docility and good temper. They made

it a bed on a box, with a piece of blanket to cover
it, and it was often seen to scratch the blanket
snugly round it, and pull it up when slipping away,
in the most cosy and civilized manner possible.
Having also a *penchant* for making its way into
any other bed from which a scrap of blanket or rug
hung down to serve as a climbing ladder, it became
an object of dislike to the servants, and the worthy
farmer determined, much to the grief of the
children, to part with the favourite, which, like all
other favourites, was fast gaining foes. He carried
it away a considerable distance, put it down in the
forest, and returned home with the story of his
success; but ere the evening was ended, a certain
well-known scratching sound was heard at the door,
and the delighted children opened it for their poor
weary wombat, who had found his way home to
them again. A second time he was conveyed away,
and to a greater distance, but still he came back;
the third time the farmer carried him across the
Mersey in a boat, and left him on the opposite
bank of the broad deep river, quite secure now that
the business was finally settled. His poor friend
was, however, still of a different opinion, and by
the time the boat had touched the home shore, the

creature had found a huge fallen tree, which lay half across the stream, and had crawled to the extreme end of it, wistfully gazing upon his departing friends, who, thinking it quite impossible that he could cross the intervening portion of the river, went away home. How the heavy fat thing *did* cross, no one knows, but he arrived as usual that night, and, as may be imagined, his kind-hearted master did not try again to drive him away. Unfortunately, he was at last accidentally burned, from creeping too close to the hot ashes of the hearth, and, in mercy to his sufferings, was killed.

Wombats are generally found on rocky places, especially the summits of mountains and gullies, where their haunts are mostly inaccessible. Their chief food consists of the roots of the grass-tree and other plants, to procure which they leave their rocky fastnesses at night, and visit neighbouring marshy flats, where they scratch for their living, like the porcupine and bandicoot. The skin of the wombat is so thick and tough that the teeth of large dogs are seldom strong enough to penetrate it, and are not unfrequently absolutely pulled out in the effort, so that some of the hunters of the Bush are in the habit of punishing their dogs for

meddling with a wombat; and after a few such
lessons, the dogs content themselves with barking
round the harmless creature when they find one,
and its stout natural coat befriends it like a suit of
armour.

CHAPTER XV.

The "Devil."—Native Cat.—Tiger-çat.—Native Tiger, or Hyena.—
In at the Death.—Musk-rat.—Platypus.—Opossum Mouse.—
Kangaroo Mouse.

THE "Devil" is the name universally given here to the *Dasyurus ursinus*, and, as I have never heard any other appellation applied to this very ugly, savage, mischievous little beast, I must be permitted to use the one hitherto bestowed on it. This species is entirely black; another kind (*D. macrourus*), sometimes called "Spotted-tail," has a white tip to the tail, and a white stripe, extending down the throat and between the forelegs, towards which it sometimes spreads, forming three limbs of a cross: the pied species is rather less than the other, and not so numerous, but in all other respects they are alike. The body is 18 or 20 inches long, and the head forms nearly a third of this, being large, broad, and flat, apparently very destitute of brains. The jaws open to a terrific extent, nearly to the back of the enormous head, and are armed with large powerful teeth, like those of a dog. The tail is so stiff and unpliant, as to seem more like a wooden than a real one; when the animal runs, the tail sticks straight out. The feet resemble those of a dog, but the paws are more spread out, and have large strong claws. The creature has an awkward wabbling gait, and its pace is slow, as compared with that of most other wild animals. Mr. Meredith has at different times caught them, by fairly running them down; one of these was full grown, and ran for three-quarters of a mile, when, just as Mr. Meredith came close up with it, it suddenly stood still, and snapped at his legs, as he, unable to stop himself, jumped over it; he, however, soon killed it. The other two were younger ones, and were killed after a much shorter chase.

The devil's cry is a little like that of the opossum, but sounds ill-natured and spiteful, instead of the pleasant merry chuckle of the latter. The devils are often fearfully destructive, killing great numbers of lambs. At one of my father's stations on the Apsley River, north of Swan Port, the shepherds caught in a pitfall, during one winter, no less than a hundred and forty-three devils. They frequently appear to roam about in small packs, and, if a lamb be killed by one, the sheep are immediately removed to a distance, and traps set in the run; these are generally successful, and seven, eight, or more of these animals are caught in quick succession, after which months may elapse without the same spot being infested with them again. They, like the more valuable native animals, are gradually becoming rare in all the occupied parts of the island. A dead one, which was brought for me to see, so swarmed with *fleas*, that they formed a continuous brown under-coat all over its body, amongst the coarse, harsh, black hair; and the place on the veranda, where it was laid down for a few moments, became covered with them in such myriads as to force me with all my natural-history inquisitiveness to make way for mops and buckets of cold water.

The " Native Cat" of New South Wales, which I formerly described, is another species of *Dasyurus*, and the " Tiger-cat" of this island, I imagine, belongs also to this ferocious family. It is larger than the " native cat," and its colour is a handsome chestnut brown, spotted with white. Its habits are of the same savage destructive kind as those of the rest of its kindred.

The "Native Tigers" (*Thylacinus cynocephalus*) are yet more to be dreaded among sheep than the " devils;" but, fortunately, they are far less numerous. The tiger is a large powerful animal, about the size of the largest kind of sheep-dog, but more muscular. I have the skin of one, measuring 4 feet 6 inches from the nose to the end of the back, the tail being 1 foot 10 inches long in addition, compressed laterally, and set on more like that of a kangaroo than that of a dog. The hind legs have the lower joints peculiarly short, more so than those of a greyhound, and the animal frequently rests the whole joint on the ground, even when in a standing position *.

The first opportunity I had of noticing the animal alive, was when a shepherd in the neighbourhood came to show us one about two-thirds grown, which he had caught in a snare. Having killed the mother and caught the cub, he came to show his prize, and receive the usual tribute of money or tobacco, which is always given

* The woodcut of this creature in " Murray's Encyclopædia of Geography" is a good portrait of it; the *best* I have yet seen.

for a tiger killed or taken. He had the animal
secured by a chain and collar, and when it was to
be carried off, slipped a strong bag very adroitly
over its head and shoulders, pushed the hind legs
in, and fastened it. I pitied the unhappy beast
most heartily, and would fain have begged more
gentle usage for him; but I was compelled to
acknowledge some coercion necessary, as, when I
softly stroked his back (after taking the precaution
of engaging his great teeth in the discussion of a
piece of meat), I was in danger of having my hand
snapped off.

I obtained a place for this tiger in Sir Eardley
Wilmot's collection; but its untamable ferocity and
savageness resisted all endeavours to civilize and
tame it, and, in consequence, the carefully-stuffed
skin was eventually preserved, instead of the living
form of my ungentle protégé.

I believe the tigers are truly untamable, and in
that respect, if in no other, merit the name sometimes given them of Native Hyena; at least, I
know several instances in which young ones have
been kept and reared up kindly (chained, of necessity); but they never could be approached with
safety, even by those who daily fed them; and so,

on the whole, are perhaps rather ill adapted for pets. Their colour is very light brown, handsomely marked across the hind-quarters with ten or twelve straight bands of black, the hindmost ones about an inch wide on the top of the back, and tapering off on either side. The stripes become narrower and less distinct as they approach the shoulders, where they cease entirely. The head is much like that of a dog, and would be far from ugly were its expression less savage. The ears are short, open, broad, and erect, and look very soft; but I did not attempt to touch them, my previous attentions having been so rudely repulsed. The feet are also like those of a dog, and the legs thick and muscular; but the tiger is by no means so swift as its appearance would indicate.

The common pace of the tiger is a measured, steady canter, and, from various anecdotes I have heard, it appears that they pursue the object of their chase wholly by scent, and win (literally) "in the long run" by their long endurance. On one occasion Mr. Adam Amos, of Swan Port, had made his way, by a new track, to the top of the encompassing tier of mountains which separate the Swan Port district from the interior; after he had travelled for some time along the ridge of one of the numerous narrow steep "saddles," as they are termed, among the hills, the ground became so rocky that the fat cattle he was driving could not proceed any further, and he and his party encamped for the night. The next morning, about daybreak, they prepared to return, and were getting breakfast, when a brush kangaroo came along the ridge where they were, and hopped past, within a few yards of their fire. In ten minutes after this, a female tiger came cantering along in the same line, with her nose close to the ground, scenting out the kangaroo, and passed round the fire exactly in the same track, not noticing the cattle-party, who were observing the chase with some curiosity. About twenty minutes now elapsed, when two young tiger-whelps appeared, holding the same course, and, passing round the fire, went on after their mother, who, with her steady pace, would finally run down the more swift but less enduring kangaroo, and the cubs, following on her track, if not actually "in at the death," were no doubt in excellent time for the dinner.

Mr. Meredith, whilst one day gathering wild

cattle, having followed them into a thick scrub, dismounted, and sat down for a while to let his horse rest after the hard chase; shortly after, on hearing a loud heavy crashing amongst the sticks, he thought that some of the cattle had turned in that direction, when a very large tiger burst through the thicket, and came close by him, paused an instant to look at him, and then, dropping its nose again to the ground, followed on along the track of the cattle. They will, when hard pressed by hunger, attack even man. A servant being engaged, some years since, in a thick scrub, cutting "tea-tree" poles, an old tiger came up, and would have attacked him, but, being weak and apparently half-starved, was quickly knocked down and secured, and the man brought him home, where he was chained up and well fed, and so lived for some time. Being old and nearly toothless, the poor beast had been unable to procure his usual food, and was thus rendered daring and desperate.

The Musk-rat is a pretty little harmless animal, common in most rivers in Van Diemen's Land, and I have often watched them swimming about of an evening. They live in holes, which they

burrow in the river-banks, and seem to be of
similar habits to the English water-vole, but are
fully twice its size. Their fur is soft, and of a
reddish brown, paler beneath; the tail is well
furred, like the body, and is white at the end,
like that of the ring-tailed opossum. The head
is an enlarged portrait of the water-vole, with
similarly rounded nose, and long whiskers, very
pretty and gentle-looking: an odour of musk pervades the whole animal. The noise they sometimes
make, when playing in a river on a dark night,
would half induce one to fancy a shoal of porpoises were floundering there, instead of these
frisky little creatures; plopping in from the high
bank, scuffling along the water, and splashing
loudly about, they seem to glory in their agile
nimbleness; and I have often regretted that the
darkest nights were the seasons of their chief
revels, when they could only be heard and not
seen; for a musk-rat, swimming staidly and stilly
across the river in the dim twilight, evidently
charged with business of grave import, wears a
totally different aspect from the mad, frolicsome,
dissipated fellows of the night's revelry. One
morning, in passing along a path near a creek,

we espied one of them couched under a log,
amongst some scrub; he had, doubtless, stayed
out too late over night, and was overtaken by
daylight before he could reach home. Be this as
it may, the opportunity of seeing one of his species on dry land was too rare to be neglected, and
he very quietly permitted our scrutiny, only creeping more closely under the log when we threw
leaves or chips at him to make him move, and
uttering, by way of remonstrance, a sound something similar to that of the opossum. As soon
as we left the place, we saw him dart across the
path in the direction of the creek.

Another species of water-rat frequents the river
Mersey, on the north coast of Van Diemen's Land,
which is like the musk-rat in its habits, form, and
size, but has no white spot on the tail, nor is it at
all scented with musk.

The Platypus (*Ornithorhyncus paradoxus*) is
not common in Tasmania, but a few are found in
some of the northern rivers, the Mersey, Forth, &c.,
precisely similar to those in New South Wales.

The two rarest and most beautiful little animals
in the island are commonly known as the kangaroo
mouse and the opossum mouse. Of the latter, I

have seen three specimens, and most lovely, soft, curious little things they are; about the size of, or rather larger than, an English dormouse, with gray fur, soft as down, bright, full black eyes, wide transparent mouse-like ears, and prehensile tail, naked on the under side. The little face has the gentle expression of most of the kangaroo and opossum tribe; but during the daytime it is so snugly nestled round in its warm fur, and the closely-curled tail laid so carefully over it, that until the little creature is disturbed, it looks like a round gray ball, which, on being gently moved, gives to view the delicate little head; and this, looking imploringly at the intruder, utters a low kind of grumbling sigh, and tucks itself out of sight more completely than ever. At night it grows more lively, and, when so kept as to permit in some measure the display of its natural habits, is very active and graceful. A few fresh branches hung from the ceiling of a room, with the box or cage in which the mouse is kept placed among them with its door open, form a contrivance that sometimes answers, if the house be free from cats; the elegant movements of the agile sprightly little creature are then exceedingly amusing.

In their natural state, they inhabit holes in trees where they form exquisitely neat nests of grass and fibres, lined with soft down or web, and are seldom discovered until the tree is felled which contains their tiny habitation. Of the three I have seen, one was so found at "The Bogs," on the Swan Port tier, and given to our friend Mr. J. B. Jukes, who, I believe, kept it alive on board the "Fly" for nearly a year. Another jumped out from an old charred tree at Port Sorell, which Mr. Meredith set fire to; he caught the mouse and brought it to me in his hat; but, after looking at it awhile, we gave the poor little terrified panting creature its liberty, near its old haunt. The third was chopped out, nest and all, from a tree which one of our servants was cutting up for firewood, near the same place, and this one travelled to Hobarton in a tin wafer-box, lined with flannel and wool, to join Sir Eardley Wilmot's collection of native animals. During the time I kept it, it frisked about merrily at night, and ate heartily of bread slightly moistened and well sugared. I also provided it with fresh green food and rose-leaves, but the bread and sugar alone were eaten.

A fourth specimen was destined for me by our

head shepherd, who kept it for some time in his hut, where it lived in a tin canister on the chimney-piece, going in and out of its small dwelling as it pleased, and becoming quite tame; but being allowed so much liberty, it apparently wished for more, and ran away.

The female has several young ones at a time, which are most beautiful diminutive little morsels of animal life.

The Kangaroo Mouse I only know from description, never having been fortunate enough to see one. I believe it is much more slender and long in the limbs than the opossum mouse, but with the same general appearance and habits. One was lately caught near the Mersey by the settler whom I have already mentioned as having the tame wombat; seeing the little animal darting between his feet, he closed them at the instant and captured it. This was a female, with seven young ones in her pouch; all suffered the usual sad fate of such prizes, being doomed to imprisonment, and in a short time they died.

All the opossum tribe, when in a state of captivity, are very fond of sugar, and if suffered will eat it to excess. They will also eat tea-leaves, tobacco, and meat, all of which are unnatural to them; and I have no doubt that the usual very early deaths of tamed opossums are chiefly owing to such injudicious variety of food.

These "mice," as we call them, belong, I believe, to the genus *Phascogale*, and are marsupial, and with the pouch opening anteriorly, as is the case in all those which sit upright, jump on the hind feet, and use the fore-paws as hands, such as the kangaroo and opossum families.

END OF VOL. I.

MY HOME IN TASMANIA

LATH HALL.

FROM A SKETCH BY THE BISHOP OF TASMANIA.

MY HOME

IN

TASMANIA,

DURING A RESIDENCE OF NINE YEARS.

By Mrs. CHARLES MEREDITH.

Deloraine-Bridge.

Combining two volumes
VOLUME TWO

LONDON:
JOHN MURRAY, ALBEMARLE STREET.
1852.

CONTENTS.

CHAPTER I.

PAGE

Opossums not Sluggish. — My Tame Opossum. — Mischievous
Pranks.—The Opossum at Supper. — Awful Thunder-Storm.
—Varieties of Opossum.—The Ring-tailed Species   . . 1

CHAPTER II.

Wild Cattle.—The " Milking Bail."—" Mob."—Sheep-shearing.—
Harvest.—Wages.—The Bronze-winged Pigeon.—Quail.—Snipe.
—Native Hen.—Bittern.—Presents of Pets   15

CHAPTER III.

Green Parrots. — Rose-hill Parrots. — Parakeets. — Snakes. — A
Snake Charmer.—A Tame Snake.—Poison-fangs of Snakes.—
Lizards.—" Blood-sucker."—Spiders' Nests   . . . 28

CHAPTER IV.

Destroyers of Poultry.—Native Cats.—Hawks. —Crows.—Miner.
—Great Comet.—Excursion to the Coast.—View of the Schou-
tens.—Oyster Bay Pine.—" The Two Peterses."—Apsley River.
—Pacific Ocean.—Whaling Station.—Cray Fish.—Return Home   40

CHAPTER V.

Garden laid out. — " Water laid on."—Heavy Gale.—Itinerant
Threshing Machine.—Spring and Summer Flowers.—Acacia.—
Eucalyptus.—Epacris.—Native Lilac.—Lilies.—Stylidium.—
Orchidæa.—Sun-dew.—Native Rose.—The Tea-tree.—Berry-
bearing Shrubs   61

CHAPTER VI.

Improvements.—Fishing.—Water-fowl.—Bush-rangers.—Who's
there?—Domestic Security   79

CHAPTER VII.

PAGE

Unwelcome Changes.—Preparations for Removal.—A Dripping Guest.—Our " Family Carriage."—A Conjurer.—Departure.— Passage over the Tier.—" Hop-pole Bottom."—Economy of Government Officials.—Mount Henry 89

CHAPTER VIII.

Saint Paul's Plains and River.—Bog.—Ben Lomond.—Sojourn at the " Stony Creek."—" Deoch an Dorich."—" Eagle's Return." —Coaches.—Great Western Tier.—Perth.—Approach to Launceston.—Sojourn there.—Arrival at Carrick.—Old Water-mill . 101

CHAPTER IX.

Westbury.—Deloraine.—Wooden Bridge.—Bottled Ale and Porter. —Hospitality.—A New Friend.—Last Day of the Pilgrimage. —Avenue Plain.—Crossing the Rubicon.—The Forest.—Midday Halt.—Leech.—Night Ride.—Difficulties of the Road.— Safe Arrival 117

CHAPTER X.

General Sketch of " Lath Hall."—Cockatooers.—Poverty at Port Sorell.— Potatoes.— Port Sorell Horse-keeping.— Fences.— Dutch Barns.—Model Stables.—Police Station.—Pleasant Sea View.—" Clarissa."—Cottage Sites 134

CHAPTER XI.

Our New Neighbours.—Golden Rule for Ladies.—Touchstone and Audrey.— Veterinary Conversation.— Excursions.— Walk to the " Sisters."—Sea-Birds.—Pelicans and Porpoises, &c. . . 149

CHAPTER XII.

Expedition to an Enchanted Valley.— Lichens.—Nettles.—Ferntrees.—Small Ferns.—Natural Temple.— The Tallow-tree.— Sassafras.—Mischances by the Way.—Clematis.—Orchidaceous Flowers.—Native Laburnum 159

CHAPTER XIII.

Tasmanian Eagle.—White Hawk.—White Cockatoos.—Superb Warblers' Nest.—Strange Insect.—Venomous Guests.—Burning Trees.—Stinging Ants.—Flies.—Wood Tick . . . 170

CHAPTER XIV.

PAGE

Church-Building.—Public Worship.—Deficiency of Religious Instruction.—Rustic Costumes.—Leather "Leggings."—Progressive Love-tokens.—Marriage 185

CHAPTER XV.

A Winter at Port Sorell.—Four Months' Rain.—Voyage to Launceston. — The Town Wharf. — Journey to Hobarton. — Sir Eardley Wilmot.—Sketching Epidemic.—Exhibition.—A Fern Valley.—Cabs.—Mrs. Bowden's "Anson" Discipline.—Female Servants.—Religious Instruction 194

CHAPTER XVI.

Return Home.—Route over Badger Head.—The Asbestus Hills.— The New Cottage.—Goats and their Kids.—Garden.—Bees.— Native Wasps.—Flies versus Spiders.—Wasps' Nests.—The Dark Avenger.—Rose-tree Cuttings.—Wasp Stings . . 212

CHAPTER XVII.

Fish.—The Blue-head.—Sting-ray.— Bathing.—Crabs.— Shells.— Echini.—Starfish.—Sea Anemones.—Handsome Cuttle-fish.— Jelly-fish, &c.—A Marine Mrs. Gamp.—Elephant-fish . . 230

CHAPTER XVIII.

Improvements at Poyston. — The Harriet. — A New Bird. — Diamond Birds. — Dragon-flies. — Green Frogs. — Rabbits.— Great Owl.—Small Owl.—Mawpawk.—Bush Fires.—Providential Escape 243

CHAPTER XIX.

Resignation. — Removal. — Voyage. — Contrary Breeze. — Great Peril.—Anchor at George Town.—Overland Journey to Swan Port.—Arrival of the Harriet.—Riversdale.—Improvements. —The Veranda.—Pigeons and Fowls.—Plenty without Profit. —Conclusion 259

LIST OF ILLUSTRATIONS TO VOL. II.

LATH HALL	Frontispiece.
DELORAINE BRIDGE	Title-page.
SPIDERS' NESTS	Page 28. 39.
BEN LOMOND	,, 103.
POYSTON	,, 212.
ELEPHANT FISH	,, 230.
BADGER HEAD AND THE SISTER ISLANDS, FROM POYSTON	,, 243.
VIEW FROM THE GARDEN, POYSTON	,,, 258.

NINE YEARS IN TASMANIA.

CHAPTER I.

Opossums not Sluggish.—My Tame Opossum.—Mischievous Pranks.—
The Opossum at Supper.—Awful Thunder-Storm.—Varieties of
Opossum.—The Ring-tailed Species.

HAVING in my former "Sketches" alluded to the
common opossums, which are alike denizens of New
South Wales and Tasmania, I need not minutely
describe them again, but must beg to point out
what seems to me a lamentable error in the account
given of their habits in a recent and generally very
interesting work*, of which only a few of the
earlier numbers have reached us. They are there
described as "*sluggish and stupid!*" Perhaps I
ought, in the first place, to acknowledge my own
former ignorance in calling them "opossums" at
all, seeing that the zoologically learned have de-

* "The Pictorial Museum of Animated Nature." London : Charles
Knight and Co.

monstrated them to be "Phalangers," as I learn
from the work in question; but it is so hard to know
a thing suddenly by a new name, whilst every day
brings the familiar use of the old one, by which the
creatures are known here, that I fear it will be long
ere I learn to adopt readily the new and proper
appellation of my old favourites.

And now as to their sluggishness and stupidity.
That a poor imprisoned animal, shut up in a small
box or cage, fed on unwholesome and unnatural
food, and removed to an ungenial climate, where
it is never permitted to enjoy the free use of its
limbs, may seem stupid, is very possible, especially
if only observed in the daytime. When in its natural
state, it is always fast asleep in its nest in some dark
hollow tree, or coiled up in a thick tussock or
bush; but this same creature, in its own mild
climate, and in full possession of its liberty and
health, is as far removed from the "sluggish" or
"stupid" as any in the whole glorious creation;
and if the unconscious writer of that sad libel
could mark, as I have done, the scampering,
climbing, and chattering, and the headlong frolicsome gambols of the woolly elves in our forests on
a moonlight night, or witness the havoc which

morning shows, after their exploits in the harvest-
field, which was over-night as neatly laid out as a
newly-set chess-board, he would instantly re-cast
his unfair paragraph.   At harvest-time they are
specially provoking : I have seen one of our fields
left in the evening ready for the next day's carting ;
the rich heavy sheaves nicely set up and " capped "
in compact shocks, running in even lines from end
to end (and in a " paddock " of thirty acres and
upwards, as this was, the sight is a most pleasant
one), and I have visited the same field in the morning, to be reluctantly convinced that my favourite
opossums were really the mischievous imps they
are considered.   Scarcely a line of shocks remained
as it was, but numbers of them lay prostrate, the
sheaves scattered, the bands untied, and the heavy
corn beaten and trampled down, partly eaten, and
scratched about in woful waste and disorder.   The
chief scenes of the destruction were within wide
circles round several very large dead gum-trees,
which had been " ringed " and left to perish (a
ring of bark taken off all round causes a tree to
die, although the breadth of an inch left entire
saves it); and up and down these trees, and among
their great bare branches, and round about amongst

B 2

the shocks of corn, it appeared that the maddest of the revel had gone on. No doubt the kangaroos had been of the party, and had taken their share in the mischief, but the opossums were pronounced to be the principal delinquents.

I kept one of the common species tame for some months, and know their troublesome activity but too well. One of our servants, when out at night shooting them, killed two does, each having a young one in her pouch, and these he brought to me. They were then about two-thirds the size of an English squirrel, grayish brown, softfurred, sweet-faced little creatures; and I, as delighted with my prize as a child, directly ordered a large tea-chest to be made into a cage, with thin bars, and a door at one side to put them in. As the man went on preparing the new abode, he observed quietly,—

"Ah! ma'am, I've known a many people as kep' tame 'possums, but never a one as wasn't glad to be quit of 'em again!"

This, however, I treated as a most unworthy prejudice on the part of our good servitor, and diminished nothing of my zeal for the comfort of my poor little orphan pets. I gave them a warm bed of wool and fresh hay, in which they com-

pletely hid themselves during the day, clasping
each other with their paws and tails into one round
ball. I fed them with bread soaked in milk, and
slightly sweetened, but for the first few evenings I
had to give it to them very carefully with a small
spoon, not noticing their sharp little claws and
teeth ; and afterwards they fed themselves, picking
a piece out of the saucer and holding it in their
fore-paws, which, as well as the hind feet, have the
toes so long and slender as to seem just like fingers,
and in these little creatures the texture and colour
of the skin was soft and fair, quite a delicate pink,
like a baby's fingers. They grew fast, and played
with each other at night, as well as their roomy
cage would permit, and after a time began to eat
fresh young ears of corn, grass, parsley, &c., in
addition to their constant meal of bread and milk.
One day, when I was clipping the thyme-edging of
my flower borders, I unfortunately offered them a
small bit of it in blossom. One of them refused it,
but the other ate a young sprig about two inches
long, and coiled itself to sleep again. A friend who
dined with us that day, hearing me mention having
given some thyme to the opossum, immediately
said that it would die, as he had known others

killed in a similar manner. At night, when the cage was as usual carried in from the veranda to the hall, I saw that the one which had eaten the thyme was ill, and would not touch its food; its eyes were dim, its nose hot and dry, and its stomach frightfully distended. My attempts to remedy the evil I had so unconsciously done were all unavailing, and I put the poor little creature back into its cage, hoping, but not expecting, to see it recover; its companion seemed greatly distressed and puzzled by its sad condition, and tried to rouse it up to play as usual, but it grew worse, and in the morning was dead.

The survivor continued growing and thriving well, and soon got so clever as to open the fastening of his cage and let himself out into the hall, as soon as he had finished supper, and then such a scampering and scrambling and leaping and scuffling began, as no decent household, who did *not* keep "tame 'possums," ever heard before! Up the wall, and along the row of hat-pegs, knocking off all the hats and parasols to begin with; then, before you have time to catch a glimpse of the madcap, down he pops, and, with a half-jumping half-cantering sort of run, takes advantage of the door being left ajar for a moment, to frisk past you into the parlour; then climbing up the back of a chair, he twirls his long tail over the top, and swings by it gently to and fro, looking about him the while with a sly upturned face, till suddenly he takes aim at the sideboard, springs upon that, kicking off anything in his way, such as a stray decanter or flower-vase, and runs round the raised back to the centre scroll-work, where he sits a moment or two, and, while glancing round with his bright, glittering, black eyes, you see he is plotting new mischief, though he pretends to be wholly engaged in combing his whiskers with a fore-paw, or surveying the curling end of that mysterious proboscis-finger-hook-like tail. Some one moves or speaks, and off he flies, with a slide along the piano, and a scramble round the architrave of the door, and there he is, hooked up above it to a picture-frame; dangling again by his tail for a second or two, before that sudden *plop* down to the floor, and the quick scamper up the drawn curtains by his claws, till he secures a safe and unmolested seat on the top of the cornice, whence he complacently surveys all below: and all this in a quarter of the time it will take to read it! Never surely was there such

a beautiful, graceful, innocent-faced, sly, wicked
little piece of mischief! If my open work-box
were on the table, he made it a rule to spring up,
hook his tail to the lid, and straightway upset the
whole apparatus, flying before the scattered contents
into a corner, and peeping out like a sly, spoiled,
half-shy, half-frightened child; or if, determined
not to notice him, we sat still and silent, he would
slily climb the back of my chair and gently claw
my shoulder or bite my elbow; whilst his favourite
method of attracting Mr. Meredith's attention was,
to bite his toe, or pull the skirt of his coat, and
then scamper off to hide himself, only to return the
next moment and repeat the game. He stood in
some awe of the cat, with whom he frequently tried
to establish a pleasant and playful understanding,
but in vain. Mistress puss possibly considered him
a rival in her share of my affections, and always
repulsed his advances very rudely: when she
merely clawed at him, he ran away; but if she
forgot herself so far as to spit or growl, he instantly
turned back, and looked at her very earnestly, as if
debating within himself how such an indignity
should be received, or whether the offensive de-
monstrations were really directed to him!

At last we made a rule, never to admit Willy*
of an evening, until we were disposed to be idle;
for to read, write, or work, with this spirit of fidget
in the room, was impossible ; and he was restricted
to the hall and passage, with a fresh young wattle-
tree (perpetually renewed), set upright in a stand,
for his especial comfort: this was a kind and clever
contrivance of his master's, that our favourite might
enjoy something of his native habits, in swinging
amongst the branches.   Perhaps the drollest thing
was, to see him at supper, after he had attained the
size of a cat, and was quite independent in his ways
and manners.   His tree stood close beside the table
where his cage and saucer of bread and milk were
placed at night, and as he hung like a great live
pendulum, swaying about from a high branch, he
would stretch out one hand, and, taking a piece of
bread, proceed very composedly to eat it, with his
head hanging down, and his hind legs uppermost.
The sight of my little playfellow swallowing his
food in this topsy-turvy style, was enough to give
any one a fit of indigestion at least.

Willy fully appreciated the honour of being

* The name used by the natives of New South Wales for the
opossum.

B 3

admitted to our society, and used to make clamour-
ous demands to be let in, long before the appointed
hour, by running round the architrave of the
parlour door, and crying angrily from the top; one
night, as if to spite us, he contrived to slip into
our bedroom unknown to the housemaid, who had
orders to keep the door shut.   We had missed him
for some time, and, on going into our room and
looking about, I saw the bright wicked eyes peeping
at me over the cornice of the bed, and could soon
have dislodged Master Willy; but, as Mr. Meredith
had no objection to his company, he remained,
keeping up such a ceaseless scamper up and down
the curtains, rattling the rings, and scuffling about,
that sleep was out of the question, and I feared lest
he might jump down on George's cot, and awake
him in a fright; so, striking a light, and putting on
strong gloves, I watched my opportunity, and,
seizing his tail the next time it appeared, I gently
disengaged his claws and handed him into the
passage, where he grumbled and scampered round
the door-case till I fell asleep.

One evening when the weather was very sultry,
with constant lightning and distant thunder, Willy
failed to make his usual disturbance, and I searched

for him in vain. He had eaten his bread and milk, and was gone, no one knew whither; chimneys, pantry, beds—every place was examined, but no Willy could be seen, and we gave him up for lost, when, in returning along the hall, I saw something long and dark, hanging from one of Mr. Meredith's hats, against the wall; this proved to be Possy's tail, and all the rest of him lay tightly screwed up in the crown of the hat. I would not have him disturbed, and we never heard him move until near daylight. The tempest increased to a fearful height; I never heard so awful a thunder-storm, and the lightning was for seven or eight hours literally incessant; the flashes, blue and blindingly vivid, seemed to come several at once, and the simultaneous peals of thunder were deafening; their tremendous and closely-successive explosions, loudly reverberated by the surrounding mountain tiers, were truly terrific*.

Willy, with animal instinct, had doubtless known that a storm was at hand, and as, if in the forest,

---

* The aborigines of New South Wales have a great dread of thunder and lightning, and their words for these phenomena are singularly expressive, especially when uttered in their significant and earnest manner. They call lightning "mik'ka" (very short and sharp), and thunder is " moo'rooboo'rooboroy," with a lengthened rumbling pronunciation.

he would have lain quiet in his hollow tree, so, although well housed, he sought a place of close concealment, nor tried any of his wonted vagaries, until the storm had passed over.

Latterly he often opened his cage (which was fastened by a leather loop over a nail), before the time at which it was usually carried indoors; but I felt no apprehension of losing him, as he always cantered into the house, our front door, leading to the veranda and garden, being always open during the day. One evening, the servants were otherwise occupied, and I, having fed Willy in the veranda, forgot him, until after the door had been shut for the night, and then, on seeking him, I found that my " bird was flown," and the cage opened as usual. After this, we almost nightly heard an opossum on the roof, and various things left about, outside, were tossed over, very much in Willy's scrambling style, so that we believed the house to be still visited by its old inmate; but, though tempted with saucers of fresh sweet bread and milk for many nights, he never returned to his old cage: nor, I must candidly own, should I have desired to recover my pretty plague, could I have felt certain he was safe and happy; for I *had* sometimes acknowledged that keeping one "tame 'possum" had given me quite a sufficient insight into their manners and habits in a domestic state.

If any of my readers find this memoir of a pet "Phalanger" somewhat prolix, they must attribute my tediousness to my zeal for science, and my desire to make known whatever knowledge I may possess on this interesting subject: judging from the work before alluded to, which is the only recent book on natural history I have perused, these creatures are not very well known. Should I ever return to dear old England, I seriously contemplate bringing with me a large "consignment" of young opossums, for the especial solace and consolation of such of my friends as are now constrained to pamper apoplectic lap-dogs, asthmatic cats, spiteful parrots, and disgusting apes; confident that, by so doing, I shall confer an inestimable benefit on society in general, and benevolent maiden ladies in particular.

The black, golden, and gray opossums are, I imagine, distinct varieties, although identical in nature and habits. Our barn and stack-yard were often visited by them, and sometimes they came boldly about the house early in the night; one evening Mr. Meredith shot two very large ones in a wattle-tree within six yards of the kitchen door.

The "Ring-tailed Opossum" of Van Diemen's Land (*Phalangista viverrina*) is a smaller species than the common one, and still more elegant and agile, although I have seen them the size of a full-grown cat. Like their kindred, they sleep by day and play by night, when they hop and swing among the branches of trees with even a greater degree of rope-dancer buoyancy than the others. One which was kept at Cambria some years since, was occasionally admitted to the dining-room at dessert time, and once, desiring to lower himself down over the table's-edge, and at the same time hold on to it, he clasped the end of his tail tightly round the stem of a wine-glass, and boldly swung off, wofully surprised to find his frail support and himself on the floor together.

The ring-tails are gray, the under parts being of a lighter shade than the back, and about two inches at the tip of the tail is white; they seem to possess more sagacity than most of their kind, as they are never caught sleeping on the ground in the daytime, a situation in which so many opossums are killed by dogs.

CHAPTER II.

Wild Cattle.—The " Milking Bail."—" Mob."—Sheep-shearing. Harvest.—Wages. — The Bronze-winged Pigeon.— Quail. — Snipe. —
Native Hen.—Bittern.—Presents of Pets.

I WELL remember the extreme wonder and amusement with which, years ago, we read in England
the accounts of chasing the wild cattle here, and,
with something bordering on incredulity, heard of
" milking cows leaping five-barred gates like fox-
hunters." I have since discovered that there was
no romance whatever in the story, for some of our
wild herd here would in the Bush outstrip the
fleetest horse; and when "yarded," that is, put in a
stock-yard of massive logs, five or six feet high,
would frequently clear the top-rail at a bound. I
dreaded the periodical " collecting of cattle," more
than any other duty attendant on the farming
operations; suffered great anxiety while it lasted,

and always thankfully rejoiced to see "Master,"
men, and horses return home without serious
injury, after one of their campaigns of a week or
fortnight's duration; a station at some distance
from home being the usual centre of action. The
poor horses rarely escaped being hurt by severe
falls, besides being nearly ridden to death. Not
that a helter-skelter chase is the method adopted,
for, if the cattle are once suffered to start off at the
top of their speed, they become perfectly mad, and
very little chance remains of regaining them that
day at least. The utmost care and skill are
required to avoid alarming them; and the grand
object is, not to make them run, but to prevent
their doing so. Four horsemen are usually sufficient to collect a small herd of two or three
hundred cattle.

When near the place where they expect to find a
herd, they ride quietly and silently along in
"Indian file," through the Bush, and the first
person who discovers the cattle gives a low whistle,
when all stop, and, observing their position, separate, and endeavour to surround them, but more
especially to cut off their retreat into a thicket or
swamp, or other hiding-place, where pursuit would be

impossible; the chief endeavour being to get them into a piece of open country, where the stock-riders can circle them round and round, so as to narrow the space they occupy, and get them to stand, which is the great difficulty, and care is taken not to scare or alarm them in any way. Sometimes one or two or more dart away, and, if not recovered immediately, are suffered to gallop off, as, whilst pursuing them, the rest might be lost. Other "lots" belonging to the herd are collected and joined to these, and the whole driven, or rather manœuvred, in the direction of the station or stock-yard, where the calves are to be branded with the mark of the owner, and steers, cows, and "beef" selected for use. On approaching a "scrub," with only a narrow cattle-path through it, one or two of the stock-keepers ride on ahead to the clear ground, so as to be in readiness to check the cattle when they emerge upon it, otherwise they would again set off at full speed. They are then conducted along, with one horseman ahead, to keep them from going too fast, one on each side, and one behind; and if this, the proper routine, can be observed, the gathering is thought to be very easily accomplished.

Horses accustomed to the task understand the whole programme as well as their riders, and will pursue a run-away beast through an intricate forest, or avoid the attacks of the infuriated animals, with the most nimble adroitness.

As may be supposed, these wild animals have a strong repugnance to enter a gate, and care is taken, on their approach, to leave all open and clear for them, and to remove out of sight all dogs, people, and everything that is likely to alarm them. I have often seen the drove selected for use, and not considered wild, as compared with many others, brought within a few yards of the gateway leading to our farm-yard several hours before they could be got through it. They would often approach tolerably near, as if about to trot quietly in, when, with a start and a snort, they would burst off, some one way, some another, through the river, into the scrub, " o'er the hills and far away," and the poor weary horses be compelled to gallop furiously after them, till the " lot" was again collected, and perhaps with the same result, again and again. Sometimes a party of more civilized animals were turned out to meet and mix with the strangers, who might possibly be beguiled into rushing in with them altogether, but this plan would only answer occasionally.

Extreme activity, nerve, and presence of mind are essential in the business of the stock-yard, where fifty or more of these raging creatures are pent up together, and it is necessary for persons to go in amongst them to draft certain of them off, "rope" them (*i. e.*, catch them by flinging a noose over their heads), &c., avoiding, as they best may, the apparently inevitable fate of being impaled on some pair of the entangled mass of horns threatening them on all sides, the only mode of escape being by a leap over the stock-yard itself, when a stumble, or a moment's hesitation, might be fatal.

Some of the cows from such a herd are very troublesome before they can be quietly milked, and it is necessary to have a kind of pillory, called a "milking bail," in which, without hurting them, their heads are held fast, and a leg of the refractory ones tied also, to prevent them from injuring both themselves and the milkman, who, with the aid of this simple contrivance, seldom fails in soon making them quiet. Sometimes they have an incorrigible desire to run away back to the hills, leaving their

calves, and the rich pasture, and a life of ease, to
go galloping about with the herd.

"Milkmaids" are out of the question among
such cattle as these, so that the pictures, so
common at Home, of buxom damsels tripping about
with pails and three-legged stools, would find few
living resemblances here.

A number of cattle together is here usually
termed a " mob," and truly their riotous and unruly
demeanour renders the designation in this case far
from inapt; but I was very much amused at first, to
hear people gravely talking of " a mob of sheep,"
or " a mob of *lambs*," and it was some time ere I
became accustomed to the novel use of the word.
Now, the common announcements that " the cuckoo
hen has brought out a rare mob of chickens," or
that "there's a great mob of quail in the big
paddock," are to me fraught with no alarming anticipations.

December being, with us, midsummer as well as
Christmas, brought with its warm sunny weather
the summer tasks of sheep-washing and shearing.
The former part of the business was easily and
efficiently performed in a bright running pool in the
Swan River; and as we had as yet no suitable

buildings erected for the latter, a temporary boarded
floor was laid in a stable, around which the sheep-
pens and yards were arranged with hurdles. This
brought the busy scene rather close to the house,
but in our young establishment we could not have
all things fit at first, and I was too well pleased
with the progress already made to find room for
complaint. Master George was, of course, in a
great state of delight, and tumbled over hurdles,
got knocked down by the sheep, hugged the dogs,
made friends with the good-natured shearers and
shepherds, and got in everybody's way with impunity, as long as the, to *him*, charming disturbance lasted.

The lambs of our flock were all shorn at the
same time as the old sheep, a far more humane
method than that usually practised here ; most
persons choosing to leave the lambs' fleeces to grow
a month or two longer, so as to obtain a larger
" clip," thus stripping the poor animals of their
warm natural clothing just as the cold autumnal
and wintry weather approaches ; and, although
great numbers of lambs perish miserably in consequence, the cruel and short-sighted custom is still
obstinately adhered to by many, to whom interest,

if not humanity, might teach a wiser course. We
had the satisfaction of seeing our fat frisky lambs
with good warm winter coats on again by the time
they needed them, and their healthy lusty condition
was an ample compensation for the temporary
sacrifice of a few pounds of wool.

Sheep-shearing ended on the 11th of January,
and harvest began on the 26th of the same month.
Heavy and luxuriant were the crops our new land
yielded us, and most pleasant it was to see wide
fields of golden grain waving in the sunshine, and
rows of sturdy reapers busily plying their gleaming
sickles, where, only the year before, we had with
difficulty threaded our tortuous way through scrub
and forest.

And pleasant, too, was it to see the goodly stack-
yard fast filling with the plenteous store, hard by
the little spot where our first modest wheat-rick had
gladdened our grateful hearts. Now, instead of one
small one, five large portly stacks stood in brave
array, and the erection of a capacious barn and
straw-yard gave the finishing touch to that portion
of our farm arrangements.

The extra " hands" engaged for the harvest each
received a dollar (4s. 4d.) a day, with the same

unlimited allowance as our own servants, of meat,
flour, vegetables, tea, and sugar, and a bottle of
wine a day each. To each of our own men, Mr.
Meredith gave £2 after harvest, as a reward and
encouragement for good behaviour and diligence.
These were prisoners, not better than the average;
but they were industrious, well-conducted men,
who, though under strict discipline, needed not a
day's punishment whilst in our service *.

Numbers of the beautiful bronze-winged pigeons
frequented our corn-fields and stubble, affording
Mr. Meredith a little shooting, in which murderous
diversion I must not deny being an accomplice, for,
by walking up the lands of the field, I put up the
birds, whilst he shot them as they flew over towards
the scrub. They are considerably larger than the
common tame pigeon, and their plumage is a soft
purplish dove-colour, with a reddish glow upon the
breast, and the resplendent prismatic hues on the
wings from which they are named. In some the
preponderating gleam is green, and in others red,

---

* Wages were at that time high, good ploughmen and farm-servants
receiving from 35l. to 40l. a-year, with rations, &c.; but as wheat was
then worth 10s. a bushel, and wool 1s. 6d. a pound, the farmer's pro-
spects were far better than since (1847-8-9), with wages from 10l. to
15l., wheat 3s., and wool 10d.

but always bright and lustrous, like a peacock's back, or a pearly shell in the sunshine. They have pretty pink feet and ruby-ringed eyes. I have often thought of trying to domesticate some, by rearing them with my tame pigeons; their rich plumage and handsome shape would be very ornamental. A friend of ours had one so tame that it flew about his house, sat on his shoulder, and, when he went from home, would accompany him for a considerable distance, and then fly back again. The poor bird was at last accidentally destroyed, to its master's great regret.

When cooked, the bronze-winged pigeon is excellent, being plump, tender, and well-flavoured, very nearly the size of a good partridge, and here, where those birds are not to be had, is our best substitute for them. The meat on the breast is of two distinct colours, white and brown, in two separate layers.

A few quail bred among the corn, but they are always scanty in number; the native vermin, as well as hawks and snakes, and cats of the domestic breed, become wild, are all terribly destructive to them.

Before the marshes were drained, snipe were often plentiful in them, but are now very rare.

Our dogs often found a bird commonly known
here as a native hen, and chased it out of the
scrubs or long grass; but unless a gun came to
their aid, they did not often succeed in catching
one, for the bird is exceedingly swift afoot. It is
something like a common fowl in shape and size,
of a dusky copper-tinged colour, with long powerful legs, and dark, generally tough flesh. It is
eaten and relished by some persons when skinned
and nicely stewed, but requires good cooking to
render it palatable. The noise the native hens
make at night exactly resembles that made in
setting a saw.

One evening Mr. Meredith was looking for wild
ducks beside the river, when a rustling flight from
the tall sedges near induced him to fire, and he
shot a fine bittern, much to our regret, for we had
long known by the strange " boom," heard at night,
that we had one for a neighbour, and would not
willingly have had it destroyed. Its long fringed
neck and crest, and tall slender legs, reminded me
of the heron, and, for old acquaintance' sake, I
should have rejoiced in having it about us alive.
Its plumage is a sober brown, with markings and
shades of darker and lighter hues, altogether much

more grave and ancient-looking than the bright array of the blue cranes.

All kinds of wild things used to be brought to me by our servants, for pets, until the very unlooked-for ways in which I disposed of most of them had the desired effect of damping their well-meant ardour in making captures. One man brought me a hatful of beautiful young quail, which he found among the corn, and I felt very much tempted to try to rear them; but knowing that such experiments usually ended fatally for the poor little birds, I contented myself with looking at the lovely, tiny, little helpless things, and had them straightway carried carefully back to the place whence they were taken, so that the old birds might find them again, and, as the young brood was well-grown, fledged, and active, I am fain to hope they did.

Another man brought me a nest of wild ducks, which, by the time he had drank the tumbler of wine I gave him, I had determined to dispose of exactly as I did the quail. A third caught for me a pair of robins, but my love for the bright little birds is much too great to permit me to imprison them, or indeed any others. Birds in cages are

to me most distressing and melancholy objects;
I never keep pets that must be so utterly deprived
of their freedom; for my pleasure in possessing
them would be outweighed tenfold by the sight and
knowledge of their unhappiness.

SPIDER'S NEST.

CHAPTER III.

Green Parrots.—Rose-hill Parrots.—Parakeets.—Snakes.—A Snake Charmer.—A Tame Snake.—Poison-fangs of Snakes.—Lizards.— "Blood-sucker."—Spiders' Nests.

ONE family of birds may invariably be found in this island wherever there is grain for them to steal, and these are the handsome, merry, impudent, wicked, rainbow-plumag'd, thieving parrots. The common kind, attired in shaded green, with a yellowish breast, and a few blue feathers in the wings and tail, is the most daring and incorrigible. These beset the stack-yard in legions, literally covering some of the

ricks, and terrible is the havoc they commit, clawing off the thatch and scooping caverns beneath,
into which they retreat when attacked, and peep out
in the most provoking way imaginable, crying
continually "cushee—cushee—cushee!"—and, when
assailed by volleys of sticks or stones, will often
only bob down their round saucy heads, or hop
aside to avoid a blow, and go on coolly pecking the
ears of corn they hold in their claws, as if the
assault were a most unprovoked and unwarrant-
able one.

They are not deemed worth powder and shot,
but may be knocked down with sticks, and when
skinned are tolerably good in pies.

All our parrots here have long tails, and are what
I should in England have called parroquets. The
stuffed specimens in museums, and in Gould's
magnificent work on Australian birds, have probably
made the chief of them familiar to my readers.
The Rose-hill, or Rosella parrot, is the gayest of the
family indigenous to Tasmania; the brightest and
most positive colours are distributed over its
brilliant attire with such startling contrasts as would
be unpleasantly gaudy in anything but a bird.
Only imagine a lady dressed in a scarlet turban,

green shawl, scarlet and yellow stomacher, green
dress (a different shade to the shawl), and long
purple train, edged with sky-blue! Yet all these
clear and distinct colours are united in this bird's
radiant plumage. A group of them daintily pacing
about in the sunny garden, climbing among the
plants, picking flower-seeds, and performing all the
elegant, affected, coquettish antics which only
parrots can do, is a sight that well repays me for
the loss of many a half-hour which I cannot but
waste in watching them.

They are very easily tamed to follow their master
about the house, or sit on his hand; but they
cannot be taught to speak or sing so well as the
larger kinds of parrots: I have never heard any
here which are comparable, in point of accomplish-
ments, to the large gray and green parrots I used
to know in England.

The most exquisite of all the Tasmanian species
is the little green parakeet, which is not much
larger than a fat sparrow. Its plumage is of two
colours only, green and red, but the green is a
living emerald, and the red is like that of moist
coral; it is sparingly displayed about the head and
tail. A flock of these radiant little creatures

skimming past—for they fly very swiftly, and are much more shy than the larger species—can scarcely be exceeded in beauty by the gorgeous lories of New South Wales. They appear to live on the honey of flowers, chiefly gum-blossoms, and are very short-lived in captivity, none, that I have heard of surviving more than a year.

The ground parakeet is a singular species, never being seen to perch on a tree, but always alighting on the ground. Its colour is clear bright green, barred and spotted with black; it is described to me as very beautiful, but it is so rare that I have not yet seen it.

I had feared that we should suffer much alarm and annoyance from snakes at Spring Vale, judging from the numbers destroyed there during the first year of its occupation as a farm; but, with the exception of one found in the stable litter, and two killed in the cellar at different times, we saw none very near the house; and the number destroyed by the men on the farm was not a quarter so large as during the previous year.

A very thick black snake was brought home one day, and, on being opened, was found to contain a nearly full-grown kangaroo-rat, quite entire, all but

the head, which was already digested; the snake
was not quite four feet long, and the kangaroo-rat
measured ten inches in length, with proportionate
girth.

Several well-authenticated instances have been
related to me of snakes being killed, which had
half-swallowed other snakes very little smaller than
themselves, the lower portions of which were in
process of digestion in the devourer's stomach,
whilst the yet unswallowed half hung out of its
mouth.   One of these was discovered by a boy
treading on it, when, to his horror, the reptile
instantly coiled itself round his leg, but without
biting him, and, on a person coming to his aid,
it was found that the snake's mouth was fully
occupied and distended by the body of another
snake.

The extreme coolness with which some persons
will attack snakes is, to me, perfectly terrible.   One
of our men-servants had a peculiar talent in this
way, and would, after peeping into a snake's hole,
thrust in his bare hand and arm, deliberately draw
out the deadly inmate by the tail, and, holding
it up for a few seconds, swing it round, and dash
its head to pieces against a tree or log, with as

much *sang froid* as any one else would crack a whip!

It is said that when a snake is held up by the tail, and gently swung round and round, it cannot turn up its head so far as to bite the hand. I can hardly imagine any one trying the experiment.

Considerable interest has been excited here lately by the wonderful performances of a prisoner named Underwood, who professes to have the power of "charming" any kind of snake, so as to render it gentle and innoxious; and he has exhibited his extraordinary faculty before the Lieutenant Governor, the Bishop of Tasmania, several medical men, and many others of the most intelligent persons in the colony, all of whom bear testimony to his evident power over the reptiles. He handles the most venomous snakes with impunity, tying them in knots, or putting them in his bosom, and suffering them to make their way down over his body, taking them up from the leg of his trousers. All such feats, however, are merely surprising; but he also declares that he possesses an effective antidote for the bites of all venomous reptiles; it consists of a liquid, a drop or two of which is to be immediately applied to the wound. I believe that its efficacy has been tolerably well tested, and Underwood has obtained permission from the Government to compound and sell his antidote for his own advantage. He says he learned the secret of its composition when at Callao, and would disclose it if his pardon were granted to him in return. Should the remedy prove really as valuable as at present represented, the inestimable benefit it confers on all dwellers in these and other snake-infested countries does indeed demand a most generous reward.

Many years ago Mr. John Amos, one of the oldest settlers in Swan Port, whilst ploughing, with his feet bare, accidentally trod upon a large black snake, close to its head : with admirable and surprising presence of mind, knowing it could not hurt him while in that position, he let go of the plough, and stood fast, whilst the reptile twined itself tightly round his leg and struggled to get away; but he held on stoutly until a knife could be brought to cut off the snake's head, and free him from a situation which very few would have nerve enough to endure, notwithstanding the prudence of doing so.

Differences of taste are proverbially great, but perhaps in few instances more strikingly shown than in the choice of tame pets, some persons patronizing hens, some mice, and some monkeys, and it seems even snakes have their patrons, for Mr. Meredith was once absolutely horror-stricken at seeing an old servant exhibit to him a tame snake, which he kept in an old tea-kettle; and, when desirous of enjoying its company, would take off the lid, put his hand in, and pull out his strange friend as unconcernedly as a boy would fetch out a tame guinea-pig! The precaution of a cork was adopted, to prevent the possibility of the reptile's absconding by going up the spout.

The black snake seems unable to give many mortal bites in quick succession, the venom, as it would appear, becoming exhausted. Some years since a large snake was seen to bite three dogs, one after the other, as they attacked it in turn. The dog first bitten died almost immediately; the second in about two hours; and the third, after being very ill for some time, eventually recovered.

I am not aware how many kinds of snakes infest Van Diemen's Land. Most of those killed come under the two denominations of "black" and "diamond" snakes, but I have observed varieties in the shades and marking of their skins, which probably constitute several distinct species; both these are sometimes found five feet in length, but more commonly three-and-a-half, and four feet. A smaller kind of snake, of a green colour, is also known, but is less common.

In examining the heads of snakes, the venomous fangs are distinctly visible, two or three being placed together on each side of the upper jaw; and, in a newly-killed snake, they can be raised or depressed with a pin or needle, the bag of venom at their base being also seen. The teeth, when examined with a microscope, appear transparent, with a tube traversing nearly their whole length, and opening on the side, leaving one-fifth of the tooth like a solid point, which pierces the thing bitten, whilst the venom-bag, squeezed by the pressure of the tooth, ejects the poison through the tube into the wound. The mechanism of this terrible weapon of destruction very much resembles that of the spines of the stinging-nettle.

The length of the venomous fangs in the head of a snake which Mr. Meredith destroyed a few days since was about the sixth of an inch. We were walking over a wooded rocky point above the sea-beach: I had lingered a moment behind, gathering flowers, and was hastening on again, when a very large diamond snake darted almost from beneath my feet; when struck with a stick, and severely hurt, it turned fiercely upon us, with its hideous head flattened out, and its throat distended, looking as nothing but a snake *can* look; unable to reach us, it seized its own body in its teeth, and held it tenaciously for some seconds; then, suddenly loosing, fastened on another part, and bit again in a most savage and determined manner.

Several kinds of little harmless lizards are found here, similar to those in New South Wales; one of them frequented our dining-room at Riversdale, often amusing me, when I have been sitting alone and silent, by its swift movements, and adroit capture of flies on the floor and wainscot, into a crevice of which it disappeared when alarmed.

Another description of lizard is here vulgarly called the " blood-sucker," and is supposed to be venomous, but I think this is probably an error, the extreme ugliness of the unlucky little reptile being, with most persons, deemed ample evidence against it. Its body is dark gray, marked with black above and white beneath; in shape it is broad and squat, rather toad-like in aspect; both the body and the long tail are rendered somewhat formidable by longitudinal rows of larger scales than the rest, set up like spines. The head of one species of blood-sucker is hooded, of the other, bare, but both are very ugly. They are six or eight inches long.

Some of our spiders form most ingenious nests of gum-leaves, webbed together at the edges. I annex a sketch*, which I made long ago, from a very pretty nest formed of five green leaves, perfectly closed up at both ends. After I had had it some days, a flock of tiny spiders came out and ran about. I have often, since then, seen what appeared, at a first glance, to be a spider's web scattered full of coarse pepper, hanging to the threads, but the slightest touch transformed the grains each to an active little spider. The two other clever nests, each formed of a single gum-leaf, were also the habitations of spiders. Ground-

* See page 28.

spiders are likewise very numerous, with beautifully-
formed cells, in the earth, but they are less often
seen with doors to their houses than those of New
South Wales.

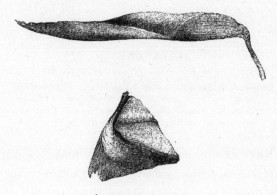

SPIDERS' NESTS MADE OF GUM-LEAVES.

CHAPTER IV.

Destroyers of Poultry.—Native Cats.—Hawks. —Crows.—Miner.—
Great Comet.—Excursion to the Coast.—View of the Schoutens.—
Oyster Bay Pine.—" The Two Peterses."—Apsley River.—Pacific
Ocean.—Whaling Station.—Cray Fish.—Return Home.

NEXT to my perpetual horror of snakes, I may
rank among minor colonial troubles the annoyance
suffered from the various depredators amongst our
poultry. Hens which would not sit in the fowl-
house, but chose to select their own nests in the
Bush, were frequently taken by native cats, and
most often just as the young brood was hatched.
A trap, baited with some meat of rather high scent,
was sometimes successful in catching the delin-
quent, but as often failed. Hens with young
broods under coops were in great danger at night,
even though I always took the precaution of
placing them close to the house. We well knew, by
their cries, when cats were near them, and many

a midnight sally to the rescue took place in consequence. One poor partlet was attacked thrice in the same night; and, being unable to see and shoot the enemy, Mr. Meredith left a lighted lantern in front of her domicile, to prevent further molestation; but in the morning we found she had been so much hurt, that it was necessary to kill her. The thin, wiry, native cat had, apparently, squeezed itself in and out through the bars of the coop.

Cats of the common domestic breed are now wild in the colony in considerable numbers, and are fully as destructive among poultry as the native vermin. One, which had been reared on the farm a demure and respectable kitten, and had taken to disorderly and predatory habits in her mature age, committed sad havoc among my half-grown chickens and sitting hens, and for a time eluded all our vigilance. One evening Mrs. Puss was detected stealing crouchingly along under the shadow of a fence, when a shot from a gun, so often vainly devoted to her service, in a moment cut short her hopes of " chicken-fixings."

The hawks, as a matter of course, rank prominently among my poultry-perils, and I truly

grieve that they are so terribly mischievous, for
their noble stately beauty almost disarms one's
enmity; and, shameless freebooters and tyrants as
they are, I cannot help sorrowing for every one
that I see killed.

The common brown hawk of this island is a
noble and powerful bird, and, when perched,
stands sixteen or seventeen inches high, with an
immense span of wing. The plumage of the back
and tail is rich hazel-brown, barred with a darker
shade, and that of the breast a soft pale tint of
gray, warming into fawn-colour, also barred across
with deeper hues: very grave, but exceedingly beautiful; a chaste, quiet, tasteful dress, well suiting a
bird of his ancient and aristocratic race.

"Old times are changed" for the glorious-eyed
bird; in these railroad days, and this matter-of-
fact colony, the once favoured of courts, and the
caressed of rank and beauty, is simply regarded
as an arrant thief and most impudent marauder.
Very many were killed at Spring Vale. During
one of our morning rambles round the fields, Mr.
Meredith shot four; the first was one of a pair,
which rose from a dead bandicoot, or other like
delicacy on the ground, as we passed. After

shooting another at some distance farther on, two
more appeared, high overhead, approaching the
place, and Mr. Meredith, having reloaded his gun,
flung the dead bird high in the air, when instantly
the two stooped towards it, and the two barrels,
fired in quick succession, killed them both.

The boldness of hawks in pursuit of their prey
is well known, and I have seen them follow our
fowls or tame pigeons so close to the house,
that, as the frightened creatures darted within for
protection, the hawk's wings nearly brushed the
door.

The crows, too, were most audacious in their
forays for eggs and chickens; the former species
of theft I might perhaps have been tempted to
overlook, by my admiration for their beautiful
sable plumage, and their identity of kind with
their English brethren; for, to resemble anything
which speaks to me of *Home*, is a royal road to
my favour. But after procuring, with some pains
and trouble, a set of white turkey-eggs, and after
all the cares and anxieties inseparable from the
duties of poultry-rearing—after seeing my eight
interesting little chickens thriving well, and beginning to chase ants and grasshoppers on their

own account—after all this, could human patience (*feminine*) endure to see one—two—three—four successively pounced upon, and carried squeaking away by the same grave, solemn-looking culprit? So the gentleman in black was one day ignominiously shot, in the act of chasing a young chicken into a wattle-bush, and his body formally nailed to a tree, near which I usually placed my young broods, as a rather pointed moral lecture to his surviving relatives on the fatal consequences of such evil courses.

A very amusing and pretty bird, here called the miner, often assisted us in detecting the hawk, when the latter had taken refuge in a tree out of sight. These miners, or minors (for the etymology of the name has often puzzled me), are nearly the size of a blackbird; their plumage is a delicate French gray, with darker shades on the wings and tail, and a little black cap, and touches of yellow about the head; and their general air and expression are extremely piquant and saucy. They are evidently great gossips, perpetually hunting out and interfering with every bird in the neighbourhood; and a whole troop may frequently be seen chasing a marauding hawk or egg-steal-

ing crow, flying all round in the busiest manner,
and uttering their quick, sharp, distinct cry of
"Thief! thief! thief!" Their own morals being
none of the purest, we might expect them to be
chary of abuse; but, apparently, their individual
experiences in theft only render them the more
alert in detecting the peccadilloes of their brethren, and we have often traced out our poultry
foes through their agency.

Their depredations in orchards are really serious,
and their impudence is so imperturbable, that nothing short of mortal wounding will scare them
from their stolen banquet. A fine bearing cherry-
tree, one of our richest prizes from the Cambria
orchard, was planted close to one end of the veranda, in the belief that there the fruit would be
safe, as persons were constantly passing to and
fro; but our busy friends took up their daily
abode in it as soon as the cherries began to
ripen, and continued to partake of our store, in
the proportion of the lion's share, as long as any
remained. Yet was it well worth the loss of a
few cherries to witness the impudent *nonchalance*
of these miners—how they would hop and creep
about the branches, and, instead of flying off when

pelted with gravel or shouted at, would pop out
their bright-eyed saucy heads from amidst the
clustering leaves, and cry "thief! thief!" as loudly
as ever, straightway making a fresh onslaught on
the fruit with such honest-looking confident as-
surance, that I almost began to doubt whether they
or we were the rightful proprietors of it.

A rather suspicious circumstance occurred one
day, not reflecting much credit on the miner as a
kind or charitable neighbour. Mr. Meredith, in
shooting at a wattle-bird in the top of a high
tree, only winged it, and, as it fluttered down, it
alighted in a bush, whither he watched it whilst
reloading his gun, and then ran to the spot,
where he found the wounded wattle-bird fluttering and struggling in the claw of a miner,
which would not loose its hold until struck and
driven away.

The sudden appearance of the great comet of
this year (1843), which we first saw on the
5th of March, was a glorious incident in our
somewhat monotonous life here; which, with its
ever-recurring digging, clearing, and "grubbing,"
ploughing, sowing, and reaping, perhaps does
tend to make our thoughts savour "of the earth,

earthy;" but this stupendous visitant gave them, for a time, a loftier impetus.

Mr. Meredith determined to measure the apparent length the comet subtended on the sky, although we did not possess a single fit instrument for such a purpose. But not even Sir James South, or her Majesty's Astronomer Royal, ever set about an investigation with more zeal and high resolve! Firstly, there was made, with all possible accuracy, a "cross-staff" and plummet, and thus we proceeded to work:—At night, and when the comet was brightest, with the nucleus just above the mountain tier, we "set up our instruments" (*i. e.*, laid them on a chair), on the lawn. My office was that of worthy Master George Seacoal, "to bear the lantern," carefully darkened until required. When my better and cleverer half had fairly shot the nucleus, at which he took deliberate and deadly aim with the cross-staff, I brought the lantern to bear on the latter, and marked with a pencil where the thread of the plummet fell; ascertaining the altitude of the extremity of the tail in like learned and scientific manner: and then, after taking the respective bearings by the compass, also aided by the lantern, and repeating the whole ceremony twice or thrice, to test the accuracy of the results, our astronomical observations ended for the night. If not very grave or dignified, the style of the proceeding was infinitely diverting; and, as it eventually proved, some of the greater lights among the learned here were less correct than we and our lantern, for, after the comet's length had been calculated, and published in the colonial papers, to our no small mystification, as 23° only, it was finally declared to be 42°, the same result as that we had arrived at in our primitive method of measurement, which was, of course, highly gratifying and satisfactory.

The popular responsibilities of comets in general are known to be heavy and various, and this being a comet of such vast and startling dimensions, had naturally a great deal to answer for, with some of the simple good people around us. If the sun shone pleasantly out, the comet was bringing " terrible hot weather;"—if a shower of rain fell, the comet brought that too, and would most probably favour us with a flood;—if the hens ceased laying, the comet had frightened them;—if an apple-tree died, the comet had blighted it;—and, whatever

domestic accident occurred, whether a baby cut a
tooth, or its mother spoiled a batch of bread, it
was "all along of that comet!"

To us its rapid progress was a source of great
interest; night after night we traced it, changing
its direction, and traversing one constellation after
after another, waning in brightness as it receded,
until first a doubt arose whether we *could* discern
it, and then came the reluctantly-acknowledged
certainty that we could *not*. We felt as if some
friend and companion, who had for a while spoken
to us, with stirring eloquence, of the glory of Nature, and of Nature's GOD, had departed from beside us.

Mr. Meredith had long projected an excursion to
show me the river Apsley and the eastern coast
north of Oyster Bay, about thirty miles distant
from Spring Vale; and this year, after harvest, we
arranged our little plan, which involved the necessity for an absence from home of two nights. I
fabricated for myself a nondescript kind of valise
or knapsack, to hang over the pommel of the
saddle and fasten with the girths, which contained,
in marvellously small space, the essentials for a
travelling toilette, besides a pocket telescope and

sketch-book; and, mounted on the gentle and beautiful Arab dedicated in her old age to my especial service, I set forth with Mr. Meredith, on a fine autumn afternoon early in March, to cross the tier, and remain the night at the house of a settler eight miles on our way, so as to enable us to reach the coast and return thither the following day.

On the verge of our own land we passed the cottage and busy blazing forge of our tenant the blacksmith, whose forty acres had yielded him a good return; and a bonny wheat-stack, a well-filled garden, and oxen, poultry, and pigs in plenty, made a pleasant show of homely comforts all about it. Beyond this, the road entered on the property of the Amos family, who deserve honourable mention at the hands of any chronicler of this island, as being among the best farmers it contains. I know not any spot here which so vividly recalls to my mind the scenery and character of an English village, as the group of homesteads and the surrounding cultivated land occupied by different members of this family. The substantial buildings include several good houses (now embosomed in Home-like gardens), a large water-mill on the bank of the Swan River, barns, and all other requisites ; and the strong neat fences, in many places lined with thick hedges of sweetbriar, the perfectly-cleared and well-farmed land, and the air of abundance and comfort pervading the whole, form a most striking contrast to the slovenly, improvident style of farming prevalent in some other parts of the colony.

Shortly after fording the river, we began to ascend the hills, over which a very rough and stony track passes, certainly not worthy to be called a road, as by all, save colonial travellers, it would be pronounced totally impassable.

We gained a few very pretty peeps of wild mountain scenery, wherever the dense forests around afforded an open vista; particularly a foreshortened view of the Schoutens, which was very beautiful, with a foreground of densely-wooded hills and ravines glowing in the full-golden radiance of an afternoon sun. In due time we crossed a "saddle" of the tier, and began to descend again, traversing some very wild and picturesque glens and gullies, where the "Oyster-Bay pine" flourishes in great luxuriance. This species of tree is only known within a well-defined boundary, of about forty

miles from north to south in this particular district;
it is not found either northward of the Apsley
River, or south of Oyster Bay, or in any other
explored part of the island. It is a very handsome
tree, not so densely verdant as the "scrub" or
"brushy pine" before described, but much more
lofty and picturesque, and so perfectly straight and
taper, that the larger trees resemble the entire mast
of a vessel, from deck to sky-sail. The lower
branches curve downwards, and turn up again, with
a most graceful bend; the cones are small, each
consisting of four or five hard scales, and a few
small ones between them; they grow in clusters,
sitting close to the branches, and their polished
dark brown shells are beautifully conspicuous
amongst the vivid green foliage.

Although known here universally as pines, yet I
imagine that both this tree and the "brushy pine"
belong to the cypress family. Some of the largest
grow to the height of from 90 to 120 feet, but the
average size varies from 30 to 80 feet. They are
found on the most rocky hills and gullies, and,
being useful for many purposes, are much thinned
in the more accessible regions. As I did not
penetrate beyond these, I have not seen the finest

specimens, but the common road-side groups of them are very beautiful. We frequently sent men and teams into the tiers for pine spars to make ladders, rafters, fence-rails, &c., and, when sawn and well laid, they make excellent floors.

Emerging from this region of woods and glens, we came out at the head of Moulting Bay (so named in days of yore, when swans were abundant), and reached the house which was our night's destination. It commands a fine view of the ever-grand Schoutens, Great Swan Port, two conspicuous eminences called "St. Peter" and "St. Paul" (or more commonly "the two Peterses"), and various other hills and inlets.

We set forth again early the following morning, and cantered briskly along through thick woods of gum, pine, and wattle trees, and then, climbing another rugged stony hill, came in view of an extensive lagune, a drained flat of rich land, formerly a fresh-water marsh or lake, but now chiefly under cultivation: the owner of it has a good house-garden and farm buildings on the slope of a hill commanding a fine view; also a large orchard, producing a hundred or more hogsheads of cider annually.

The next pleasing object in our landscape was the river Apsley, a deep, clear, beautiful river of fresh water, which, if it went on its way like other orderly rivers, and rolled its waters onward to the ocean, would be of the greatest advantage to the neighbouring settlers in shipping their produce; but, after running for a considerable distance of sufficient depth to float a frigate, it suddenly makes a full stop, and finishes off abruptly in a low flat, over which, when floods occur, the superabundant waters flow into the bay, and the river itself is no more seen: the produce of the adjacent farms has thus to be conveyed some miles overland to the east coast.

The striking change in the outline of the hills as we advanced, gave quite a different character to the scenery here; instead of widely-spread sloping hills, fine wooded ridges of most picturesque form, and with almost precipitous sides, bounded the prospect in every direction. Many bright flowers enlivened the Bush, among which the most conspicuous were, the large crimson epacris and a small snow-white-blossomed "tea-tree" (*Leptospermum* —— ?)

We soon reached my father's sheep station on

the Apsley, where the overseer in charge had a
considerable quantity of land cleared, neatly fenced,
and under cultivation. His barn-yard displayed
some comely stacks of wheat, the produce of the
recent harvest; and his cottage, garden, goats, pigs,
poultry, and a swarm of sturdy, healthy, shouting
children, made a pleasant busy scene to greet us
after our quiet ride through the silent, wild, primeval
forests.

Being anxious to achieve our chief purpose of
reaching the sea in good time, we declined for the
present the hospitable offers of the overseer's wife,
but promised to call on our return; and, again plunging into the forest, journeyed on as usual along a
bush road, which after some distance quitted the
dark "trap" rock we had hitherto travelled over
from Spring Vale, and entered upon a range of
granite hills, comparatively low in some parts, but
rising in others to a considerable elevation. From
the last of these we gained a view of the magnificent
Pacific, which truly then deserved its name! It
was pure intense blue, even to the beach, where the
little waves rippled on fine sand, white as driven
snow. This beautiful beach extended for a distance
of many miles along the coast, only interrupted

by crags and huge heaped-up masses of granite,
sparkling like gems in the sunshine, as the transparent blue waves broke in endless dazzling succession, and the feathery spray flew high over the
rocks.

Long high headlands stretched away to the north,
in the vicinity of the river Douglas and St. Patrick's
Head, and a bright bare granite island, called Diamond Isle, lay almost close in-shore. The creeping plant called here the "Macquarie Harbour
Vine," spread its long chaplets of broad verdant
leaves in a thick net-work over the high sand-bank
above the beach, together with the common Mesem-
bryanthemum (known here as "pigs' faces") and
a few low green shrubs, vividly contrasting with the
more sombre tints of the lofty mountains behind,
all thickly clothed with wood, except where some
grotesquely-shaped granite mass protruded in the
form of an ancient tower or rampart.

We dismounted and walked along one beach in
the hope of finding shells, but saw scarcely any;
then rode over an intervening point to another
beach, when we left the horses tied to a shady tree,
and enjoyed a scramble amongst the rocks, which were
very beautiful, exhibiting great variety of colour and

crystallization: in some of the masses were cubes
of red felspar nearly two inches square, with equally
large scales of mica; in some places the granite contained schorl, and was covered with large black
patches of that mineral. A very minute red lichen
clothes some of the rocks so completely as to appear
at first their natural colour, whilst numbers of the
bright deep little pools among the crags were gay
with many-coloured sea-weeds; vivid green, rose,
crimson, purple, and other less showy hues floating
together, gay and changing as a living kaleidoscope.
Some of the Algæ were new to me.

Remounting our horses, we rode on over another
point, to another beach, close to which a spring of
pure fresh water rises in a green grassy hollow, and
here Mr. Meredith unsaddled and tethered the horses
to graze, whilst we sat under a scrubby old honeysuckle tree, and comfortably discussed our own
luncheon, in as lovely and lonely a spot as can well
be conceived. This important matter satisfactorily
disposed of, we again rode forwards and southwards
to "Wabb's Boat Harbour," where a granite island
lying very near to the main-land affords shelter to
the narrow channel between them, which is much
frequented by the small vessels visiting this part

of the east coast to receive the corn, wool, and other produce of the settlers *.

This little harbour of refuge being the only shelter in a stretch of many miles of rocky coast, it is often occupied during the winter as the station of a whaling establishment, although at the period of our visit all was silent and deserted. Skeletons of huts and skeletons of whales stood side by side, and with greasy barrels in long and black array, and remains of putrid carcasses steaming in the sunshine, formed one scene of dirt, desolation, and disgust, contrasting powerfully with the clean bright crags, snow-white beach, and the pure brilliant character of the surrounding scenery.

As we looked over the rocks into the still deep water of the little strait, great numbers of cray-fish were seen clawing about amongst the floating kelp, rather provokingly, for we had no means whatever of catching any, and they are particularly nice, although I suppose they act in the capacity of sea-scavengers in this place, their presence here in

* The recent discovery (1849) of a coal-field, supposed to be of great extent, near this place, will no doubt speedily effect a great change in the aspect of the neighbourhood, especially if the promised Government tramroad be formed, for the conveyance of the coal to Wabb's Harbour for shipment. A company has been formed for working the coal, and operations are expected to begin immediately.

such quantities being, at the least, suspicious. They resemble the lobster in flavour, size, and shape, except that they are destitute of the large claws, and the back-shell is very rough with sharp tubercles; their colour is a dull dark red, which becomes the common lobster-red when boiled. A string with a piece of raw meat, or even a bit of red rag, is a sufficient decoy to bring the cray-fish to the surface, when they must be seized with the hand and pulled out. They are plentiful in many parts of the coast, where the water is deep and still, with a rocky bottom.

Bidding a reluctant farewell to the blue Pacific, we turned homewards, traversing a better road than we had done in coming, the decomposed granite forming a fine white gravel path across the hills.

On arriving again at the overseer's cottage, we found the unfailing mark of hospitality—a steaming tea-pot of gigantic capacity, ready to give us welcome. The good wife had been busy too, making that favourite bush dainty, a "fat cake," which was hot and brown, and of a most savoury and unctuous smell, although rather too rich for my inexperienced palate (its composition being that of pie-crust, with abundance of dripping or "fat" kneaded into it,

and then being made about an inch and a half
thick, it is baked slowly in the frying-pan); but the
nice bread and tea were very acceptable, and we
discussed those, and all matters connected with the
farm and the garden, and the large family of small
clean sturdy children, at the same time.

We reached our resting-place of the previous
night about sunset, and rode home the following
morning, two nights' absence from our little boy
seeming to me a scarcely excusable act; and divers
visions of perils from nursery-fires, snakes, ponds,
horses' heels, and cows' horns, had begun to haunt
me most reproachfully, when, as we neared the gate,
the joyous little voice came ringing forth to greet
us, praying for a ride before me on "old Dainty,"
which being duly granted, our pleasant little excursion was happily ended.

CHAPTER V.

Garden laid out.—"Water laid on."—Heavy Gale.—Itinerant Threshing Machine.—Spring and Summer Flowers.—Acacia.—Eucalyptus.—Epacris.—Native Lilac.—Lilies.—Stylidium.—Orchidæa.—
Sun-dew.—Native Rose.—The Tea-tree.—Berry-bearing Shrubs.

ALTHOUGH our new garden had been planned, and
many trees planted in it, even before our removal
from Riversdale, it was not neatly and artistically
finished until the June of the present year, 1843.

A great lightwood tree, very green and well-
formed, grew at the lower end, and a drain, through
which a bright clear stream always flowed, traversed
one side; the banks were well planted with raspberries, currants, stone-fruit trees, and nuts, whilst
in nice moist corners we cherished some weeping
willow cuttings, and encouraged a few groups of
the elegant white-blossomed tea-tree to grow up in
kindly companionship with the strangers.

The valuable gifts we received from the paternal
orchard at Cambria included the finest kinds of

grafted fruit trees of all sorts, many of them bearing
well, so that even before our garden was finished it
yielded us fruit, and at once assumed a pleasant
and promising aspect when made neat and trim :
the walks smoothly laid, and sown with English
grass-seeds, showed green and fresh, and in fancy I
saw the China-rose cuttings I had carefully planted
vis-à-vis beside them at intervals, grown up into
verdant and blooming arches and bowers. But my
speculations on the future glory of our garden were
suddenly checked by a tremendous winter flood,
or rather two successive floods early in July, which
caused the rivers to overflow in new places, and
drove a raging roaring torrent directly through our
neat, precise, and just-completed garden.

Among minor losses and troubles, I do not remember one which ever annoyed and grieved me so
much as this. We had been so long striving to
achieve what we now saw ruthlessly destroyed, that
my eyes grew dim with positive tears, as I stood
watching the resistless stream come sweeping on,
driving the stout paling fence before it, bending
down and uprooting tree after tree—plum, and
peach, and apple—and washing off whole beds of
vegetables and flowers. Finally, after surging

heavily for some time against the ponderous dead-
wood fence at the bottom of the garden, it burst
the massive barrier, which it flung open on either
side like great gates, and rushed uninterruptedly
onwards to the Swan River. About the middle of
the flood, we saw the " seed-lift," which the man
sowing had left the day before in a wheat field
nearly a mile distant, come sailing along over the
drowned flower-borders, till it lodged in the boughs
of a cherry tree; and this told very plainly that the
work of destruction was carried on to a still more
serious extent elsewhere. We afterwards found
that eight or nine acres of rich ploughed land had
been washed away out of one field, and three acres
out of another, leaving the unploughed subsoil
smooth as a floor.

Two of our men-servants, with their wives and
one child, lived in a cottage about half a mile from
us, on a little plot of land which they cultivated for
themselves, and on which, at the time Mr. Meredith measured it for them, not a trace or vestige of
flood or "wreck" was visible, such indications
being always accurately observed in choosing a
building-site; but during this terrible inundation
(the highest known here for nineteen years), the

water rapidly rose round them, leaving the cottage
awhile as on an island, until towards night, when it
flowed over the floor, and, all retreat to the higher
ground being cut off, the men proceeded to set up
a kind of perch or rude platform in the nearest tree,
upon which they hoisted their few stores and
clothes, and then helped the terrified women and
child up also, the woman who had no child carrying her favourite cat with her for safety; and thus
they passed the dismal night, water rushing and
roaring all below, and the rain still pouring heavily
down.

Late in the evening, our shepherd, in taking his
last circuit to see that the sheep were safe, hailed
the two men from a distance, as he saw them wading
about, with the help of long poles, and learned
something of the state of affairs, although the noise
of the water prevented his comprehending much
that they told him. Both of the women had been
my servants, one being the nurse who was so much
affected when "Bill" was "up a tree" in the
former great flood, and I was truly concerned to
learn that she was now "up a tree" herself; but no
aid could be safely afforded them until day dawned,
and the waters fell, which they did during the

night, so that the poor, wet, cold creatures contrived to make the ever-comforting "pot o' tea" before daylight, and soon after were able to re-enter their soppy dwelling, which their dog had never quitted, having made himself as comfortable as circumstances would permit on the top of the bed-place.

After the flood had wholly subsided, and we could again walk about, we found that the Swan River had risen between twenty and thirty feet above its ordinary level, and that several spots which we had formerly thought of as sites for our cottage had been overflowed to a considerable depth, and heaps of wreck, huge ponderous trees, and pieces of fencing, left on the banks at a scarcely credible height above the usually placid river. My poor garden was long ere it recovered from the devastation, and the necessity of making another broad drain through it, and of laying down a portion of the borders in a long grass-plot, to prevent future floods from carrying away the soil, considerably affected my favourite plan.

Not long after this watery desolation, we were visited by one of the most furious gales of wind I ever remember, and as Mr. Meredith had started for Hobarton the day previous, and was then travelling through the Bush, where, in such a tempest, trees are continually falling, and huge limbs of others are rent off, and driven about with terrific force, I felt no small degree of apprehension on his account. So many reports of damage done around our own homestead poured in upon me, that I resolved to sally forth and superintend the preventive and remedial forces in person, though sorely buffeted and breath-spent in the attempt.

The barn displayed a miserable appearance; the thatch, rent off by yards, left nothing but bare rafters between our threshed corn and the threatening skies; and the mischief, so far from abating, was still making rapid progress. All the stacks were likewise stripped " to windward," and partly ripped open; pig-sties, stable, cowsheds, calf-pens, and all such buildings, perfectly neat in the morning, exhibited now a most dishevelled and deplorable condition; whilst fences blown down in all directions, laid the corn-fields open to the forays of horses, sheep, and cattle. Many and ingenious were the contrivances proposed and put in practice to arrest the injuries on all sides, the gale raging with unwearied vigour and intensity until nightfall,

when it moderated a little, and relieved my appre-
hensions lest the house itself might be unroofed.

When, from the state of the markets or other
causes, it becomes desirable to thresh corn out
speedily, we young farmers, who have not yet erected
a threshing machine, are obliged to hire one of
those which are kept to go out to work in most
districts (the "char-women" of their species);
those who employ such assistance paying three-
pence or fourpence per bushel for all the grain
threshed, and furnishing twelve men and some or
all of the four horses required in the operation,
which must be hard and weary work for the poor
animals; and I always rejoiced when the business
was over, and the deafening, clattering, factory-like
din, and the suffocating clouds of dust, subsided
together, and the great reeling rumbling machine
rolled away from our peaceful home.

The month of November is the chief season for
our Tasmanian wild flowers, and consequently the
pleasantest time of the year for a ramble in the
"Bush," and our many long wandering walks
made me acquainted with various new faces among
the delicate and fragrant denizens of our woods
and meadows.

The notion that our flowers have no scent is as ridiculous as the idea that our birds have no song; both assertions must have been made by people too much prejudiced to admit the natural impressions of their senses. Without enumerating the less conspicuous blossoms of the colony, there is the wattle or acacia tribe, contending species multitudinous, and *all* fragrant, if English hawthorn or meadow-sweet be fragrant, both of which they resemble in perfume, and are, like them, almost too strongly scented to be pleasant for any length of time in a closed room, although out of doors the rich odour is most delicious. All the *Eucalyptus* family bear an abundance of bloom, in constellated wreaths of starry flowers, sweet as the rich honey which the labouring bees suck from the crystal stores that lie deep within the fringe-bordered cups; and as you pass a tree full of blossom, the fragrance it diffuses seems to hang around so lusciously as to be almost palpable to taste as well as smell.

The *Epacrida* are here usually called heaths, although we have not any true heaths in the island; all of them bear honey-laden flowers of sweet scent, but not very powerful. The lovely *Epacris pulchella* is well known in English green-

houses, and the crimson and white varieties are
scarcely less beautiful, growing as they do here in
such lavish abundance.

A little purple flower, which is equally common,
so vividly recalls to my mind, both by its scent and
colour, an Old-World favourite, that I always know
it as the native Lilac (*Tetratheca juncea*). The
flowers have four petals, partially closed, so as
often to give them a bell-shape; the stamens,
united in a spire, are black or nearly so; the
flowers form pendulous clusters of six or eight; the
foliage is small and hard, and the slender stems are
from six to eighteen inches high. It grows in
every part of the colony with which I am
acquainted, and flowers in November and December: I have sometimes found specimens nearly
white, and some pink; but the usual colour, and
the universal scent of this lovely little flower, are
those of the lilac blossoms.

Another very fragrant flower is the common white
lily, *Diplarrhœna Morœa*, which is as universal a
guest here as the daisy in England, but more
especially occupying rocky gravelly banks, where
its great tussocks of long reedy leaves flourish all
the year round, and in the spring and summer are

abundantly adorned with the elegant white flowers. These are much of the Iris form, the three larger petals snowy white, and the small inner ones delicately tinted with yellow and lilac. Each lasts one day only, but they appear in a long succession, emerging singly or in pairs from the sheath, which terminates the long slender stalk, where the little buds lie closely hidden, like shy young birds, till fully fledged to flutter and dance in the breezy sunshine.

Our children always exult in the first bunch of lilies they can find for me, and bring them home in great triumph. The lilies are our true heralds of summer, and seem to me the most generous and loveable of all our wild flowers.

The sadly prosaic, dull, matter-of-fact habits of mind, and apathetic want of observation, which characterize so large a proportion of colonial young people, are to me lamentable, and we guard against such habits in our own children as we would against the symptoms of some mortal distemper of the body, at the same time offering perhaps the best antidote in the shape of our own opposite habits and active interest in all things around us.

One day, very long since, whilst engaged in

drawing one of our commonest wild flowers, with the name of which I was then unacquainted, I accidentally made a discovery, which seemed to render my botanical immortalization inevitable, until, shortly after, I found that my new wonder had been known, printed, and published in England years before! The flower was the *Stylidium* (*graminifolium?*), and whilst sketching it, I gently raised the singular central column of one blossom with my pencil, in order to examine its form more accurately, when, the instant it was touched, it leaped over to the other side of the flower, as if I had suddenly moved some hidden spring which previously confined it. Greatly surprised and interested, I touched the columns of all the other blossoms, and all performed the same jump with greater or less vigour; and, believing in my simplicity that what was so new to me must be also new to every one else, I was prepared to receive the honours due to my wonderful discovery, until a chance reference to page 1480 of "Murray's Encyclopædia of Geography," published in 1834, nipped all my vain aspirations in the bud.

The *Stylidium*, or, as we named it, the "Hair-trigger," is common all over the colony; the flower stem springs from a low tuft of grassy leaves, and grows from a foot to eighteen or twenty inches high, the upper half of it being adorned with purplish pink flowers, which succeed each other during several months in summer.

Many very pretty orchidaceous flowers dwell amidst our woods and wastes; among these the golden *Diuris* holds a conspicuous place, with its singular long-petalled bright yellow flowers, grotesquely marked with rich brown, and, as they are viewed in different positions, may be fancied to be dragons' heads, snakes, or nondescript creatures with long horns and beards. *Diuris umbellata* has darker amber blossoms, also clouded with patches of brown.

Some of the Thaladenias are yet more fantastic; one, viewed in front, always reminds me of the picture of an ancient court jester, with a tall conical cap, gay crimson doublet, and long partycoloured legs; but I never could persuade any one else to see more than the likeness of a spider in this odd little flower. Other species of Thaladenia are pale lavender colour, pink, &c. One small kind, very delicate in form, and daintily shaded pink and white, has an unpleasant odour very similar to that of mutton-bird feathers.

I have often found the curious little *Neottia Australis*. The stem is ten or fifteen inches high, with one or two small leaves at the base, and a multitude of little bell-shaped flowers without foot-stalks, circling closely round and round the twisted stem, corkscrew-wise, to the top; each flower being partially sheathed in a curving green leaf or bract; the tiny bells are bright pink outside, and white within, with a pleasant but slight odour, like new hay. In the same meadow where this little beauty dwelt, I have also found an eccentric relative of an old Home friend, namely, the forked-leaved sun-dew of Australia (*Drosera binata ?*).

Every one knows the common English species of the sun-dew, with its rosette of round leaves sitting close to the soil, and sparkling like a cluster of little rubies, as the light glistens on its dew-tipped crimson fringe: but its Tasmanian cousin is totally the reverse of this compact character. The plants I have gathered have usually six or more leaf stalks springing from the root, of from two to six inches long, the leaf seeming merely a continuation of the stalk, divided into two thin portions, forming a fork of one or more inches in length, and the whole greatly resembling in shape an old bent pitchfork with a crooked handle, for the leaf stems have always some twist or bend in them. The forked leaf is richly adorned with the fringe of crimson threads and sparkling dew-jewels peculiar to this curious family of plants; the young leaves first appear like closely-curled tendrils; the flower is white, very similar to that of the English sun-dew. In the bright pools of the Cygnet River I have seen the plant growing much more luxuriantly than on land, the flower-stalk being a foot and a half high, and the leaf fork three inches long.

On the banks of these same bright pools, too, dwells the loveliest of all the Tasmanian flowering shrubs, the *Banera rubiæfolia*, more commonly known as the native rose. Its clear green foliage is nicely disposed in starry circles round the slender waving stems, and the exquisitely-delicate flowers which appear among them are something like a wild rose or apple-blossom in form, but are smaller and far more airy and slender in character; whilst the closed, round, red buds are the prettiest little coy green-hooded fairies imaginable. The flowers are a soft rosy pink, passing into white towards

the centre of each petal, and the anthers are
golden yellow. After gathering a few sprays of
the native rose, I always glance around, and rarely
in vain, to find a Tea-tree, and straightway pil-
lage its snow-laden pyramids of some dainty little
branches, which form a lovely contrast, in their
chaste lily-like purity, with the blushing little
rose.

The tea-tree (*Leptospermum*) blossoms may be
somewhat likened to those of hawthorn, in their
individual form, although longer; but, instead of
being grouped in detached clusters, they form tall
continuous pinnacles of flowers, most graceful in
form and motion, and charmingly enhanced by the
rich myrtle-like foliage and the scarlet-brown tints
of the sepals, shown between the bases of the white
petals.

Grouped with these is often seen another handsome shrub, which I used to call a Yellow Metro-
sideros. but is, I believe, the Crested Calistemon;
its great bottle-brush flowers of pale yellow, and
its long sharp-pointed leaves, show well beside the
more delicate proportions and tints of its gentle
neighbours.

The steep rocky banks of the rivers, as they

E 2

recede among the mountains, produce many beautiful shrubs, which are wholly absent from the more level parts of the country. Our pretty Cygnet River often afforded me a treat in the discovery of some new flower. One, which we especially admired, was a species of *Hovea*, a long, scanty, scrambling kind of shrub, with a very large proportion of stem, and only the terminal sprays adorned with much foliage, the leaves being small, oval, and of the darkest green, with a rusty down on the under side; but the clusters of small papilionaceous flowers were of the loveliest pale lilac or French gray colour, with an eye of deep violet, whence slender veins of the same hue went wandering over the whole flower. We were at great pains to remove some of these plants, but they grew in such wild craggy places, and with their strong iron-wiry roots so knotted round and amongst the rocks, with no apparent soil near them, that the task was a somewhat tough one; and of the four we succeeded in detaching, only one, planted in a hole in the rocky bank by our cottage, survived the removal.

Many of these mountain shrubs are more beautiful in their seed-time than whilst in flower, as their berries are very ornamental. One very prickly bush bears inconspicuous little greeny - white flowers, succeeded by quantities of berries, the size of currants, but painted like peaches, shaded and tinted with the brightest and clearest hues. with a soft tempting bloom on them; but, alas! the beauty is to the eye alone! The apples on the Dead Sea shore are not more deceptive in promise than my pretty peach-berries of Tasmania.

A very handsome shrub, or small tree, the *Notelia*, bears glossy bright berries of a rich morone crimson, deepening to black; the leaves of this shrub are also beautiful, being long, and of a deep. rich, polished green. Some species of *Leucopogon* bear transparent berries, called native currants, but none of all these are good to eat.

Wandering among my favourite river-side dingles and dells over again on paper is so pleasant. that for my own part I could very complacently loiter on, until every leaf and blossom I loved were duly presented to my readers; but, remembering that paper and ink can make at best but a sorry description of my bright sweet flowers, and their wild, still, beautiful dwelling-places beside the rip-

pling river, or under the cypress shade, I must
leave them, although reluctantly; for I would fain
show how wondrously fair they are, and how possible it is to enjoy their beauty, and the beauty of
much more in this favoured land, without a thought
or dream of the horrors and terrors, and other uncomfortable inventions, which it seems customary
now to associate with the idea of poor Tasmania.

CHAPTER VI.

Improvements.—Fishing.—Water-fowl.—Bush-rangers.—Who's there?—Domestic Security.

OUR pleasant little home had assumed a tolerably civilized aspect by the summer of 1843-4. The principal rooms were plastered and finished; the veranda erected along the front was by this time partially hidden by roses, native clematis, and other plants; the garden was thriving and productive; and behind the house, on the same bank, stood a goodly barn, surrounded by other farm-buildings. A granary was built of wood, supported some feet from the ground on thick posts, in the vain hope of excluding the destructive little mice from the corn; but in an incredibly short time they infested it, as they do every building in the colony, and I think to a greater degree than in England, our mild climate here no doubt favouring their more rapid increase. Even our fields abound with the little creatures, and in barns and stacks they literally swarm. Rats I have heard of as having been seen here, but am happy in not yet having myself made their acquaintance.

Among other of our improvements, a rampart of huge logs and an embankment were raised, to defend the garden, in future, from the devastating sweep of the river-floods, by restricting the entrance of the water to a certain breadth, and preventing the wide tearing rush of the torrent: to shut out the flood was impossible, but the spread of the still water did comparatively little mischief, especially after the main track of the floods had been laid down with English grass-seed, which in time made a firm sward, and saved the soil from being washed away and scooped in holes.

Our bright rivers often yielded us a nice dish of fish, for which, however, we were most frequently indebted to the skill and patience of some of our servants, not being ourselves much skilled in the " gentle craft." When we did make an onslaught among the delicate trout that abounded in the Cygnet's crystal pools, I much suspect our proceedings would be pronounced positively heretical

by any proper orthodox angler. Walking across
the verdant grassy marshes (*Anglicè*, meadows) to
the Cygnet River, each armed with a "stick and
a string," and some lean raw mutton for bait, we
selected our several pools, some of which were as
much as four yards across! George being stationed
beside his papa or me, we began to bait and bob;
our rods being sticks, four or five feet long, and
our lines not much longer.

The chief charm consisted in our being able to
see distinctly down into the pool, and watch every
movement of our finny victims; and great was the
excitement when, from amidst the waving shelter of
some long-tressed clustering water weeds, the round
head and winding body of a wriggling eel would
glide into the sunlight, and manœuvre round the
bait among the lesser fry, which instantly lost value
in our eyes, as every energy was devoted to the
capture of the greater prize, the achievement of
which won a shout of delight from George. The
trout we usually caught were a small species, from
four to nine inches long, and very nice and delicate.
A larger and less firm kind of fish, called "Black
fish," was also numerous; but these seldom began
to bite until after sunset, when the mosquitoes

E 3

began to bite too, so vehemently that I could not remain after that time. Poor little George's bare legs were terribly attacked, and we were thus driven home just as the proper fishing time approached, for our men always began to fish after dark, lighting fires on the banks of the large pools in the river, and often remaining out half the night, having excellent sport.

Fine bream abound in the lower parts of the Swan River, where the salt water prevails, and a small delicate fish, called "cucumber fish," from its peculiar odour, is sometimes found in great abundance in the rocky pools and basins higher up towards the mountains.

Of the water-fowl of this colony, many species, like the poor swans, have been so much destroyed and disturbed as to be almost exterminated in most of the settled districts; we rarely see more than a few wild ducks or teal in a season, although formerly every lagune teemed with them, and with legions of bald coots, but the latter are now so rare, that I have not yet seen one. The musk duck is a large, heavy, beautiful bird, of dark sombre plumage, pervaded with a strong scent of musk; of these I have seen two only, and those were dead.

The mountain duck is a magnificent creature, with the clear blue and chestnut brown of the king-fisher, added to all the bright metallic hues of its other plumage. Sea-eagles, gannets, gulls of various species, pelicans, divers, shags, cormorants, kingfishers, and other aquatic birds, frequent most rivers and inlets in greater or less abundance, in proportion to the populousness of the vicinity, and the disturbance they suffer.

In December, 1843, our then new governor, Sir Eardley Wilmot, paid Swan Port a passing visit, in a tour he made on the east coast, and I, a true lover of my native Warwickshire, naturally felt more than common interest and pleasure in welcoming one so well and deservedly esteemed at home, to our lowly abode in his new dominion. Another connecting link seemed woven at once between my new home and my old one; little did we then dream it would be so soon and so cruelly broken!

Several parties of bush-rangers excited considerable alarm about this time, and some of them came into our immediate neighbourhood, robbing remote shepherds' huts of food and clothing, and attacking other dwellers in lonely places. One night, or rather morning, about two o'clock, a violent rapping and thumping was heard at our kitchen door, and of course the first half-dreaming thought was of "Bush-rangers," although they are not in the habit of besieging houses exactly in that style. Nevertheless, a parley was held (with bolted doors), and the noisy visitor proved to be a settler from a small farm about three miles distant, whose cottage had been ransacked, and himself and servants "bailed up." As soon as he could escape, he ran to warn us and other neighbours to be on our guard against his lawless guests, who were, he supposed, still lurking about. The fact, well known around us, that plenty of loaded fire-arms were always kept ready for use in our house, may have preserved us from like disturbances.

For several months at this time, ominous rumours were constantly floating about, of the deeds and desperation of these marauding parties, most of whom, it appeared, were making their way towards our neighbourhood, in the belief that they would be able to seize and take off some of the coasting vessels, which were always trading to and fro, or lying at anchor at Swansea or Wabb's Harbour; but no abduction of the kind took place.

A small party of soldiers was stationed on our

farm, as being a central situation, whence all the upper portions of the district were readily accessible, in case the robbers were again heard of; but no opportunity occurred for the display of their military prowess, although the persevering activity they exhibited during their abode at Spring Vale, in the capture and demolition of eggs from our poultry-house, gave us a most impressive conviction of their foraging capacities.

During this season of alarms, Mr. Meredith, who had been detained at an out-station, was returning home on a Sunday morning, and called at the house of a settler on the way. He found the doors closely shut and fastened, and knocked stoutly for admittance. Presently a face appeared at a window, and, beside the face, there peeped out also the muzzle of a double-barrelled gun; whilst, from within the door, a voice, accompanied by the peculiar click of cocking a pistol, demanded "who was there, and what was wanted." The peaceful cause of this warlike display being instantly admitted, was ushered into the family sitting-room, where morning prayers had just been read, and on the table (round which the old gentleman and his wife and their patriarchal assemblage of sons and daughters and grandchildren had been seated) lay, side by side, bibles, prayer-books, guns, pistols, and an old yeomanry sword: it was like a meeting of the Covenanters of old. A report had, as it appeared, reached them that morning, that a most daring and notorious fellow, whose name had been the terror of the whole country population for months, had been seen near their house, and hence the preparations for defence in case of an attack, which, however, was never made.

Fortunately this unpleasant condition of things was not destined to continue. A new chief police magistrate arrived, in the person of Mr. F. Burgess, and, in an incredibly short time, his active vigilance and well-organized system of pursuit effected an entire change; so that, instead of parties of armed absconders being tamely permitted to harass the defenceless country settlers for months and even years together, their escape was so rapidly and invariably succeeded by their recapture and punishment, that the terrors of bush-ranging became absolutely almost forgotten in the colony; and at the very time when the ridiculously-exaggerated accounts of our lost and outraged condition were being diligently circulated at Home, every country house in the island, however lonely, was in far less danger of molestation and robbery than those of any English city. How well I remember the nightly preparation at Home, the fastening and barring of shutters, locking, bolting, and chaining of doors, sticking up of spring-hung bells, and all the elaborate defences of English houses, both in town and country! whilst the loneliest dwelling here has neither shutter nor bell, the French or sash windows are merely closed with hasps, and the outer doors with a single bolt; and on many occasions our lower windows have been left open, and the front door unfastened all night.

It seems doubly hard on us, not only to suffer the odium of receiving the majority of England's felons here, but also to have the credit of keeping them as worthless as we get them; and, so far as one small voice may serve to disprove it, I am by no means disposed to let the false and injurious impression continue dominant. True it is, and must be, that, out of the many thousand convicts sent hither, some do remain wholly incorrigible; but, for each one of such, are there not scores of good, willing men, who, thankful for the opportunity afforded them here of leading a new life, and enjoying in abundance all necessary comforts, are quiet, orderly, industrious, and trusty servants ? If this be not generally the case, then we must have been singularly fortunate; but I believe the old axiom, that "good masters make good servants," meets with more corroborative cases here than elsewhere. The low mean spirit which loves to domineer over and taunt its fallen brother with the perpetual upbraidings of his errors and degradation, does more than check his onward struggles towards amendment—it drives him forcibly back, and perchance further on the road to perdition than he ever went before.

CHAPTER VII.

Unwelcome Changes.—Preparations for Removal.—A Dripping Guest. Our " Family Carriage."—A Conjurer.—Departure.—Passage over the Tier.—" Hop-pole Bottom."—Economy of Government Officials.—Mount Henry.

I HAVE before alluded to the heavy and calamitous losses which the almost universal insolvency in New South Wales, and the unprincipled conduct of persons whom we believed trustworthy, had inflicted upon us. For a time we had ardently hoped, and earnestly striven, to remedy the consequences; and, had the prices of farm produce continued even moderate, we should, probably, have succeeded; but wheat at 2s. 6d. a bushel was a sorry help to remove mortgages at 10 per cent.

Reluctantly—most reluctantly—did we at last acknowledge the necessity for some new plan of exertion; but having once resolved, we lost no

time in endeavouring to carry out our determination.   Our kind friend Sir Eardley Wilmot
offered Mr. Meredith the police magistracy of
a newly-formed and remote district: it was accepted thankfully; and, just as the pretty and
loved home of our creation was assuming an appearance, and a reality too, of comfort and com-
pleteness, and all the rough and arduous work
of a new place was merging into mere pleasant
cheerful occupation, we were destined to leave it
to the care of a few small tenants, the farm servants and overseer.   Unsettled as our former life
had been, we had taken up our abode at Spring
Vale with the comfortable feeling that *there* our
wanderings had finally ceased, our weary way-
faring ended.   The conviction that all was about
to begin again, came upon my heart with most
sorrowful and dispiriting anticipations; I felt as
if there were some evil spell upon us, dooming
us always to go on wandering, as if for us earth
had not a home.

Our new settlement was to be in a district called
Port Sorell, of which previously we had scarcely
so much as heard.   We found that it occupied
the central portion of the north coast, about

150 miles from Swan Port; and its sea-side vicinity was a potent charm in reconciling us to our migration thither.

Mr. Meredith set out to enter upon his new duties in the beginning of May, leaving me at Spring Vale with our two children. My husband's letters descriptive of the new country were indeed discouraging: the scenery, except that on the sea-borders, was one vast dreary forest—damp, dark, and dismal; the inhabitants, with a few exceptions, miserably poor, so that the contrast to our comfortable and substantial neighbours of Swan Port was somewhat striking. Another unpleasant peculiarity I soon perceived—that of the extreme wetness of the climate, for every letter I received, whether one or more reached me in a week, contained some similar paragraph, such as, "The rain has not ceased for four days;" "It is raining heavily;" or, "I have just come in, wet through." The place seemed to be the constant scene of a partial deluge.

The impracticability of a winter transit for our children and myself, and the difficulty Mr. Meredith found in procuring a residence for us, combined to delay his arrangements for our removal; and at the end of June he came home for a brief

visit, and again returned to Port Sorell, without
being able to end, as I had hoped he would, my
lonely sojourn in single uncomfortableness. Most
dreary were the long winter evenings, which had
never seemed long before, and perfectly intolerable
were the floods, when they prevented my receiving
the "post."

My chief occupation was the gradual packing
up and removal of our goods and chattels down
to Swansea, in readiness for the vessel which was
to take them round to Port Sorell, and as the winter
rains rendered the roads and rivers often quite impassable, and always nearly so, we could only cart
down small loads at a time. Accordingly all
articles not essentially useful, such as pictures,
&c., were first taken down and put away in cases,
then most of our books, and by degrees every
piece of furniture that could be spared, until the
baby was put to sleep first in a drawer, and, when
the drawers departed, in a clothes-basket.

Towards the end of August, when I was in daily
expectation of Mr. Meredith's arrival, to take us
back with him to Port Sorell, one of our terrible
floods arose; the inundated lowlands became,
as usual, one vast lagune, and the raging rivers

swept angrily along in swollen rapid torrents.
Knowing that the streams on the inland side
of the mountain-tier frequently show no indication of rising, even when ours are flooded,
I feared greatly for my husband's safety, as he
could not arrive near home before late in the
evening, and then might rashly venture into
danger. I had scouts out until after dark, and
the head shepherd, a faithful old servant (albeit
formerly a *prisoner*), went wading across the
flooded lands, up to his middle in water, hoping
to meet or hear his master, so as to assist him;
but he at length came in, satisfied that no one
who knew the place as Mr. Meredith did would
attempt to cross the flooded Cygnet that night;
and I tried to persuade myself that it was so,
although more than half inclined to feel cross
with the good man for giving up his watch,
and very much disposed to go forth in the pelting rain and resume it myself, when the noise
of a finger lightly tapping at the window sent
me in one bound to the door, where, wet and dripping as a merman, stood my own good man!

Instantly the whole quiet household was joyously
astir; and when the streaming guest had been

all comfortably arrayed and refreshed, he told his story, as benighted wanderer should. The whole country was partially under water, and the Cygnet River formed a wide outspread stream, with several deep channels, and broad intervening shallows, all which he had to traverse in the dark, on foot; it would have been impossible to ride, as he trusted to his memory of certain fallen trees to aid him in crossing some of the channels. In one or two instances, after cautiously wading to the spot where he remembered a fallen tree-bridge, it was not to be found, except by *probing* the gully with the pole he carried, when the log was discovered two or three feet under water: at length the last deep channel was crossed, the inundated marsh splashed through, and he gained our terrace-like bank.

As one preparation for our transit, a strong easy vehicle, something of the jaunting-car genus, an invention of Mr. Meredith's, which had been some time in progress, was now quickly completed, and fully answered our expectations. The seat, a *dos-à-dos*, and very roomy for four persons, being made movable, to shift on the body, according to the number conveyed, enabled the weight to be always

placed centrally over the axle; and this arrangement, with four excellent springs, and high wheels,
gave an easy uniform motion like that of a good
Stanhope, instead of the agonizing spasmodic
shaking to and fro of the cars commonly in use
here, which have only two springs, and are the
most perfect instruments of torture conceivable.
The springs and axle were procured from a good
coachmaker, the body was very neatly made and
painted by our own carpenter; a neighbouring
blacksmith and wheelwright, who was quite an
artist of a Vulcan, made the wheels and remaining
ironwork, and put all together; whilst the cushions
displayed my proficiency in the upholstery department: so that our "family carriage" was truly
home-made, and did us all infinite credit; not the
least useful part of it being a large square box,
fitting in beneath the double seat, and capable of
containing a very tolerable travelling equipment for
our party. All Long Acre could not have furnished
us with a conveyance so well adapted to the service
we required; whilst its perfect originality, and the
curiosity and diversity of opinions it excited, were
infinitely amusing. Its first appearance in public
was on the occasion of our farewell visit to Cambria,

when the rivers were still almost dangerously high; but our stout tandem, good horses, and skilful driver overcame all obstacles.

An itinerant conjurer, who was engaged to perform before the party in the evening, afforded our George the extremest delight. He, unsophisticated child of the Bush, had never beheld anything of the kind before, and gazed with fascinated astonishment, as each respectably ancient piece of legerdemain was exhibited, clapped his hands with joy at the disclosure of the impromptu pancake, shouted aloud when a cauliflower tumbled from his papa's hat, and contemplated the fire-eating process with a comical mixture of curiosity and horror; but the climax of his mystification and amazement arrived when the pistol, which George had *seen* properly loaded with a ball, was deliberately fired in the necromancer's face—and, coolly taking the bullet from his mouth, the marvellous man showed it, slightly flattened, to the spectators! Poor little boy! I began to debate within myself whether such a blissful state of ignorance deserved more my commiseration or my envy. Not that *I* was an uninterested witness of the good old tricks; they were too pleasant, as reminders of bygone

times, and my own childish wonderment, to seem at
all despicable now.

Returning home the following day, our final
arrangements were made, and next morning we
set forth from our dear cottage-home, to cross the
mountain-tier to the north, in order to get into
the main road to Launceston. Our party consisted
of Mr. Meredith and myself, the two children
and nursemaid in the car, our old house-servant
on horseback, and several others to assist us over
the tier.

For the first five or six miles our road was
comparatively good; we then reached a ford of
the Swan River at the foot of the hills, where a
saddle-horse was waiting for me; George also was
mounted before one of the men on horseback,
the baby carried by another, whilst Mr. Meredith and a third led the tandem horses, with the
nearly empty car, up the steep ascent. After a
fatiguing climb of several miles, we paused for
a few minutes on a high point of the mountain
range, whence we gained a last beautiful farewell
view of the grand Schoutens. We then continued
our journey over rough abrupt masses of rock,
varying from the size of a waggon to that of a

hat-box, heaped together in one chaotic wilderness
of mounts and ravines, thickly covered with both
growing and fallen timber.

By about three in the afternoon we had accomplished the descent of the mountains, and forthwith prepared for dinner. The horses were taken
out to graze, a fire made to leeward of our grassy
dining-table, and our commissariat unpacked, which
contained a cold turkey, ham, cakes, wine, &c., and
we brought that best relish, a good appetite, to the
banquet. This over, the supernumeraries from
Spring Vale and the horse I had ridden over the
tier turned again homewards, and we journeyed on,
through bogs, logs, mud-pits, and quagmires, as we
best might, in a hollow denominated " Hop-pole
Bottom," which, being full of deep holes of water
and fallen timber, was perilous to traverse, after
so much rain, and amply tested the safe qualities
of our stout vehicle, and the strength and docility
of our good horses.

In this valley, the first sign of a human abode
we had seen since passing the Swan River greeted
us in the shape of a large assemblage of huts and
other buildings, almost like a village, erected for
the accommodation of a Probation road-party, who

the neighbouring settlers innocently expected would
have made the fearful track we had traversed conveniently passable; but, according to the usual
custom of the late Comptroller-General, the convicts were ordered for removal elsewhere, so soon
as all the expense of building their abode had
been incurred by the Government, and without
their being suffered to become useful, as they
might and ought to have been in this and
many other places: thus affording another notable
instance of the obstinate reckless obstructiveness
of the officer in question.

" Mount Henry," a hill of picturesque outline,
but provoking situation, lay before us, and our
road, or rather track, made four-fifths of a circuit
round it, affording us a long series of monotonous views; " Mount Henry" being to us, as
Salisbury Cathedral was to Mr. Pecksniff's pupils,
the object of contemplation from all points of the
compass.   The short twilight ceased ere we approached our destination for the night, which was
the cottage of a friendly settler acquaintance; but
after manifold groping examinations of fences, in
search of an entrance gate, we at length succeeded in making our way on foot into a ploughed

field, and thence to the garden gate, not without being in some jeopardy from the numerous dogs of all kinds and sizes, which our nocturnal invasion had aroused to full vigilance and wrath. Our kind reception within-doors seemed doubly pleasant after so rough a salutation without, and the hospitable attentions of our good friends were not a little enhanced by the fatigue and difficulty of our past day's journey.

CHAPTER VIII.

Saint Paul's Plains and River.—Bog.—Ben Lomond.—Sojourn at the "Stony Creek."—"Deoch an Dorich."—"Eagle's Return."—Coaches.—Great Western Tier.—Perth.—Approach to Launceston.—Sojourn there.—Arrival at Carrick.—Old Water-mill.

THE first part of our next day's journey was through a beautiful valley, between fine ranges of wooded hills, one of which, from its high round form, is named "Saint Paul's Dome." Our road lay along the opposite declivity, overlooking the vale, with its snug farms and cottages, green lawn-like fields, and the bright winding river ("Saint Paul's River") outspread in fair array below us.

We had frequently to get out of the car, whilst Mr. Meredith drove it over some dangerous gully or steep ravine, and then, with his and the manservant's help, we scrambled over too, and reseated ourselves; but as sometimes we were obliged to seek for logs or stones, to build a foot-bridge or make stepping-places over brooks or creeks, these interruptions greatly delayed us. One most horrible black morass spread out before us over a length and breadth of some acres, rendering any avoidance of it by walking over utterly hopeless, and, after a brief contemplative pause, Mr. Meredith. urged the horses straight on. In they plunged, nearly up to the shafts, in a sable sea of something very like bird-lime; and I cannot now remember, without horror, my (by no means groundless) dread lest we should be smothered, or that the traces should break, as the good horses dragged, and struggled, and floundered on; but at last they rose again upon the hard ground, and pulled us safely out.

As we drove pleasantly along "Saint Paul's Plains," fully appreciating the comfort of hard firm ground, albeit sometimes rough with rocks, my attention had for some minutes been engrossed by the graceful outlines of the distant hills on our left, and in watching the changes of effect caused by the passage of clouds across the sunlight, when, on looking again to the right, I involuntarily uttered a cry of astonishment and delight :—beyond a sort of promontory, in which one hilly

BEN LOMOND, FROM ST. PAUL'S PLAINS.

FROM A SKETCH BY THE BISHOP OF TASMANIA.

range abruptly ended, had arisen, as if by enchantment, a living picture of the snowy Alps!
a distant lofty expanse of crag, and battlement,
and peak, all white and dazzling in silvery snow,
amidst which the steep sides of some mighty but-
tress-like rocks showed black as jet, and the deep
blue unclouded sky crowned this glorious scene;
which, I suppose, was yet the more charming
to me as being wholly unexpected. My new
mountain friend was the Tasmanian Ben Lomond, the lordly chief of a great mountain group
in the north-east of our beautiful island.

We drove on, still along the plains, with no
living thing near us, save the wild birds and some
scattered sheep; the grand snowy mountain changing, but not waning, in its stately beauty as we
proceeded. Soon after midday we halted in a little
isolated grove of trees, affording both shade from
the sun and shelter from the wind (which sweeps
keenly across these wide plains), and also yielding
us some dry firewood, a bright fire being, whether
needed or not, an indispensable part of a bush
bivouac. I contrived to gain time for a slight
hasty sketch of Ben Lomond before the order
for our onward march was given. For foreground

there was the wide plain, only varied by a few
stray straggling trees, and one or two indistinct
tracks across it; beyond, ranges of hills, covered
with sombre forests, rose dark and abruptly, and
above these the snow-clad summit of Ben Lomond
rested against the clear blue sky.

Changes of the same landscape accompanied us
in the afternoon, until near the lonely inn where
we intended sleeping; and, just as we had alighted
to walk down the steep rocky bank of the " Stony
Creek," we heard a hearty joyous cry of " Here
they are! Here's the master!" and two of our
own servants, who had gone with a cart-load of
our trunks and bedding to Campbell Town, and
were staying a night at the inn on their way
back, came running to meet us, ready to carry
the children, or lead the horses, or draw the car
themselves, if it would benefit us, all eager alacrity
and good humour.

On the top of the high bank, and facing another high hill which rose before it, stood the
narrow tall brick house, which rejoiced in the
sign of the "Deoch an dorich" (my Gaelic is
most probably ill-spelt). Being very new, the
sepulchral odour of fresh plaster was rather pre-

dominant within, varied at intervals by a gush of
fragrance from yet more recent paint; and the parlour was drearily cold and cheerless, fire never
having been as yet introduced to the new hearth,
whilst all entrance of sunshine was carefully prevented by a grenadier regiment of tall geraniums
and fuchsias, trained and woven upon high triangular wooden ladders, reared against the windows, apparently with the laudable purpose of
enabling the flowers to peep over the opposite
hill; the lower panes being also defended by an
outpost of spiteful prickly cactuses, forming a
compact *chevaux-de-frise*. Still, when the chimney had smoked its best to dislodge us, and finally
given up the attempt as hopeless, and a blazing
fire in some measure thawed the icy vault-like
atmosphere, we found our quarters by no means
despicable, especially when the customary dinner
tea-and-supper meal overspread the ample table,
and the pleasant fumes of tea and coffee over
came even the damp plaster and fresh paint.

"Mine host" of the "Stirrup-cup" did us good
service the following morning, by accompanying,
or rather preceding us, on horseback, to show
us a way through the Bush by which we could

F 3

avoid a notoriously dreadful boggy lane in the
neighbourhood.   We had still some unpleasant
"creeks" and watercourses to traverse, but all
were easily passed, and soon after noon we, to
our great joy, emerged on the fine main road,
and felt all difficulties at an end for a while.
Sitting on the bank, we discussed our luncheon,
and then smoothly and merrily drove along the
hard broad metalled road through Epping Forest
to the Snake Banks, where we halted for the
night at a very good comfortable inn, with the sign
of the "Eagle's Return" on the signboard; and in
a duplicate copy over the door of each room,
the same design appeared, representing an eagle
pecking at a very bare bone.   What hidden mean-
ing might be attached to this picture, I am not
aware, but the feeling it naturally excited was
one of compassion, that the noble bird, whose
"return" seemed an event of some interest and
importance, should not have found better fare to
welcome his arrival.

Whilst the waiter was bringing in dinner, I
observed him endeavouring to drive something
out of the room, and thinking it was our spaniel,
I said, "Do not drive the dog out, let him stay."

"Oh! ma'am, if you please it's our missis's tame jackass, and he's sometimes so rude, he gets upon the gentlemen's heads; I'd better put him out, if you please, ma'am."

But the jackass did not seem inclined to be so easily dismissed, and I had the pleasure of his amusing company for some time. Talking a little, and hopping about a great deal, the poor bird appeared very happy, and was equally entertaining. It had perfect liberty, and flew in and out and all about the house at pleasure; sometimes chattering upon the banisters upstairs, and then flying out to hail the arrival of new guests.

The bird so ridiculously named a jackass is about the size and shape of a starling, with dark shaded brown plumage, and, being easily reared and tamed, is often kept as a pet; it learns to whistle tunes, and to say a few words tolerably plainly, and is a merry sociable bird when allowed its freedom, as this one was, which seemed quite a popular character in the establishment.

The arrival of the mail and other coaches was a great event for George, to whom the whole busy affair of changing horses was a most amusing novelty; and I confess I was far from an apathetic spectator myself, for the bright handsome vehicles, the good horses, and orthodox-looking guards and coachmen, were all pleasant lively reminders of Home, although now, I fear, almost obsolete there. The substitution of hideous smoking steam-engines, dark tunnels, and sooty stokers, for the gay, brisk, well-horsed coach, is, in my mind, as unpleasant an offering upon the altar of utility as the equally-prevalent change from beautiful graceful sailing vessels to clumsy thick-chimneyed sputtering steamers. The saving of horse-torture would, however, be a weighty argument, with me, in favour of steam and iron, were not the luckless omnibus and cabhorses driven more furiously and mercilessly then ever, in consequence of the generally-accelerated speed of travelling. Doubtless we far-off colonists are apt to think of English railways with feelings a little embittered by the unnecessary fatigues and deprivations we suffer here, from the lamentable mismanagement of an amount of labour which, if wisely and honestly directed, would leave us little to envy, in the item of roads, in any country. But in the present state of things, the contrast is tryingly great, between English people at home, for whom journeys on turnpike roads like bowling-greens are now too tardy and difficult, and English colonists here, who (except the few residing near the one main road) have little else but mountain and bog in a state of nature to scramble over, whether for business or pleasure; so that the most amiable of us cannot restrain an occasional growl, or a wish, however bootless, that the despised turnpike-roads of the mother country could, like other despised and condemned things, be transported hither as a bequest to her daughter.

We left the Snake Banks after a night's sojourn, and drove on to Perth; the whole of the land on either side being inclosed for sheep-runs, farms, pleasure-grounds, and gardens, with pleasant houses and cottages seen at intervals, and my grand favourite Ben Lomond lifting his snowy head above all the eastward scenery   On our left lay a wide extent of inclosed and cultivated lowland, dotted with houses and settlements, beyond which the great western range of mountains stretched in a long dark shadowy chain of snow-crowned peaks and wide bleak moorland heights, which may be considered as the vertebræ of our Tasmanian mountain system, which sends out limbs that traverse most of the eastern half of the island, and almost wholly occupy the western. Embosomed in these dreary mountain wilds are several large and beautiful lakes, of whose lonely grandeur and picturesque scenery I have heard their explorers speak in terms of high admiration; and in the summer, numerous flocks of sheep are sent to depasture in the grassy valleys and lowland in their vicinity.

We entered the flourishing town of Perth on the south-east, over a handsome stone bridge of eight arches, with bold stone parapets, and quite an imposing aspect, more like a good old English bridge than the usually flimsy colonial constructions, which seem for the most part built on the principle of children's card-houses, for the pleasure of seeing them tumble down again. The broad rapid river, the signs of population and industry on its banks, the many good finished buildings around, and many more in progress, gave a pleasant cheering aspect to the place; and during the hour's halt we made at one of the inns, whilst the horses rested, we walked down, after luncheon, to the bridge, to sketch and look about more at our leisure; we then drove on to Launceston.

After living for five years in the "Bush," and
having a personal acquaintance with nearly every
human being we were in the habit of meeting
on the road, and almost with every team of cattle,
I found quite a childish amusement in seeing so
many new people, new horses, and new vehicles
of all descriptions, as we approached the town.
Neat suburban cottages, veritable "cottages of
gentility," with coach-houses complete, abounded
by the road-side, with their strips of garden and
smart green gates. Carts full of cut wood were
travelling townwards for sale, a sure indication
of our advance towards a denser population.
Brewers', bakers', and other trades-peoples' errand
carts were jogging about; waggons nodded drowsily
along, loaded with the furniture of hapless people,
"flitting" like ourselves; gigs, pony chaises,
phaetons, and Irish cars of all kinds, all full of
people, in spruce dresses, driving briskly to and
fro, mingled with numerous equestrians of all
grades, and divers quadrupeds being led forth
towards Campbell Town, in readiness for a grand
"hunt" on the morrow.

Nor were we, whilst observing, unobserved. Many
a curious glance and earnest stare were bestowed

on our original turn-out; the good horses, correct
harness, and clever character of the whole, rather
enhancing the interest awakened by the novelty
of our carriage itself, and the family group it
contained, with our handsome little dog gravely
looking out in front; and then the wandering
eyes next rested on our short stout old servant,
in his new suit of velveteen and tall shiny black
hat, with his shot-belt and double-barrelled gun
carried rather defiantly than otherwise, and mounted
on a horse too tall to be easily ascended in haste:
altogether, we must have borne unmistakable
evidences of our country rearing, and I can only
hope that we proved as amusing to the good folks
we met as they did to us.

From the brow of a hill down which the road
passes into Launceston, we commanded a full view
of the town and adjacent "swamp" (as it is.
for a miracle, rightly named). Dense fogs are
so prevalent in this ill-situated place, that I believe
there are not many days in the year when this
view can be enjoyed; the usual prospect which
awaits the expectant traveller on this spot being
a rolling mass of thick white vapour, below which,
as if at the bottom of a mighty steaming cauldron,

lies, he is told, the populous town of Launceston, which, as we saw it unveiled, with its shipping along the wharf, and the far winding river lying bright in the sunshine, formed really a very pretty picture. The beauty, unhappily, is only perceptible at a distance, and on entering the town vanishes entirely amidst the dirty streets, where the handsome churches and other buildings, and good large well-stored shops, are interspersed with mean squalid hovels, unpleasant even to pass.

We found roomy apartments prepared for us at a quiet hotel, and took up our abode there for two or three days, Mr. Meredith having business to arrange. The portion we occupied had been added since the original building of the house, and, from some contrivance or whim, the windows of our drawing-room, which were not above a yard high, rested nearly on the ground, so that the only comfortable way of looking out was by sitting on the floor beside them, a mode of proceeding much more congenial to George's tastes than my own.

So far we had had no choice as to our mode of transit, but now the question arose, whether we should go on the remaining sixty or seventy miles by land, or take a passage in one of the little coasting vessels, and ship the car with us, sending the horses overland, the way, for *road* there was none, being deemed by every one but Mr. Meredith as totally impracticable for the tandem. *He* said he could drive over it, having carefully noted all the difficulties in his former journeys, and gave me my choice.   In furtherance of my decision, we went to the wharf, and looked down into two of the Port Sorell vessels : they were very small, very dirty, and gave out such a potent compound odour of stale tobacco, grease, and bilge water, that I stepped back and gave my casting-vote for a land progress ; thinking that even a night's lodging in the forest, under or within the hollow trunk of an old gum tree, would at any rate be a cleaner and sweeter kind of penance than an incarceration, perhaps for a week or more, in either of the cabins I had peeped into.

Accordingly, our business being ended, we remained no longer in Launceston, but gladly drove out again on the third afternoon of our sojourn, though half drowned in a pelting thunder-shower which fell just as we started ; and, after a boggy progress for ten miles, we stayed for the night at the little village of Carrick, where we found the neatest of all possible inn-parlours, and the prettiest and most obliging of all nice amiable landladies (a colonial Mrs. Lupin, with teeth and eyes that a duchess might have envied), and were as cosy and comfortable as we could desire.

Having an hour's daylight to spare, Mr. Meredith took me down the muddy road to see an old mill of which he had become enamoured in his lonely journeys this way; nor was I at all disappointed in it. All buildings in these new countries are so completely the things of yesterday, and generally look so glaringly and obtrusively new and discordant amidst the surrounding scenery, that it is especially pleasant to see anything of human work which has really mellowed into something like an harmonious character, and so this crazy old weather-board mill won its way to our admiration. We stood on the rather frail wooden bridge which the road crosses, and looked up the narrow rocky bed of the stream, which came foaming and chafing down towards us, overshadowed in many places by graceful bending trees, and an infinite number of lovely flowering shrubs, growing on the steep banks and little islets of the noisy turbulent river, the "Liffey," a tributary of the Meander. A portion of the water turned aside a short distance above these rapids was conveyed along a wooden trough, supported on stout tall mossy props, which displayed an infinite variety of angles, according to their respective lengths and the inequalities of the ground. This "lead" brought the water to the mill, where it poured down in a glassy sheet on the dark shining old-fashioned overshot wheel, that brought to my mind the many old water-mills I had loved to loiter beside at Home; and, as the vexed stream flowed onwards, lodging its creamy wreaths of foam on the rushes as it hurried along, it seemed like the strange links of a dream, to unite the long-ago with the more recent scenes of my life; till it rushed madly down a little ravine, and tumbled again into the parent stream, carrying all my retrospective romance along with it, and leaving me ready to walk back to tea. Since my visit a tall, sharp, grievously-neat, new mill has taken the place of the picturesque old wooden building, and I am thankful that I am never likely to pass through Carrick again.

DELORAINE BRIDGE.

CHAPTER IX.

Westbury.—Deloraine.—Wooden Bridge.—Bottled Ale and Porter.—
Hospitality.—A New Friend.—Last Day of the Pilgrimage.—
Avenue Plain.—Crossing the Rubicon.—The Forest.—Mid-day
Halt.—Leech.—Night Ride.—Difficulties of the Road.—Safe
Arrival.

LEAVING our neat inn and our pretty hostess after
breakfast the following morning, we struggled on
through the quagmire roads as we best might, sometimes waiting whilst the servant rode on ahead to
fathom the depth of any very threatening bog
before we ventured into it, but generally trusting to
good driving and stout horses to pull us through.

A bridge over the South Esk had a toll-house and gate upon it, and this would have been a pleasant scrap of Old-World ways had the road in the vicinity been worth paying for; but as, on the contrary, it appeared to me that we deserved rather a handsome premium for enduring the risk and misery it involved, the charge seemed adding insult to injury.

The snow, which lay thick and white along the higher ridges, gave a piercing keenness to the bleak southerly wind, as it blew aside cloaks and shawls and furs; the poor children looked pinched with cold, through all their mufflings, and we were glad to sit by the inn fire to thaw, when we stopped for a few minutes at Westbury, a watery, dreary, muddy place, and the coldest part of the island I have yet visited.

The roads became gradually but evidently worse as we approached the forest. Often I thought we must relinquish the idea of taking the car further, and travel on upon the horses in the best way we could, but still we advanced, and before evening reached Deloraine, on the river Meander.

We passed through a great part of the settlement, which, with its recently-erected raw brick and wooden buildings, has very much the character of the ugly irregular suburbs of some fast-growing manufacturing town, with square patches of ground fenced for gardens, but as yet producing little besides a scattered crop of brick ends, old mortar-pits, and sawdust, with here and there a huge black stump remaining unburned, to tell of the departed forest.

A singularly picturesque wooden bridge crossed the Meander here, formed of several piers of logs supporting the causeway, each of the piers being built of even logs laid crosswise in a square, partially bedded into each other at the corners, but leaving space between each so as to offer less resistance to the water when floods occurred. The causeway and railing of the bridge were considerably out of repair when we crossed it, but the ponderous piers had every appearance of stability; and the river was then considered very high. Since then a heavy flood of rain came, bringing down immense quantities of fallen trees from a neighbouring " clearing," which blocked up the openings of the bridge, and the tremendous weight of the timber and the body of impeded water behind it entirely carried away the whole fabric. It has been replaced by a new one, which I have not seen.

Close to the bridge was our destined inn, a square red-brick house, looking older than most others in the settlement, and the property of its landlord, a tolerably wealthy man, but who, finding his circumstances thriving, and his inn receiving abundant custom, seemed to think all improvement in attendance or refinements in accommodation wholly unnecessary; yet he practised genuine liberality in the *stable* department—a golden virtue in country innkeepers.

A good fire was our first desideratum on our arrival, and then, being warmed, we requested to be fed. A large round table stood in the middle of the parlour we occupied, and presently the elderly good wife of our host came in with a huge loaf of bread in her arms, which she deposited in the middle of the bare table, and hurried off (to fetch a tray or dish and a tablecloth, as I innocently supposed); but in a few seconds she returned, carrying an enormous cheese, which promptly descended, with a heavy sound, beside the loaf, also on the bare wood; then I began to understand the style of things a little better, and looked on in no small amusement to see what would follow. Next came a heap of large blue plates (the dear old

inexhaustible " willow pattern "), and on these a fear
ful mass of gigantic wooden-hafted knives and forks;
then a very small tea-tray, with a very large crockery
teapot, and a tall shaking tower of capacious blue
cups and saucers, skilfully packed together; with
some table-spoons of German silver, or some other
equally unpleasant composition.   A basin of black
sugar, and some coarse salt, completed the display,
until the entrance of a great dish of hot fried
mutton-chops and rashers of salt pork.

Spirits and excellent English bottled ale and
porter are kept in the meanest public-houses in
the colonies; but of their wine, the white is cape,
and the port of that peculiar vintage for which
" Punch" gave us the recipe some years ago,
prescribing a decoction of logwood, brown paper,
and old boots.

Some cases of well-stuffed native birds adorned
our parlour, and after tea we had a most unexpected
and unlikely treat in such a place, being the company of a very large and excellent musical box,
which played some brilliant airs from new operas
very pleasingly.

We were dismayed the following morning to find
a thick heavy rain falling in a steady determined

way, as if to preclude all chance of our proceeding ; and our host prognosticated " a big flood," which was a remarkably cheering and pleasant augury ! Our breakfast was the tea over again, minus the cheese, and I obtained a few eggs for our own servant to boil for us, frying being the only popular mode of cooking them here.

We had slept very comfortably ourselves, with everything sweet and clean, though bare and rough in the extreme, and the other beds looked equally well ; but when poor George came to me, the odour of the abominable " mutton-bird" pillow on which he had lain was most sickening ; and it is retained so strongly in the hair, that the most elaborate washing, aided by " Macassar" and Eau de Cologne, is all unavailing : time alone will remove it. I believe a little careful preparation renders these offensive feathers quite inodorous, but, being cheap, they are used commonly without. It is impossible to be in the same room with any person, or even any garment, that has passed the night on such a bed, without being most unpleasantly aware of the scent.

As I could not find any books to read, save the " Newgate Calendar," I sat at the window sketching

the bridge, whilst the rain forbade our walking
about.

The worst thirty miles of our journey now lay
before us—the passage through the forest; and, as
it seemed scarcely possible to achieve it in one day,
short as they were at that season, we thought of
hiring some mattresses and blankets from Deloraine,
and sending them to a vacant cottage which we had
permission to use, ten miles on the way, that we
might rest a night there, and divide the stage; but
the account we received of this place, which was in
the "care" of an Irish stock-keeper, and the abode
of untold legions of all varieties of vermin, put
a stop to that plan. The only other house on our
way was but four miles beyond Deloraine, but even
that distance it was desirable to subtract from our
last long stage; and a note to the hospitable owner,
requesting the aid of a night's lodging, speedily
brought him in person, as its reply, to escort us
back with him at once. Just as we were starting,
our groom arrived from Port Sorell, with Mr.
Meredith's saddle-horse, equipped with a side
saddle, which enabled me to travel more pleasantly,
and also to lighten the car. Four miles of boggy,
rocky, slippery, sloppy progress brought us to our

new friend's cottage, where all that the kindest hospitality could suggest was done for our comfort.

Bidding a grateful adieu to our worthy entertainer the next morning, we set forth on our last day's pilgrimage, about eight o'clock, with a slight drizzling rain falling, which happily did not increase, and at intervals wholly ceased, but the day continued damp and gloomy.

We plodded on, through dreary woods and swampy plains, now fording a lagune, now scrambling over a gully, till a steep channel containing a broad stream of black liquid mud lay before us, bearing the cheerful appellation of "Dead Cow Creek." Setting down the children and the maid, Mr. Meredith drove into it, and our poor leader instantly disappeared, all but his head; but floundering on, he emerged, and the wheeler went in, and finally the car; all clambering safely out again, in process of time, on the opposite bank. The maid crossed over by walking along the rails of an adjoining fence; the children were carried; and I made my way down the bank of the gully, till I found a place narrow enough for my horse to jump across. Then we hastened on again, for many such

obstacles beset us, and our general progress could
very rarely exceed a walk.

Suddenly, on passing through a gate near to a
lonely stock-hut, we were surrounded by fifteen or
twenty great fierce dogs, growling and barking
furiously ; but before any worse effect was produced
than that of making our valiant little dog, Dick,
look as bold and angry as if he seriously contemplated fighting the whole party himself, they were
called off by the stock-keepers, who very civilly
offered us some refreshment, and were very anxious
that I would at least take a " pot o' tea ;" but it
was too early for luncheon, and I am not sufficiently
imbued with the genuine bush predilections to
admire the composition usually known here as
" tea," among the labouring class.

Soon after passing the hospitable stockmen, we
reached the Avenue Plain, which in summer must be
a beautiful spot, but was then covered with water,
from a few inches to a foot or more deep.   Its
name tolerably well describes it ; a wide, long, open
space, intervening between the belt of fine verdant
lightwoods and other trees skirting the river
" Rubicon" and the great forest ; so that it is a
grassy flat, surrounded by high wood, and in

summer is a valuable grazing ground. We did not
pass the Rubicon until some time after, and then
crossed only a branch of the classic stream, of
very insignificant dimensions.

From the Avenue Plain we turned aside, and at
once plunged into the dark forest. Gigantic gum-
trees rose on every side, and in every variety that
such tall, straight, bare, gaunt things can exhibit;
for handsome as *single* gum-trees frequently are,
and thick-foliaged and massive in their sombre
hues, those which grow clustered in the forests are
almost invariably ugly, and these were so close
together that it was only possible to see around for
a short distance, and so destitute of leaf or branch
for a height of fifty or seventy feet, that nothing
but timber seemed to shut in the view, except where
a stray lightwood or wattle brought the welcome
relief of foliage to the drear gray wall of upright
trunks. Unhappily, they were not all upright; the
fallen ones giving us infinitely more trouble than
the serried ranks standing; the car often having to
make long détours to get round them, amidst dead
wood, holes, bogs, and all imaginable obstacles.

At last, for every mile of our difficult progress
through this dismal, dreary, and most monotonous

forest seemed like a dozen leagues at least, we
made our mid-day halt for nearly an hour; watered
and fed the horses, for whom we had brought some
oats from Deloraine, and made a good fire to cook
our provisions and make some tea, which, being hot,
was more coveted than the ale or wine we had with
us.   Everything around us was cold, damp, dark,
and gloomy. Hideous fungi, of all varieties of shape
and colour, clustered beneath the wet half-charred
logs, or inside the hollow trees, as if they knew themselves to be unfit to meet the light of day, or even
the twilight of the forest, so disgusting were they,
in their livid, bloated, venomous-looking swarms.

Our allotted rest was soon over, and we set forth
again; on, on went the car, jolting, bumping, and
splashing along, over logs, rocks, lagunes, and
bogs; whilst, as I followed its erratic course, I often
reined up my horse, and waited, almost breathlessly,
to watch its passage over some unusually threatening "bad bit of road," but providentially no
accident happened.

Occasionally we came to some semblance of a
bridge, rarely more than the skeleton, the holes and
gaps in which had to be temporarily stopped with
leafy boughs of trees and shrubs and bundles of

cut reeds and grass, so that the horses' feet might
not slip through in crossing. All these delays
hindered us exceedingly, and we found the short
winter afternoon advancing fast, whilst we were yet
far from our destination. A few plants of the
beautiful large crimson epacris began to appear at
intervals, and soon became abundant; but before,
behind, and on all sides, spread the dreary vast
forest, an interminable continuance of the same
sombre desolate picture, till I began to doubt if the
existence of meadows and open country were not
altogether a mere pleasant fiction.

I was riding at some distance from the car,
when I heard a scream from the nursemaid, and,
on hurrying up, found her in great terror and
wonder to know what could have hurt the baby,
who was bleeding fast from a wound beneath the
chin, evidently the bite of a leech. These creatures are very numerous in such damp cold places
as those we were traversing; our dogs were often
afterwards seen with several hanging to their
legs whilst out hunting; and one had probably
been brushed into the car from some of the moist
shrubs, and, after satisfying its appetite, had dropped
off again, for it could nowhere be found.

Soon after this little fright, a horseman was seen approaching us, who proved to be a kind friend's servant, coming to meet us and assist us in any way he could; and as he was a clever "bushman," and a most useful intelligent fellow, we were right glad of his addition to our party.

By the time we arrived in sight of a lonely stock-hut, supposed to be six miles from our future residence, the sun set; and as to drive in the dark through the standing forest and over the prostrate one was a sheer impossibility, it had been determined to leave the car here, in the care of our old servant and his gun, until the morning, and make our way on in the dark on horseback. Our new ally, "Sydney Bill," led the way, and kindly volunteered to take charge of the baby, who had at last wearied of his jolting journey, and for some time had cried piteously; but his new rough-looking nurse held him so tenderly, and the walk of the quiet horse was so much more easy a motion than the unequal one of the car, that the poor weary child went quietly to sleep for the remainder of the journey, and worthy "Bill" won my enduring thankfulness. Mr. Meredith took George before him, on his fine

G 3

tall horse, and rode next in the cavalcade; I followed, and the maid and boy, mounted on the tandem horses, closed the procession. We proceeded in " Indian file," endeavouring to keep on the narrow track of little more than a foot wide, which was all the road our bush-route displayed.

In the forest the usual half twilight is after sunset so rapidly changed to perfect darkness, that my somewhat short-sighted eyes soon lost Mr. Meredith, whose dark horse and dark clothes were undistinguishable to me from the rest of the palpable gloom around; and I several times got off the track until I sent the groom on before me, and as the horse he rode was a light gray, I could then just discern a patch of something less black than the surrounding inky void, moving ahead, which I followed with literally blind confidence. Every now and then my husband's voice reached me, giving some direction or warning : sometimes sounding from below, crying, " Mind this steep gully! When at the bottom, keep to the right for a few paces, then turn to the left, or you will be in the bog!"

A little further on came another mud-hollow, and with it the good advice, not easy to follow in

the dark, "Keep in the middle here!—there are
deep holes on both sides!"

Shortly after, a quick, sharp "coo-ee!" and
"Stoop your head well—here are some very low
branches to go under," and as I could not possibly know the exact whereabout of these treacherous boughs, I lay almost with my face on the
horse's neck, till the next order arrived from
head-quarters, with directions for the mastery of
some new difficulty.

I soon learned to trust more to the sagacity
of my good horse than to my own inferior instinct,
and, in some way or another, he scrambled safely
through all the gullies, and jumped well over
all the innumerable logs; and as I could not
see one of them, my ride was altogether a series
of surprises and mystifications, which would have
been amusing enough, had I felt less weary; but I
had been ten hours on horseback, tiresomely creeping at a foot pace, and had become so thoroughly
chilled, cramped, and drowsy, as to be scarcely
capable of feeling the reins in my hand, and
began to fear that I should drop off my horse
before we arrived at our destination.

Sometimes, looking straight upwards, I could

catch a passing glimpse of a few bright stars, showing that anywhere but in the horrible forest it was a fair clear night; but whilst we were buried in that waste of wood, groping our way like the explorers of some subterraneous world, we were shut out, or rather shut in, from all cheering skyey influences. I scarcely know anything more thoroughly wearisome, both to mind and body, than a slow progress through these dreary dark forests, with their huge, tall, gaunt, bare, half-dead trees, standing around you in apparently the same hideous skeleton shapes, however far you go; as different from the verdant, leafy, shadowy depths of an English wood as a decaying mis-shapen skeleton is from a perfect human form in vigorous life.

Suddenly, the loud barking of several dogs came most pleasantly upon our ears, and in a few more paces a span of starry sky opened out before us, and the outline of some building was visible.

"Here we are at last!" cried my husband, but it seemed unlikely we should be there long, for half a dozen immense dogs were raging round us, apparently only discussing who should be eaten up first, until their master, our valuable assistant "Bill," called them off, and we reached the garden gate of our new domicile. The poor children, both fast asleep, were quickly carried in, beside a good fire, and I followed as soon as I could walk, for, on first alighting from my horse, I was too much cramped with cold to stand.

The good bachelor friend from whom Mr. Meredith had rented the cottage (and our friend Bill's estimable master) having kindly left us his furniture until some of our own should arrive, we managed admirably, making children's beds of car cushions, cloaks, &c.; nothing seemed worth thinking a trouble or annoyance, now that our difficult and weary journey was safely over.

CHAPTER X.

General Sketch of "Lath Hall."—Cockatooers.—Poverty at Port Sorell.—Potatoes.—Port Sorell Horse-keeping.—Fences.—Dutch Barns.—Model Stables.—Police Station.—Pleasant Sea View.—"Clarissa."—Cottage Sites.

I WAS somewhat curious, the next morning, to judge for myself of the situation of our new dwelling, after the very unfavourable accounts Mr. Meredith had given me, but I found his descriptions most faithful. The cottage occupied the top of a slight slope, which was so far cleared that the chief of the great trees had been cut down, but not cut up, and the enormous dead trunks, lying over and under and across each other, made a most melancholy foreground to the everlasting forest, which bounded the narrow view on all sides, like a high dense screen. Two avenues, which had been cut through it in front of the house, gave distant peeps of two other cottages on two other slopes, and gum-trees again, behind. No one who has any

regard for health would, I should think, venture to
live in the hollows or flats of the forest, which seem
the very strongholds of ague, miasma, and all the
other pleasant progeny of swampy woods.

From the back of the house, the close dense
forest was the only view; so close, that any one
looking for sky from the kitchen door must gaze
up to the zenith for it! Altogether, as may well
be imagined, our new home was not a cheerful one
in its external characteristics; and we soon found it
to be exceedingly damp throughout, and very cold.
The walls were built of upright "slabs," that is to
say, of thick pieces of rough split timber, six or
seven inches broad, two or three inches thick, and
about nine feet high, fastened to logs at the
bottom, and wall-plates at the top. These slabs
were lathed and thinly plastered within, and lathed,
but not plastered, without; whence, as the cottage
had no name, I bestowed upon it the sobriquet of
"Lath Hall." The slabs were in many places some
inches apart, and the inside plaster displayed
multitudes of capacious crevices, which enabled the
external air to keep up a friendly and frequent
communication with that within. Five doors and a
French window, all opening into our only parlour,

were not calculated to diminish the airiness of the apartment.

By suspending a thick curtain across one recess, we screened off three doors at once; and another curtain hung over another door, excluded a copious volume of wind from an opposite corner.

Fortunately, fire-wood was abundant, and our liberal use of it in every room which possessed a hearth contributed not a little to clear the near portions of the forest of masses of dead wood.

The instalment of our household goods which had been sent overland to Launceston safely reached us in about a fortnight after our own arrival, and the main body in some weeks afterwards, but in a most deplorable condition—broken, dismembered, and destroyed; casks of well-packed china and glass produced little besides fragments, and all the furniture was maimed, wounded, and disfigured for life. We found, on inquiry, that when the goods were put on board the vessel engaged to convey them from Swan Port to Launceston, her captain and crew were all alike intoxicated, and tumbled our unlucky goods pell-mell into the vessel's hold; and hence the serious and very annoying loss we suffered.

" Lath Hall" being about five miles inland from the police office and township on the shore of Port Sorell, I took an early opportunity of accompanying Mr. Meredith in one of his daily rides thither, to see what manner of place the coast of our new district might be, for I certainly was not enamoured of the inland portion I had seen. Our way lay through the forest, dark, dismal, and dreary as ever, for about three miles ; the only variety of scene was afforded by a few wretched-looking huts and hovels, the dwellings of " cockatooers," who are not, as it might seem, a species of bird, but human beings ; who rent portions of this forest from the proprietors or their mortgagees, on exorbitant terms, and vainly endeavour to exist on what they can earn besides, their frequent compulsory abstinence from meat, when they cannot afford to buy it, even in this land of cheap and abundant food, giving them some affinity to the grain-eating white cockatoos.

The mere clearing off the timber from such land usually costs at least 10*l.* an acre, and the im practicability of a man without capital clearing it, paying rent for it all the while, and maintaining himself and family till the crop comes in, is too evident to any rational mind to need a comment.

The common course is this:—Some industrious
servant who has saved a few pounds from his wages,
if he has been so unusually fortunate in this
peculiar district as to receive his earnings, or a man
with a little money and farm stock, blindly agrees
to pay a high annual rent for a piece of dense
forest, covered with the heaviest timber, the land
itself being of the richest description. With a
large portion of his small capital, he builds a hut
for his family, and then goes on clearing a field for
the plough. Meantime, nothing is coming in, and
money for food constantly going out; rent-day
comes round, and if the remaining savings are
enough, they pay the rent; if not, the cart, plough,
or bullocks must go as well. The coming crop is
offered as security for other inevitable debts, and is
swept off when harvested, leaving only the promise
of the next to carry on the work with until it
comes; and when it does, in all probability the
demands exceed the receipts; the sad finale being
that the wretched family goes forth again, bereft of
every shilling they possessed, and the place where
their all lies buried is let as an "improved
property" to some other adventurer at an advanced
rental. Until I came into the district of Port

Sorell, I could not conceive such poverty as I saw there, to be possible in this land of plenteousness; nor is there, I imagine, in the whole island a similarly-conditioned neighbourhood. It was something quite new again to me, to find the poor people around us thankful for any victuals or other little helps we could give them, such as our comfortable small settlers of Swan Port would have scorned to accept had they been offered. One poor industrious man near us declared afterwards that the scraps of meat and rusty bacon, &c., he had from our kitchen were all he had to eat during one winter, except some cabbages from his garden; every saleable kind of produce, such as wheat, potatoes, &c., having gone in part payment of his debts and rent.

As compared with the extremities of famine recently suffered by thousands of our miserable fellow-creatures in Ireland and England, a winter's subsistence on cabbages may not appear to merit much commiseration; but here, where good fresh meat sells for twopence or twopence-halfpenny a pound, and is used thrice a day in every labourer's or shepherd's hut, besides tea and sugar, and abundance of good wheaten bread, vegetable diet is felt as an unusual hardship.

Much of the penury of Port Sorell may be traced to the high price which was obtained for potatoes some few years ago. Those persons who cultivated them in this district sold their crops one year for 10*l.* and 12*l.* per ton, and as the produce varies from six to ten tons an acre, according to soil and aspect, the simple people fancied they had nothing further to do but plant and dig potatoes, and count gold, (if indeed such gains as they expected *could* be counted!) not taking into consideration the possibility of a depreciation of prices. Lavish expenditure in clearing, cultivating, and building was rapidly made; little estates were mortgaged beyond their value, for funds to carry on the improvements; and, after the whole small population of the neighbourhood had become deeply involved in the fatal potato speculation, prices sank, more rapidly even than they had risen, and, instead of 12*l.*, the faithless root fetched only 5*s.* or 10*s.* the ton. At the period of our residence at Lath Hall, they were deemed scarcely worth even carriage. Horses and pigs were fed on them, and some scores of cart-loads, stored in an inclosure on one side of the cottage we occupied, were deemed worthless, and left there to perish, until the insufferable odour arising from their putrescence compelled us to require their removal.

On Mr. Meredith's first arrival in the district, he one day called at the cottage of a settler, who very civilly inquired, "Would you like your horse put in the stable, Mr. Meredith?"

"No, I thank you," was the reply, "he will do quite well where I left him."

"Then," rejoined Mr. Smith, "shall I send him a few potatoes?"

Such an extraordinary suggestion as offering a dish of potatoes to a horse seemed very like a quiz; but the grave earnestness of the querist proved his perfect sincerity, and, on inquiry, Mr. Meredith was duly initiated into the Port Sorell style of horse-keeping; a bucket of small raw washed potatoes being as usual a "feed" there, as a "quartern of oats" at Home, and the animals seem to relish and thrive on them.

And now to return to our cockatooers' farms, from which the great potato question has too long detained me. Four or five of these little excavations in the forest lay near our route to the beach; each with its one or two small patches of cultivation, surrounded by the forest wall (like a child's garden of a foot square, with a paling a yard high), and a low dilapidated hut and some hovels, usually crouching in one corner of the clearing, shadowed from all but a vertical sun by the gigantic tree-barrier around.

In a place where timber of the best descriptions for sawing or splitting is so superabundant as it is here, we should expect to see particularly good fences, as, if the labour of making posts and rails were too expensive, a perfect rampart of a dead-wood fence might be erected with ease, and the advantage of saving labour in clearing the ground : but the common fences all through Port Sorell would convey the idea that timber was an almost unattainable article ; for, save in one or two instances, I rarely saw any but the most deplorable imitations of brush fences ever attempted, and as these are no defence against the inroads of cattle on the growing corn, perpetual disputes and bickerings arise, which a little good fencing would wholly prevent. Undoubtedly, uncertain tenure and small gains tend not a little to such negligence in tenants, but the proprietors are scarcely better farmers themselves.

At one time I engaged a "cockatooer's" wife in the neighbourhood to come to our house two days in the week, to wash and iron, and gave her 5s. each time and her board; but she shortly sent me word she could not come again, as she must stop at home to keep the cattle off the wheat. A day or two after, I had the curiosity to go and look at the fence of their field. It consisted of a few boughs of shrubs laid on the ground, vary-ing from a few inches to two feet in height, and at intervals forked sticks were stuck up with long thin "tea-tree" poles, like fishing-rods, resting in the forks, and these by no means continuous. It would not have kept a sheep out, in any one place, far less resist the determination and strength of half-wild cattle. Yet these people were content to plough and sow, and then leave their crop with no defence but the vigilance of an old woman; whilst a couple of men and a team of oxen would in less than a week put such a wall of logs round it as should be impregnable for years, and had this been done, I need not have lost my washerwoman, nor she her wages.

The majority of the barns in the district exhibit an equal economy of timber and industry. The

most popular are denominated Dutch barns, and
consist of a roof, supported on posts, with the
sides and ends open. I have also seen stables
there, constructed in the same style, but with
the spaces between the posts walled up with heaps
of manure two or three feet thick! The least
tidy kind of rough wall I have observed in any
other part of the colony has been "wattle and
dab," or turf at the least; it remained for the
ingenious indolence of Port Sorell to invent this
odoriferous composite order of rural architecture.

Some few bits of the forest scenery on our way
to the beach were, from being less dense, much
more pleasing than the rest, especially where magnificent lightwoods, rich in colour and foliage, and
the symmetrical native cherry trees (*Exocarpus*),
in their close massive cypress-like shape, and full
deep-shaded green hue, made pleasant pictures
amongst the more dreary realities of the eternal
Eucalyptus trunks above, and the harsh olive
green ferns below. A few flowers appeared here
and there, seeming rather like things gone astray
from a fairer home, than constant dwellers beneath
the dark gum-tree trunks.

After passing one or two swampy plains tole-

rably bare of trees—crossing "Muddy Creek,"
a clear fresh-water rivulet in a deep hollow—and
descending the next hill, a most welcome line
of blue water appeared over the distant trees,
and we entered a more open country of undulating
grass land, with belts and groups of leafy trees
scattered about, more like a Swan Port sheep-run,
than the Port Sorell forest; and soon we reached
the police station, the situation of which seemed
to me singularly beautiful, after our forest-den,
commanding a view of the calm blue waters of
the port, its pretty rocky islets, and long wooded
points, with the open sea (Bass's Straits) beyond,
bounded on the east by the beautiful range of
the Asbestus Mountains, and on the west by the
West Head of Port Sorell, and Carbuncle Island
(usually rendered Cary-bunckle)   Two or three
little vessels, including my odoriferous friends of
the Launceston wharf, lay at anchor in the port.
The name of one of these was for some time a
problem to us: first we heard of a package come
for us by the "Clara Say;" then the name changed
to the "Clara Say oh!" and then into the "Claret
Sea," which in due time was absorbed in the "Pha-
risee," an odd name for an honest little schooner,

we thought, until a sight of her stern-board announced to us that she bore, in reality, the soft and romantic appellation of " Clarissa!"   Nor is Port Sorell alone ingenious in such distortions: I have known the " Sesostris " spoken of as the " Sea Ostrich;" the " Vansittart" transformed to the " Fancy Tart;" and a man in New Zealand being ordered to name a vessel the " Crocodile," actually painted, launched, and registered her as the " Crooked Eye!"

A boat, pulling swiftly out to one of the vessels, and numerous flocks of gulls and red-bills busily flying to and fro, or fishing in the shallows, added just enough of life and motion to the calm glorious view and the bright clear sunshine, which in itself was reviving and comforting, after the watery vapoury kind of twinkle which reached our forest gloom. I sunned myself delightfully on the sandy beach, till Mr. Meredith's business was over, and then we visited three different spots, which he had thought of as pleasant sites for our own cottage.   The first was a natural terrace, with a conical hill behind, commanding at high water a fine view of the port, and with good fresh water in the vicinity; but at low tide, the view chiefly consisted of reedy mud-

flats and sand-banks, which was not pleasant.   The
second spot was most beautiful; a rocky but well-
sheltered and woody point, with a view both of the
port and its islands, and the open sea; with the
Asbestus Mountains opposite; everything in point
of beauty, but deficient in the requisite of fresh
water,—

> " Water, water, everywhere,
>   But not a drop to drink."

And our miserable experience of drought in New
South Wales made us especially covetous of an
abundant supply.   Reluctantly, we rode away to
the third selected point.   This was a prominent
corner of a natural terrace, which we had traced
along for some distance, close to a running stream
of good water, and with as lovely a view as from
the spot we had last left, although as yet only
seen by glimpses through the great trees; but we
fully appreciated the capabilities of the place, and
decided that there we would erect our cottage,
as soon as the land could be officially surveyed
for the Government, the allotments advertised in
the Government Gazette, and purchased at the
public sale, all which involved an inevitable delay
of some months.

H 2

Wooden houses are built with such rapidity that we hoped to remove into ours within a year, including all expected hindrances; but even that seemed a long time to live so completely " under the shade of melancholy boughs."

CHAPTER XI.

Our New Neighbours.—Golden Rule for Ladies.—Touchstone and
    Audrey.—Veterinary Conversation.—Excursions.—Walk to the
    " Sisters."—Sea-Birds.—Pelicans and Porpoises, &c.

THE inhabitants of our new district were highly
delighted at having their frequent prayers for a
resident police magistrate at length granted, and
the full measure of popularity was accorded to him ;
whilst I was enabled to judge of the degree of
reflected lustre which I enjoyed, by the number of
calls which succeeded my arrival : by the time these
complimentary visits were over, and in due order
returned, I had grown quite weary of answering the
same questions over and over again. I soon discovered that, although we had a more numerous list
of *visitors* than at Swan Port, we had not gained in
point of *society*.

All the residents were farmers, of greater or less

degree, and all "esquires," if not in their own right, by their own assertion, which was often very amusing, and, for all common purposes, did as well. In America, military titles seem the especial ambition of the shop-keeping and agricultural classes, and "majors," "colonels," and "generals" abound on all sides; but in our peaceful island, all such redundant ambition tends towards one point of glory, and "esquire" is the coveted and demanded distinction, *asked for*, when not accorded without, and now so universally applied, that its omission will soon begin to be the really honourable distinction of a colonial gentleman.

One crying fault of the "ladies" prevails far more in colonial than in English society—I allude to that most absurd fallacy, which seems to imagine that a lady ought to be discovered by any chance visitor, at any hour of the day, fully arrayed in her newest attire, and in a state of smartness and precision as regards flounces, ribbons, and collars, which is wholly and utterly incompatible with any kind of domestic occupation or duty whatsoever.

Now the prevalence of this monstrous belief is productive of many evils; not the least of which is, the delay which almost invariably takes place in the

appearance of the ladies of any family on whom
one calls in the country; and the period allotted
for a friendly chat thus passes in a dreary survey of
a formal drawing-room, or in constrained talk with
the unhappy master of the house, who is in a fidget
of anxiety and impatience at the absence of wife
and daughters. Thus, unless we determine to let
our own dinner spoil, or to omit some other intended
visit, we are compelled to take leave in five minutes
after the entrance of our fair friends, whose recently-
smoothed hair, horizontally-folded dresses, and red
damp hands, attest with painful certainty the trouble
which our kindly-intended call has occasioned them.

I know I am on dangerous ground, and that I
might almost as safely "patter in a hornet's nest,"
as show myself so manifestly a traitor in the
camp; yet a little exposure of such follies ofttimes
effects so much improvement, that I do not hesitate
to take my share of responsibility in the attempt.
The golden rule by which all such troublesome
transformations may be rendered unnecessary is,
of course, to avoid ever being untidy or slatternly,
let our occupation be what it may.

My own criterion of propriety in every-day dress
is a very simple one. Of all persons living, I

consider my husband to merit my first and chiefest
respect; and if my attire is such as I deem neat
and proper to be worn in *his* presence, I do not
think I ought to suppose it unfit to appear in
before indifferent people or strangers. And it seems
to me far more pleasant to imagine one's lady-friends
notably busy in a morning, as good country house-
wives must be and are, than to conceive such
useless impossibilities as ladies (some of whom in
this place, I know, keep no female servant) dressed
in new silks or muslins at noon, and seated on a
sofa, doing nothing! To my simple notions, the
latter is intensely contemptible, whilst the former is
right and respectable; and whatever may be thought
of my heretical opinion by my fair acquaintances
themselves, I am quite sure that the husbands,
fathers, and brothers, are all on my side of the
question.

The children, too! such an expenditure of soap
and hair-oil as is deemed indispensable before they
can be introduced to strangers! and then ten to
one but the poor innocents put their mamma in
an agony by instantly informing you that " This is
my best frock!" or that " Bobby mustn't come in,
he's dirty!" Whereas, if no attempt were made to

make things appear finer than they really are, all
this vexation would be spared, and the pleasant
little dirt-pie or pebble-pudding which the little
party were happily discussing, would proceed without interruption.

One of our neighbouring "esquires" one day
asked Mr. Meredith what he called the horse he
was then riding; he replied, "Oh, this is Touch-
stone, and that," pointing to mine, "is Audrey."

"Ah!" rejoined the querist thoughtfully—"Yes,
I see; Touch-stone—oh, yes, he *does* touch the
stones, to be sure, but still I think Top-log would
have been better, for he's a rare one to leap!"

Our unlucky *penchant* for classical or Shake-
spearian names for favourite horses or dogs, often
led to a similar display of incorrigible innocence in
our acquaintance, very few of our Port Sorell
friends being literary characters. A lady, whilst
looking over a scrap-book, with which I had essayed
to amuse her during part of a dreary visit, appealed
to me for some explanation of one of Liverseege's
exquisite Shakespeare scenes which passed her comprehension, and I began trying to *remind* her of the
situation it represented, by a rough sketch of the
well-known characters and locality of the play; but

she wofully checked my valuable illustrations by exclaiming, " Oh, no, indeed, I don't remember anything about it; I never read Shakespeare, I never could."

Shortly afterwards, some local matter became the topic of conversation, and, thinking that was perhaps a more congenial theme, I addressed a common-place remark to my fair guest as to her opinion of the affair; but was again repulsed and reproved by "I do n't know, indeed, I never trouble *my* head with reading newspapers; I've something else to do." The very truth being, as I opine, that such heads pass through life in the enjoyment of almost absolute sinecures.

I was sometimes rather startled by the very *veterinary* character of the conversation prevalent among some few young and (otherwise) lady-like women of our acquaintance. Good and fearless horse-women themselves, their whole delight seemed to be in the discussion of matters pertaining to the stable; and when meeting any young lady friend from a distance, the first questions were not en-quiries after parents, sisters, brothers, or friends: no, nor even the lady-beloved talk of weddings and dress; but the discourse almost invariably took a

" turfy " turn, that was, to say the least, unfeminine
in the extreme.

As the swampy road between " Lath Hall " and
the port became tolerably hard in summer, we
frequently drove down with the children, to pass the
day on the sea beach, both as a great treat and a
sanitary measure also ; for we felt how impossible
it must be to live long in that dark dank place, surrounded with such masses of growing and decaying
vegetable matter, without the children, at least, feeling the injurious effects. The perceptible change
in the atmosphere as we left the forest was always
striking. On a cool day, the air around our cottage
was damp and chilly, on a warm one, close and
oppressive, and always seemed heavy, as if vapour
laden ; but as soon as we emerged from the woods
upon the open land, the fresh light sea-breeze
brought us new life and vigour ; the very act of
breathing was a pleasant sensation, and we all
heartily enjoyed our little excursions.

One day we had established the children and the
maid in a nice rocky nook under some lovely box-
trees (a species of our tribe of myrtles), where
George could either pick shells or pull flowers,
or, what children still more delight in, scoop up

"mountains" of sand on the broad smooth beach; and as the water was at its lowest ebb, Mr. Meredith and I determined to walk across to one of the islands called the "Sisters," which we had often wistfully gazed at from the shore.

The lovely beach we mostly frequented formed at high water the margin of a bright bay, nestled amidst rocks and wooded banks; but the tide receded so far that, at low water, an expanse of hard sand, nearly half a mile broad, was left bare and dry, and apparently extended to the islands, whither we boldly directed our course; but, as we approached, a broad deep channel became visible, lying between us and our goal. Skirting it round for some distance, we found a shallow place, scarcely ankle deep, and, resolving not to be so lightly foiled in our purpose, began to step across it, when we found ourselves on a quicksand, and had to be tolerably active to get safe through. Once on the island, objects of interest abounded. Sea-birds in flocks were around us; gray and white gulls uttering their plaintive cry overhead, as they floated along with one bright eye bent upon us; busy merry red-bills, circling us round and round, repeating their sharp impatient notes; swift-footed little sand-larks skimming rapidly over the beach, like gray and white balls, whirled along in succession; and grand demure ponderous pelicans, in their silvery white and raven gray plumage, sitting asleep, or standing like statues on the broad smooth sands. Silently and stealthily we stepped nearer and nearer to see them better; but our curiosity— as curiosity so often does—defeated its own object, and aroused the pelicans to a full belief of their peril in allowing us to advance so far. Their process of taking flight was to me exceedingly droll; they began by making a short jump on both feet, then another, and another, and another, each jump becoming longer and higher, and their wings becoming gradually expanded, till they finally bounded up from the ground and soared away; and to see eight or ten of these immense birds hopping along in this measured and deliberate style, with their grave and imposing aspect and long pouched bills, was the most comic piece of solemnity I ever witnessed.

After the pelicans took flight, a shoal of porpoises came floundering by, plunging and splashing most delightfully; then we went prying amongst the crevices of the rocks, and in the clear pools, gazing at the myriads of beautiful starfish and *Echini*, and heedlessly scrambling over the sea-weedy crags in search of oysters, until a chance look towards the shore showed us the returning tide flowing rapidly in, and our retreat almost cut off; but by instantly decamping, and fording our quicksand channel, then considerably above a foot deep, we escaped all harm save a good wetting, and by the time we had walked to the car, and were ready to drive home, my somewhat mermaidish garments had become nearly dry in the sun and wind.

CHAPTER XII.

Expedition to an Enchanted Valley.— Lichens.—Nettles.—Fern-trees.
—Small Ferns.—Natural Temple.— The Tallow-tree.—Sassafras.
—Mischances by the Way.—Clematis.—Orchidaceous Flowers.—
Native Laburnum.

MR. MEREDITH used often to make long explorations in the neighbourhood of our cottage,
sometimes to shoot ducks or a kangaroo, and as
frequently merely for a new walk. One day he
returned with such an armful of beautiful shrubs
and ferns, and such exciting accounts of the singularly beautiful spots where he found them, that
I waited impatiently for his first leisure day, that I
might go with him into the new and wondrous
world he had discovered, and see its treasures growing there.

Accordingly on the first opportunity we set forth:
we rode on horseback for two miles of forest, and
then arriving at a " scrub," so thick and close that
our horses could go no further, we left them with

the servant, and proceeded on foot. We soon struck into a cattle path, which was a beaten though very narrow track underfoot, and so far a passage above, that the shrubs gave way on being pushed, but instantly closed again. Long pendulous streamers of tangled gray lichen hung like enormous beards from the trees, and on horizontal branches formed perfect curtains of some feet in depth. Funguses of all kinds protruded from the dead, damp, mossy logs and gigantic fallen trees that lay in our path, and the deep soft beds of accumulated decaying leaves and bark that one's feet sank into were damp and spongy, and chill, even on a warm summer day.

The nettles of this colony are the most formidable I have ever encountered, both in size and venom, and in this primeval scrub they flourished in undisturbed luxuriance, often rising far above our heads, and forming quite a tree-like growth, armed with a fierce array of poisoned spears, with which they ruthlessly attacked my arms and ankles; a thin print dress being a poor defence against their sharp and most painful stings, from which I suffered severely for some days after this scramble.

A friend of ours once rode after some cattle into

a mass of these nettles, which spread over a large space of ground. His horse became so infuriated by the pain of the nettle-stings, that he threw himself down amongst them to roll, which of course increased the poor animal's torture, and his master could neither lead nor drive him out; the creature was rendered mad and furious by pain, and in a short time died in convulsions.

Our cattle-track at length brought us into the enchanted valley Mr. Meredith had discovered, and not in my most fantastic imaginings had I ever pictured to myself anything so exquisitely beautiful! We were in a world of fern-trees, some palm-like and of gigantic size, others quite juvenile; some tall and erect as the columns of a temple, others bending into an arch, or springing up in diverging groups, leaning in all directions; their wide-spreading feathery crowns forming half-transparent green canopies, that folded and waved together in many places so closely that only a span of blue sky could peep down between them, to glitter on the bright sparkling rivulet that tumbled and foamed along over mossy rocks, and under fantastic natural log bridges, and down into dark mysterious channels that no eye could trace out, under those masses of fern trunks, and broad green feathers overarching it; and all around, far above the tallest ferns, huge forest trees soared up aloft, throwing their great arms about in a gale that was blowing up there, whilst scarcely a breath lifted the lightest feather of the ferns below; all was calm and silent beside us, save the pleasant music of the rivulet, and the tiny chirping of some bright little birds, flitting about amongst the underwood.

I had brought my sketch-book, and although despairing of success, sat down under a fern-canopy to attempt an outline of some of the whimsical groups before me, whilst Mr. Meredith and Dick went to look for a kangaroo, the former giving me the needless caution not to wander about, lest I should be lost, a catastrophe for which I seem to possess a natural aptitude in the "Bush."

I soon relinquished my pencil, and shut my book, half in disgust at my own presumption in attempting for an instant a subject so far beyond my poor abilities; and, fastening my handkerchief to the trunk of my canopy fern-tree, I ventured to make short excursions from it on all sides, taking care not to go out of sight of the handkerchief. Sometimes I could go as much as ten yards, but this was in the clearest place; generally the view closed in about five or six.

The stems of the fern-trees here varied from six to twenty or thirty feet high, and from eight inches diameter to two or three feet; their external substance being a dark-coloured, thick, soft, fibrous, mat-like bark, frequently netted over with the most delicate little ferns, growing on it parasitically. One species of these creeping ferns had long winding stems, so tough and strong that I could rarely break them, and waving polished leaves, not unlike hart's-tongue, but narrower. These wreathed round and round the mossy columns of the fern-trees like living garlands, and the wondrously-elegant stately crown-canopy of feathers (from twelve to eighteen feet long) springing from the summit, bent over in a graceful curve all around, as evenly and regularly as the ribs of a parasol.

Whilst making one of my cautious six-yard tours, a fine brush kangaroo came by me, and was instantly out of sight again; and then I heard a whistle, which I answered by a " *coo-ee*," and Dick soon bounded to me, followed by his master. We then shared our sandwiches with the

little birds and the ants, and drank of the bright
cool rivulet, and again went on exploring.   In one
place we found a perfect living model of an ancient
vaulted crypt, such as I have seen in old churches
or castles, or beneath St. Mary's Hall in Coven-
try. We stood in a large level space, devoid of
grass or any kind of undergrowth, but strewn with
fern leaflets like a thick, soft, even mat.   Hundreds
—perhaps thousands—of fern-trees grew here, of
nearly uniform size, and at equal distances, all
straight and erect as chiselled pillars, and, springing from their living capitals, the long, arching,
thick-ribbed fern-leaves spread forth and mingled
densely overhead in a groined roof of the daintiest
beauty, through which not a ray of light gleamed
down, the solemn twilight of the place strangely
suiting with its almost sacred character.   Openings between the outer columns seemed like arched
doors and windows seen through the " long-drawn
aisle," and stray gleams of sunshine falling across
them were faintly reflected on the fretted vault
above us.

Danby *might* paint the scene ; or perhaps one of
Cattermole's wondrous water-colour pictures done
on the spot might convey some tolerable idea of

its form and colouring, but a mere slight sketch were wholly useless.

After reluctantly leaving our temple in the wilderness, we wandered some time longer amidst the grand and beautiful scenes around, and I made a collection of small ferns and other plants new to me.

We noticed one very ornamentàl shrub, usually known as the " Tallow-tree" (from the viscous greasy pulp of the berries), growing here very abundantly, and in great luxuriance; but every one we found was growing out of a fern-tree, the foster-parent in most cases appearing exhausted and withering, whilst the nursling throve most vigorously. It seemed, generally, as if a seed had lodged in the soft fibrous rind of the fern-tree, and had sprung up into a tall, strong, erect stem, at the same time sending out downward shoots, that eventually struck into the earth; but we could not find one plant growing in and out of the earth, although I am aware that the tree is not always a parasite. Many of the stems were a foot through, and their great, coiling, snaky root-shoots clasped about the poor old hoary fern-trees. These tyrant parasites are very handsome, with rich, dark green, glossy leaves, and red blossoms, succeeded by most brilliant orange-coloured berries, which, when ripe, split open, and the case flying back partially displays the bright red cluster of seeds within, like a little pomegranate with an orange-peel husk.

The beautiful Tasmanian sassafras-tree is also a dweller in some parts of our fern-tree valley, but not in those we explored on the present occasion. The flowers are white and fragrant, the leaves large and bright green, and the bark has a most aromatic scent, besides being, in a decoction, an excellent tonic medicine. The wood is hard and white, with scarcely any visible grain, but is marked or shaded with light brown in irregular occasional streaks. Thinking that it must partake the pleasant fragrance of its bark, I procured some to make boxes of, but found it quite devoid of scent after the bark was removed. A block of it furnished Mr. Meredith with an excellent material for a beautiful toy sailing-boat, which he carved out of it for George; and the fine, close, velvety texture of the wood seems admirably adapted for carving of any kind. The sawyers and other bush-men familiar with the tree call it indiscriminately " saucifax," " sarserfrax," and " satisfaction."

We found no small difficulty in getting out of our vale of enchantment; indeed, I began to think that, having really forced an entrance into Fairy Land, the wicked sprites had bewitched us, so that we must perforce remain there. No returning cattle-track could be discovered, the scrub was too dense to observe the position of the sun, and its unbroken entanglement was most fatiguing to force one's way through. Several times we took a wrong direction, and, after a long combat with briars and nettles, were forced to " try back" again. The heat and oven-like closeness of the air were most depressing to strength and spirits, and once or twice I sank down almost exhausted; but after a brief rest I grew more resolute, and pushed on after my husband.

The impossibility of seeing what was beneath our feet caused me to suffer many unwelcome surprises, by stumbling over logs, falling into holes, and like mischances; but at length we succeeded in scrambling once again into light and sunshine, and very thankfully mounted our horses and rode home, the pleasure of our day's exploring having so im-

measurably overbalanced the fatigue, that I promised myself several more pilgrimages to the same
shrine, which, alas, were never performed.

I never saw the lovely native clematis growing
so luxuriantly as among the Port Sorell forests.
There, over the universal undergrowth of ferns,
this beautiful climber often spread over a space
many feet broad and long, in a richly-woven
mantle of loaf and flower, or, clinging to some
slender tree, formed a tangled covering all over
it, with long starry chaplets waving about. The
bright blue *Comesperma* was equally abundant,
but its abode was usually in drier and more open
places.

Myriads of strangely-shaped orchidaceous flowers
bloomed in all situations, and included various species of yellow and brown *Diuris*, lilac, pink, and
blue kaladenias, various in form as in colour;
and one very eccentric individual of the orchis
family, with a very long dark-brown lower lip, in
the centre of which rose a large protuberance like
a nose. I have shown my drawing of it to many
persons, but none had ever seen the plant, or could
tell me its name. I also found three varieties of a
singular green orchis, of a helmet-shape, growing

singly, on rather tall slender footstalks.   One of these had a long feather-like appendage protruding from the opening in front.

A beautiful shrub, with flowers and leaves very much resembling the laburnum, formed thickets in some of the damp hollows near us, and many other ornamental shrubs abounded, whilst fern-trees were plentiful near most of the rivulets; but though very Oriental and palm-like in their aspect, they were not comparable, in point of beauty or magnitude, with those of our charmed dell.

CHAPTER XIII.

Tasmanian Eagle.—White Hawk.—White Cockatoos.—Superb Warblers' Nest.—Strange Insect.—Venomous Guests.—Burning Trees. —Stinging Ants.—Flies.—Wood-Tick.

FEW varieties of birds enlivened our forest gloom; the most numerous were the crows and black magpies; but none of the sweetly-singing pied magpies are seen nearer Port Sorell than the Avenue Plain; and much as I missed my pleasant merry friends, I could not but applaud their taste in frequenting any part of the island rather than this most dreary and disagreeable district.

Now and then, two, three, or four lordly eagles might be seen soaring grandly high overhead at the same time, and once we saw as many as seven together, and marvelled much what so grave an augury portended. As all things edible were scarce in the vicinity, we sometimes thought that our goats, with their young kids, might possibly attract the attention of the eagles; but I must freely exonerate them from all charge of theft—they never molested any of our live stock. I cannot give an equally good character to their disreputable kinsfolk, the hawks, who were bolder and more rapacious than any I had seen before, coming and sitting quite composedly on the very hen-house itself, and swooping into the veranda after my pet guinea-fowls with insufferable audacity. White hawks, so rare in most parts of the island, were numerous here; they are most superb birds, with plumage soft as satin, and whiter even than snow; and radiant piercing eyes, so bold and bright! I often wished to procure a young one to rear tame, but I suppose that a revolt amongst my poultry would certainly have ensued, on the installation of such a favourite.

The Tasmanian eagle is a very large and noble bird, of grand and majestic aspect; but prejudice is here very strong against him, and scores of instances are currently related of his destructive predilections for young lambs, sucking pigs, and other dainty morsels; we, however, give very little credence to these ungenerous stories, as none of the narrators have been able to say that they themselves saw the offence committed.

One of our shepherds (at Swan Port), having on one occasion wounded an eagle slightly in the wing, caught it, and brought it to me: had I refused to keep the poor thing, it would immediately have been put to death; I therefore let him leave it, and for some days it was tethered by the leg to a large coop, and plenty of food given to it, but it ate nothing—parrots, chickens, rabbits, and offal were all alike untouched. I then supposed that my noble captive was too heroic to eat whilst in that fettered condition, and after having the feathers of one long beautiful wing cut, I set him at liberty in the garden; but, although daily tempted by fresh food, he ate nothing for *three weeks* from the time of his capture, and I began to despair of keeping him alive, when one day, to my great joy, a piece of fresh liver conquered his heroism, and he devoured it greedily. After that he always fed heartily, and roamed about the garden for some months, but never became tame enough to eat from our hands. One day a servant whom I had entrusted with a gun to shoot rabbits, saw my poor eagle sitting on a fence a short distance from the house, and believing it to be a wild one, shot it, much to my vexation.

The beak and talons, and indeed the whole form and aspect of the bird, denote enormous strength, and the span of the extended wings is from seven to nine feet, so that it would be a formidable adversary to almost any creature it determined to attack. I have heard a story here of a child two years old being carried some distance by an eagle, and then dropped, with its head severely injured; but I am unwilling to place any reliance on the tale.

The two neighbouring dwellings which we used to peep at through the streets or avenues cut in our girdle of forest, had some meadows and corn-fields on a rich marsh that spread out below them, and in our walks we often saw great flocks of white cockatoos thickly scattered about like sheep, eating up the springing grain. Unlike the clever, harmless, black cockatoos, the white ones are exceedingly mischievous, devouring immense quantities of corn; and they are so cunning and sagacious, that it is very difficult to approach them with a gun. One pair which had been shot near us was brought me as a present. They were very large handsome birds, of snow-white plumage, with crests and lower tail-feathers of the most pure and delicate yellow. Knowing that they feed wholly on grain, and are commonly eaten in New South Wales, I had them roasted, and we found them excellent, being young and tender, very much like a fat wild duck; but I believe youth is an indispensable requisite in a cooked cockatoo, the elderly birds being of rather leathery texture.

Very few parrots visited us, and those were of the common green kind, the least beautiful of all. Wild ducks and quail were tolerably plentiful, but we neither saw bronze-winged pigeons nor wattle-birds.

One or two pairs of "Superb Warblers" lived close to the garden fence, and for a long time I tried in vain to discover their nest. We often fed them, and they came boldly about us, but always baffled me when I endeavoured to watch them home. At last I felt quite sure I had found the grass tussock containing one nest, but although this was not above two feet across, I was some time still ere I discovered the entrance, for of course I would not disturb anything, and the little creatures were so artful and cautious, and in such a sad state of fluttering chirping trepidation when I was peeping about, that they distracted my attention, as they naturally intended to do. At last, I accidentally looked directly into the little tube of woven grass and web that served them as hall and ante-room— several blades of reeds waved before it, but still, on gazing intently down into the dark little cavity, I espied two or three little gaping mouths, and heard a faint small chirp. The two tiny parents of these tinier babies (which could not be much bigger than peas) were all the time flying round and round me, in most distressing terror, almost brushing my face with their delicate wings in their anxiety to drive me away; and the instant I drew back, both darted into the nest to see if all was right at home. Poor little flutterers! they need not have feared me. I only confided the secret of their abode to my husband, and so fearful was he of disturbing them, that I could not induce him to go near enough to examine the nest. In due time we had the pleasure of seeing the whole miniature family out together; the old birds in a great state of importance and flutter, feeding their droll brown little offspring most assiduously.

"Come here, and look at a strange insect," said Mr. Meredith, one day when we were in the garden; and I went, and looked, and looked again, all over the low young cherry-tree to which he pointed.

"I cannot see any insect; where is it?"

"Oh! look for it; it is at least eight inches long, so you surely ought to find it!"

And searching again, more narrowly than before, and following the direction of his glance, I observed something like a few dry sticks or twigs, hanging in a loose irregular angular style from one of the sprays, which, on a closer view, proved to be a living creature, so exactly the colour and apparent texture of a dead stick, that I could scarcely credit its being anything else, and carefully took it off the tree, before being quite convinced. I suppose —for I am wofully unlearned in entomology—that it was one of the animated straw genus. The body was of a dull brown, and about six inches long, and little more than a quarter of an inch thick, with one or two folds just like the joints of a dead reed or twig; the head had prominent eyes, and two long feelers, like thin dead rushes, which being in a line with the body, added nearly three inches to its apparent length. The six legs were like thin dead rushes too, about four inches long, divided into three joints and ending in a clawed foot. Rather nearer to the head than the tail were two very short small wings, like the bladebones of unfinished

shoulders, evidently quite inefficient as instruments
of flight to the long body and legs. The creature
seemed in a half-torpid state when I captured it,
and eventually became rigid, when I ventured to
believe it really dead, and preserved it, until devoured by insects, and utterly destroyed. Some
persons who saw it told me they had seen other
specimens, with large handsome wings; but their
kind promises to procure me one were never fulfilled.

Any one fond of entomology, or the study of the
Crustacea, might have enjoyed great opportunities
and facilities at " Lath Hall," where fine lively
scorpions were in the frequent practice of perambu-
lating our parlour walls, particularly near the fire-
place; and interesting full-grown centipedes, of a
most venomous green hue, and rarely less than four
inches in length, gracefully meandered in the folds
of the window-curtains, our dressing-room (usually
by us denominated " the tank," from its icy damp-
ness) being their favourite haunt; and as in all
the rooms save one, which we allotted to George
and the maid, the wide-apart " slabs " of the floors
afforded ample space for a lobster to pass through,
the entrance of any of the insect tribe was a matter

of no marvel whatever. My chiefest terror was, lest snakes should come in too; but although many large ones were seen and killed very near the house, I never saw one within it.

Tarantulas straggled along with impunity in all directions, unless so near that I apprehended their crawling on me; and then the idea of those eight great long woolly hairy legs, and that fat black body, traversing any portion of my own person, generally conquered my humanity, and the intruder died.

One of our few amusements was, burning trees down, and no one would marvel at such an occupation becoming quite an exciting pursuit, had they seen how cruelly the tall gaunt trees shut out the morning sun. In winter, if the sun rose at half-past seven, not a glance of his glorious face reached our chilly den before ten o'clock: we seemed to be living, as they say Truth does, at the bottom of a well, and we did what we could to excavate an opening towards the sunshine.

Selecting our victim-tree, we first made up a bundle of the driest leaves, grass, and bark inside, if it were partially hollow, as was generally the case; and after lighting this with a lucifer-match,

and fanning up a bright blaze, we carried to it
quantities of loose wood and bark, the latter commodity being very abundant everywhere, the gum-
trees shedding their outer skin yearly, which lies
about in all directions, some of it like gigantic
pieces of cinnamon, many feet long, and some sorts
in wider and flatter flakes, but all highly com-
bustible.   When a good heap rose against the first
tree, and the fire grew too fierce to approach, we
carried a " fire-stick " to another, and made up our
blazing pile there too, pursuing the same system
with five or six, by which time the first fire required
replenishing.   Many of the logs that we dragged
to our fires were the abodes of numerous kinds of
ants, most of which *nip* rather sharply, but of some
the sting is venomous and agonizing in the extreme.

We were busily employed in this way one evening
(the working party consisting of the papa, mamma,
and George, with the nursemaid and baby Charles
looking on), when a piercing shriek from poor
George alarmed us with the idea that a snake had
bitten him; he sprang up into the air twice or
thrice, far higher than he could have jumped with
his utmost exertion at another time, and then rolled

on the ground still shrieking fearfully. I carried
him away from the spot, and then saw the cause
of the mischief; a large black ant, above an inch
long, was on the poor child's instep, still stinging
him through his sock. Their sting is very long,
and Mr. Meredith describes the pain as resembling
what we may imagine would be that of a sharp red-
hot iron forced into the flesh. In twenty minutes
or half an hour it abates, and gradually goes away,
leaving a blister like a mosquito-bite. On another occasion, the luckless boy had one of these
horrible creatures in the leg of his trousers,
and before it could be removed, he was severely
stung in nine places. I have frequently detected
them running over me, but have always escaped
being stung. Once, as I lay on the sofa reading, I observed one very deliberately walking along
my collar, carrying an enormous buzz-fly in his
nippers.

A species of ant somewhat smaller than these,
black, with yellow forceps, is as much or more to
be dreaded, as they sting with equal severity, and
can jump a considerable distance in pursuit of any
one who molests them.

Our burning trees often formed very beautiful

objects at night, sometimes taking the semblance of ruined towers, with windows and loopholes defined in glowing fire, and showers of sparks falling from the summit. Some would burn internally to a great height, and then burst forth in volumes of flame, many feet from the ground, throwing out great jets, like gigantic fireworks, lighting up all the surrounding gloom.

I have not yet alluded to one of the most constant and unpleasant pests to which these colonies are subject, namely, the great brown disgusting buzz-flies, which continue to torment us all the year round, and in summer swarm most offensively and destructively. Our old English blue-bottle fly is, it is most true, a very noisy fellow, and seems fond of dissipated company, in butchers' shops, &c., and in summer sometimes greatly disturbs one's lonely reverie, by testing the hardness and reverberatory powers of our ceilings and windows in his riotous bumping flight about a room. But here, his brown ill-looking relatives are not content, like him, with a summer reign,— they bump about us the twelve months through, and in numbers incalculable. Now, as I write, some forty or fifty are careering through the room, knocking up against the windows, and buzzing most abominably; whilst the difficulty of excluding them from the larder, and the destruction they occasion in it, are two important items in the catalogue of colonial household plagues. The small house-fly is here, as elsewhere, very troublesome too; but though these swarm in immense numbers during the summer months, they are more endurable than the " brown buzzes."

A new kind of small fly has appeared in Van Diemen's Land within the last few years, which is generally known as the " Port Philip fly," and supposed to have been brought from thence. It closely resembles the common house-fly; but, instead of the outspreading sucker-proboscis of the latter, its head is furnished with a tapering black tube, the narrow end of which it inserts, with a sharp piercing bite, into the skin of men or animals, and commences sucking the blood most actively, often leaving a drop on the surface of the skin. To horses it is a terrible torment, and seems chiefly to abound in the vicinity of stables and straw-yards.

One of the insects which I most dreaded was the " wood-tick," an unpleasant-looking creature, very much resembling those which infest sheep, but possessing a great *penchant* for a residence under the human skin, into and beneath which it eats its way until nearly hidden from sight, without any pain to the person attacked for the first several hours, so that it often escapes notice until the intolerable aching of a large portion of the body surrounding it leads to the detection of the insect, which must then be pulled or cut out. These ticks live among wood, and are sometimes brought into the house with the fuel. I have frequently seen them on my dress or habit, when walking or riding in the " Bush," and have on two occasions been bitten : once on the throat, by a small one which had been several hours at work; it had buried its head entirely, and required a strong pull with tweezers before it could be extracted, the creature being as hard as bone, and very toughly jointed. I felt very little pain afterwards on this occasion ; but the second of the insidious little miners, which also attacked me on the neck, was a much larger specimen, and it had begun to cause a most dis-tressing ache in my shoulder, neck, and arm, which I attributed to rheumatism, until, on passing my hand over my dress, I detected its round hard body, which was too firmly attached for me to pull it away myself. After it was removed, I suffered great pain and numbness in the arm and shoulder for several days.

CHAPTER XIV

Church-building.—Public Worship.—Deficiency of Religious Instruction. — Rustic Costumes. — Leather "Leggings."—Progressive Love-tokens.—Marriage.

AT the period of our arrival, no church had been as yet erected at Port Sorell, and the roads of the district were so impassable from bogs, for nine months of the twelve, that had there been one, no congregation could have met oftener than ten or twelve Sundays in the year. Still, the absence of all semblance of a place of public worship for members of the Church of England (whilst, even in a yet poorer neighbouring settlement, an Independent chapel and minister were maintained, chiefly by poor sawyers) became too glaring to continue; and it was proposed to erect a cheap wooden building by means of subscriptions. This design, after considerable delay, was carried out:

one person subscribing so many "slabs;" another, a certain quantity of weather-boards; a third, the requisite "sawed stuff;" a fourth, the shingles; a fifth, the blacksmith's work; a sixth, the "lend" of a bullock-team, and so on; very few payments being made in money. Unfortunately, instead of being placed on the township, in the centre of the population, where a glebe and burial-ground might have been obtained from the Government, the little building was set up on a private property, too much encumbered with mortgages for the requisite gift of the site to be legally made without considerable expense, and consequently the consecration could not take place; but when merely the rough shell was set up, our energetic and accomplished Bishop came down and assisted at the first celebration of Divine service, before a larger congregation than could have been expected in such a place.

Nearly a year elapsed before any clergyman was appointed; and then service was only performed on one Sunday in a month, by the missionary chaplain of Deloraine, the Rev. Montagu Williams. He came to Port Sorell, a distance of forty miles, at the end of every fourth week, to officiate on the

Sunday morning at the little church, and in the afternoon at the police office.

Such, and so rare, are the opportunities for public worship in the wilds of Tasmania!

Surely the munificent gifts and bequests which so many pious persons at Home make for the purposes of church-building and endowment, in towns and cities where scores of churches already stand, might be extended to such a far-away nook as this island, where, from the peculiar condition of a large number of the inhabitants, the need of instruction is so great, and the means so small! The amount of good which might be effected by the ministry of truly Christian conscientious clergymen would be very great indeed.

Did the power and the means of supplying such rest with our earnest-hearted and benevolent prelate, it were well for us all, but more especially for the poor and ignorant of his diocese. But, if persons ever so notoriously unfit for holy orders are appointed here from Home, his judgment and conviction of the impropriety and mischief of such appointments cannot effect a change unless their commission of errors be as glaring as their omission of duties. We must, therefore, patiently endure

the evil, knowing meanwhile that, with the same
means, an infinite amount of good would result,
under different circumstances.

I have often remarked the difference which exists
between the outward aspect of farm labourers here
and in England : whether attributable to the various
trades and callings here amalgamated into the
same occupations, or to the sea-voyage, or to
both of these together, I know not; but certain it
is, that no British village ever sent forth such
nondescript toilettes as I have seen here on a
Sunday. Latterly, the increase of country shops
in the colony, and the variety of cheap ready-made
coats of all shapes, fabrics, and prices, have caused
wonderful innovations in the dress of all classes,
although still permitting a great display of original
taste.

Red or blue flannel serge shirts are universally
worn by labourers in cold or wet weather as a
working dress, generally hanging loosely over other
garments, or fastened blouse-wise by a leather belt;
and when these are new and bright, they are
sometimes permitted to form part of the Sunday
outfit.

The stock-keepers seem a perfectly-distinct class

in point of dress, a subject which I conceive costs them some pains, from the ingenious incongruities often displayed; all evidently aiming at something dashing, and of rather a sporting cast. We have often wondered where such oddly-cut and thoroughly queer-looking coats, hats, and other garments were procured, until a little circumstance which occurred lately threw some light on the interesting subject. Mr. Meredith was one day in a Jew slop-seller's shop in Launceston, making some purchases for our servants, when a labouring man came in, and desired to see some black hats. Immediately the counter displayed a selection of the most unaccountable shapes, chiefly very tall, and with scarcely any brims; but as even those were deemed too broad by the customer, he went away in search of narrower ones, the shopman remarking, " Oh! I see you are quite a dandy! you want to be *too* flash altogether."

And in reply to Mr. Meredith's inquiries, he said that they were obliged to keep these extraordinary articles for such men, who would buy no other, and were as fastidious and particular " as any fine lady ; " whilst we, in our innocence, had commiserated them for being victimized by the shopkeepers, and

having goods foisted upon them which were otherwise unsaleable.

Having thus touched on the delicate topic of
taste in dress, I must not confine my observations
to the servants, whilst their masters in many instances are yet more removed from the customary
aspect of persons in the same station at Home. The
true gentleman, whether at home or abroad, is as
certain to avoid any uncouth peculiarity of attire, as
the ambitious " snob " is to adopt it; and colonial
country life exemplifies the fact abundantly. The
most striking feature in the costume of such
worthies on the north side of our island is, a
description of rough brown leathern casing for the
legs, neither trouser, gaiter, nor boot, but a loose,
wrinkled, bagging, dirty, slovenly, hedger - and-
ditcher kind of envelope, worn both in winter and
summer, and usually slung to the waist by a multitude of straps and a belt, looking like a surgeon's
dressing for a fracture, ill put on; and in dirty
weather the loose puckers about the ankles serve
as such capacious receptacles for mud, that the exit
of visitors so arrayed is the signal for the entree
of the housemaid, to remove the evidences of their
sojourn from carpets and floors. When these

hideous leggings are companioned (as I *have* seen them, and on *soi-disant* esquires, too) by a hat of white felt or black oil-skin, a striped shirt, with a blue serge one by way of blouse, and a tremendously heavy long whip in full play, the refined and *recherché* effect of the combination may be imagined!

As to the tender question of *esquirearchy*, I am convinced that the only prudent principle now is, to bestow the envied title on every one alike—on the friend you invite to partake your dinner, and the butcher from whom you bought it. All this has a strong affinity to some of the ways of the "far West," not a little aided in effect by an odd use of old words, and a puzzling adaptation of new ones, which, although less racy and graphic than some of our American friends' ingenious coinages, are essentially un-English.

As all my prisoner women-servants have had suitors in plenty, I have sometimes been amused by quietly observing the growing symptoms of the tender passion, as exemplified (in their class of life) by the unfailing presents and love-tokens offered by the enamoured swain as symbols of his sincere attachment, and signs of progress made. The

campaign not unfrequently opens with the bold
demonstration of a gay print gown, especially if the
arrival of a hawker's cart at the kitchen-door has
afforded so excellent an opportunity for the display
of rustic gallantry. The presentation of a bonnet
and ribbons I look upon as a decidedly serious
advance, and in some cases a few yards of calico
often give a grave aspect to the affair; a shawl, too,
is considered a very affecting thing, and I have
known a lace cap on the head exercise a mighty
influence over the heart; but the grand conclusive
stroke of all, the true love-philter, the unerring
omen that bids me seek a new handmaiden, is—
when the bolt of Cupid comes wrapped in flannel!
Print gowns and new bonnets are, no doubt, shrewd
pleaders; ribbons and lace, too, are insinuating
things; and shawls and calico may mean much;
but when the courtship takes the shape of flannel,
I know the work of wooing has sped—the damsel's
heart is won; and that the next thing will be
John's awkward round-about request for leave to
" keep company with Mary;" which is very quickly
followed by Mary's sheepish presentation of the
" memorial for marriage," with—" If you would
please, ma'am, to ask the master to please to recom-

mend us!" And married they are, shortly after, if
the lover is in a situation to maintain a wife, which
the superior powers very rightly desire to know,
before authorizing the marriage.

CHAPTER XV

A Winter at Port Sorell.—Four Months' Rain.—Voyage to Launce
ton.—The Town Wharf.—Journey to Hobarton.—Sir Eardley
Wilmot.—Sketching Epidemic.—Exhibition.—A Fern Valley.—
Cabs.—Mrs. Bowden's "Anson" Discipline.—Female Servants.
—Religious Instruction.

WE had thought it sufficiently unpleasant to be
located for a whole summer in the forest, although
during that time we could occasionally make a
sortie from our wooden walls, and breathe the
sea-air. But the approach of winter, and the conviction that the whole of its dreary days must pass
before we could finally escape from our Castle
Dismal, was in truth a severe trial of endurance.
If even sunshine lost its brightness in that sombre
forest gloom, what a thrice-dreary aspect did it wear
in those days, and weeks, and months of almost
incessant rain! Sometimes it rained very hard,
and sometimes harder still; sometimes like a continuous thunder-shower, and sometimes in one

mighty sheet of water, like an upper ocean that had
burst its bounds.   The ground was always something wetter than a bog, and most often resembled
a flooded river : such were the pleasant varieties we
enjoyed ; and when Mr. Meredith's horse used to
be brought in a morning for him to ride down to
the police-office, it came beside the veranda for him
to embark, as a boat would alongside a ship, for a
lagune lay between the house and the garden gate,
where he usually mounted ; and the whole road he
had to traverse was an alternation of deep water,
shallower water, and bogs.

Four pouring months at length wept themselves
out ; spring found me slowly recovering from a
severe illness, and, by way of restorative, brought us
the official intelligence that the intended reductions
in the police department, consequent on the low
condition of the Government finances, would inevitably include the magistracy of Port Sorell—a
pleasant climax to our troubles ! more especially as
our own cottage was begun, on the land we had
purchased, and must be paid for, whether required
or not.   Spring, under these circumstances, became
rather more melancholy than even winter itself ;
but happily the sky of our changeful fortunes was

K 2

subsequently brightened by the intelligence that
the threatened reductions were postponed *sine die*,
and the hope that our pleasant sea-side home would
receive us before autumn.

A kind invitation at this time from the Lieutenant-Governor, our good and valued friend, Sir
Eardley Wilmot, to visit him in Hobarton, promised
us a most pleasant and welcome change of scene
and society; and we accordingly arranged for our
temporary excursion, and our final departure from
"Lath Hall" at the same time; determining to take
up our abode, on our return, in the new cottage
by the sea, however unfinished it might be, rather
than dive again into the depths of the forest.

Rapidly and most cheerfully was the work of
packing-up proceeded with, and within a week from
the first consideration of our removal, I and the
children and the nursemaid were, one bright morning at eight o'clock, sitting on the deck of the
smart little cutter the "Hope" (of about 15 tons),
which was cleaned out and furbished up especially
for our accommodation, and bound to Launceston
expressly in our service, Mr. Meredith remaining
behind to complete the dismantling of "Lath Hall,"
and purposing to ride up and meet us in town.

A fair wind carried our little vessel into Port Dalrymple by ten o'clock, when we got into smooth water; a very welcome change after the heavy swell we had suffered from during our short sail through the straits, which knocked our little bark about very roughly, and occasioned us considerable indisposition.

Launceston lies about forty miles from the sea-coast, and the voyage thither, up the Tamar, is very mononotous. George Town is a scattered little settlement on the low shores of a small but secure cove at the mouth of the estuary, a few miles above the lighthouse; on the opposite shore, near Kelso Bay and York Town, are some productive farms and gardens, but the George Town side is a mere barren, sandy waste, producing nothing. Although situated several miles from the sea, George Town is sometimes frequented by families from the interior of the island for the summer pleasures of bathing and boating, the weekly visit of the steamer from Launceston giving every facility of access.

The scenery on the Tamar is of the tamest possible description, although the river forms many fine bends in its course. The land on the banks is

generally low, but yet rising sufficiently to shut out
any distant view.   Here and there the quiet smooth
little slopes unexpectedly display a feeble attempt
at the romantic, in a few protruding rocks of very
mild and subdued aspect; the most striking point
is named "Brady's Look-out," after a notorious
bush-ranger of years gone by. who is said to have
been "planted" (*i. e.*, concealed) there for some
time; but the tokens of busy industry which meet
the eye at several bends of the river are pleasanter
subjects for contemplation.   Here stands a large
well-built steam flour-mill, with its owner's comfortable cottage, garden, and out-buildings; and,
close by, a very pretty little church: there is a
busy shipwright's establishment, with one fine
vessel nearly ready to launch, another standing in
its skeleton, and all the surrounding methodical
confusion of new boats and old boats of all sizes,
large and small, timber of all descriptions, smoking
and pleasant-smelling pitch cauldrons, neat cottages
and workshops, and a busy buzz of voices, and
sounds of hammering and singing coming cheerfully
towards us as we glide along.

Heavily-laden clumsily-shaped wood-boats toiled
slowly up the stream, carrying fuel to Launceston,

and making our progress seem rapid by comparison, until some neat, sharp, smart, whaleboat, with its well-feathered oars and clever lug sail, darted past us in the most provoking manner, and almost proved us to be resting motionless on the water. The wind had become so light and fitful that we scarcely seemed to make any way, and I began to think about making up our beds on board for the children; but a few friendly puffs came to our aid, and at sunset we were in sight of Launceston, which, viewed from the water at a proper distance, and no doubt a little beautified in my eyes by my anxious desire to reach it, looked positively pretty.

The situation of the town seems to me very ill-chosen, as at a short distance below it the river is crossed by a bar, over which laden vessels of any large size cannot pass; and accordingly when ships come in, they are compelled to anchor below the bar, until so far unloaded as to permit their crossing it, when they take up their position at the town wharf, until about to sail again, and then they drop down past the provoking bar, before completing their cargo. The placing a shipping port in such a position, when, for forty miles below, the river is navigable for a "seventy-four," seems an unaccountable blunder, and one which, combined with the unhealthy situation, must, it would seem, eventually lead to the decline of the town of Launceston, and the selection of some more eligible locality for the site of our northern metropolis.

The channel at the bar is so narrow that two vessels cannot cross it together, and we had to wait until another of the coasting craft had preceded us; the little "Hope" looking very humble indeed beside three great merchantmen which were waiting there to unload, their huge black sides towering up above us like great walls, and the people on their decks looking down as if they were on a tall housetop and we in the street below.

It was quite dark when we reached the wharf, and our little vessel was then compelled to take up a berth outside of the steamer and two other vessels, across the decks of which we passed to the shore, not without my suffering enough terror and anxiety for a life in the few minutes of our transit; the spaces between the vessels, and the deep water below, gaping like open traps to seize something precious belonging to me. Our good "skipper" (who knew how anxious I had been to get on shore), and all sorts of strange men, immediately began running off in the most kind but provoking way with my children and our baggage. I saw trunks, carpet-bags, and bedding dodging about in the fitful gleams, like things possessed; and, utterly despairing of being able to control matters any longer on board, I followed in the wake of a conspicuous roll of mattresses, until I found myself beside a heap of my property—children, maid, and trunks—all safely huddled together on the wharf, guarded by the "Hope's" mate, who soon called a cab for us. With a stodge of small folks and small packages inside, and a pile of trunks and bedding following, we drove to our hotel, highly pleased at having had so quick a passage, for vessels are often a fortnight in going this short distance (about sixty miles), owing to contrary winds, fogs, and other obstacles; and Mr. Meredith, to provide for such an untoward delay, had insisted on my packing up a commissariat large enough for a voyage to New Zealand at least, which became an acceptable and additional perquisite to the "Hope's" good people.

At four the next morning we took our seats in the coach for Hobarton, and arrived there the same evening soon after eight, a distance of 120 miles.

The fearfully fast driving was the chief drawback
to the pleasure of the journey: the scenery is in
many parts very beautiful, but the feeling of terror
with which I was possessed, lest the constantly-
threatened upset should take place, left me little
power to appreciate or enjoy it. The unfortunate
horses are flogged unmercifully, and driven for the
greater part of the way, up hill and down, and often
down very steep hills, too, at a furious gallop. No
such precaution as locking a wheel is ever heard of!
The result has been shown with terrible regularity
by the paragraphs of the weekly papers, recording
" serious and fatal accidents," fractures and injuries of all kinds sustained by the passengers, all
consequent on the senseless and pernicious system
so obstinately pursued.

Between two and three months passed very
pleasantly at Hobarton (Mr. Meredith joining me
occasionally, when he could leave Port Sorell), in
our delightful sojourn at Government House, with
the late—alas! that he is gone!—kind-hearted,
witty, generous Sir Eardley Wilmot, and in visiting
our relatives and other friends in the vicinity.

The utter and flagrant falsehood of the cowardly
and cruel accusations made by anonymous slan-

derers against our late Lieutenant-Governor has
long since been so well exposed, that I should pass
over all allusion to so lamentable a topic, and one
so painful now to touch upon, but that our visit
happened to take place at the very time when, as it
was wickedly declared, " *No ladies ever visited at
Government House.*" Such affirmations are always
best met by simple facts.   Mr. Meredith and myself, and two other families (husbands, wives, and
children), were resident guests there.   Sir Eardley
Wilmot's agreeable dinner-parties were attended by
all whom he thought worthy or desirable to invite ;
and a ball, the cards for which were issued during
our stay, and only gave the short notice of one day
and a half, was thronged by all the visitable world
of Hobarton and the vicinity, the company very
possibly including some of the heartless maligners
themselves, although I am rather tempted to believe
that the reports emanated from disappointed suitors
for admission to Government House.   Candid and
open hearted, perhaps even to a fault, in this world
of hypocrisy, highly refined and witty himself, and
keenly appreciating wit and intelligence in those
around him, Sir Eardley Wilmot rarely took prudent pains to disguise his feelings of indifference

towards the dull, the pompous, or the vulgar, and
consequently created some mortal foes, who, aided
by the ready credulity of a puritanical minister,
aimed but too surely the assassin's blow at his
honour and peace of mind.

*   *   *   *   *

After so perfect a seclusion as I had lived in for
years, it was exceedingly pleasant to find myself
once more in society; and the change which, during
those five years, had taken place in the thoughts and
habits and general tone of conversation among the
good Hobartians, though perhaps scarcely perceptible to themselves, was agreeably evident to me.

Among other more important matters, I found
that the prevalent fashionable epidemic, instead of
betraying symptoms of the ancient Berlin-wool
influenza or the knitting disorder, had taken an
entirely new turn, and that a landscape-sketching
and water-colour fever was raging with extraordinary
vehemence among the usually too placid and
apathetic sons and daughters of Tasmania. The
infection had been originally brought by Mr. Prout,
the fame of whose very clever water-colour drawings
of the scenery in New South Wales, and the
celebrity he attained there, had prepared for him a

glad welcome in Van Diemen's Land; and the exquisite art which he taught and practised so well at once became *the* fashion *par excellence*. All the young ladies, and many elder ones, immediately discovered (or coveted, which is nearly the same) a great taste for drawing, and all commenced taking class lessons from Mr. Prout in out-of-doors sketching. Stationers' shops and fancy repositories were straightway stripped of all their pencils, colours, and sketch-books, and Mr. Prout's absence from Hobarton for the summer vacation alone prevented me from joining his disciples.

An exhibition of paintings, drawings, engravings, &c., was opened after I left town, composed of contributions from the collections of the residents and the works of colonial amateurs and artists. I greatly regretted not being able to see it, but the knowledge that such a thing was achieved at all was exceedingly pleasant, and seemed a good omen of future advancement; and from all accounts of the exhibition which I read and heard, it was a highly satisfactory and creditable beginning. One more having taken place since, I trust we may anticipate that they will be continued at intervals, if not regularly.

There are some pretty fern-tree thickets at the foot of Mount Wellington, and I visited one with a large party; but after seeing our perfectly wild and untrodden fern valley at Port Sorell, this oft-frequented one, the beloved of sketching and pic-nic parties, seemed almost uninteresting. The ferns, as they ever are, were verdant and graceful, though rather small, and the gurgling brook was pretty; but the empty champagne bottles which bristled beside the rocks, and the corks and greasy sandwich papers lurking amongst the moss, savoured considerably more of the creature comforts than the picturesque.

Regattas, balls, dinner-parties, and pic-nics wear so much the same aspect wherever they flourish in English society, and Tasmanian society is, I rejoice to say, so essentially English, that a chronicle of my pleasant sojourn in our antipodean metropolis might serve for a chronicle of any equally pleasant sojourn in any nice town of the United Kingdom, and so, needless to particularize in a gossip chiefly devoted to less civilized matters.

The great number of very comfortable carriages which ply for hire both in Launceston and Hobarton is an essential public convenience, and a great

advance from olden times, when the one or two
vehicles of the kind in town would be engaged on
a ball night to convey thirty or forty parties each.
Now, long strings of smart clean cabs (so called,
though more of the chaise and barouche species)
stand in several of the public thoroughfares, and
can be as cheaply hired as similar carriages could
be in England : at the time I was there, 1s.
per mile, or 3s. by the hour, was the usual fare.

My nursemaid had become far too much enamoured of the charms and gaieties of the city to
think with any composure of a return to the
solitude of bush life, and I found it requisite to
supply her place. She had been my first trial of
the effects of Mrs. Bowden's system of female
discipline on board the "Anson," and for a year
and a half had been all I could desire in a servant,
irreproachable in her conduct, clean, cheerful, and
industrious, until the visit to town, and the greater
opportunities for showing her pretty face, caused
neglect of her duty, and an alarming exhibition of
pink silk stockings, thin muslin dresses, and other
town vanities. I again applied to Mrs. Bowden,
and had again cause to appreciate the value of her
influence, not so much in the fitness of the woman

I selected for the situation she was to fill (for at
first she was awkward and uncouth in the extreme),
as in the almost miraculous change which must
have been wrought in her to fit her for any decent
occupation whatever. She had, as I afterwards discovered, been reared amidst the worst of the bad
—had been imprisoned in some dozen different
gaols, and no sooner liberated than, partly from
destitution, partly from inveterate habit, she had
sinned again, to be again punished. At last she
was transported, and after remaining the usual
period (six months, I believe) under Mrs. Bowden's
government, she came to me a willing, orderly,
thankful creature, and remained with us a year and
a quarter, when she married comfortably. How
different to her former wretched, lost condition !

Simply judging from the superior usefulness,
willingness, and orderly, decent, sober demeanour of
the women I have taken from the " Anson," over
all others of their unfortunate class that I have
known, I must believe the system pursued there by
Mrs. Bowden to be an excellent and effective one,
and rendering the greatest possible benefit to the
colony generally.

The women always seem to feel great gratitude

and reverence for Mrs. Bowden, which her earnest solicitude for their well-doing, and her own exalted character and endowments, well deserve; they also express much attachment to her female assistants, or "officers," as they are termed. Once, soon after my first "Anson" girl had arrived, I was going to write to Mrs. Bowden, and called Jane to ask if she would like me to say anything from her, when I received this somewhat startling reply,—

"Oh! if you please ma'am, to give my best thanks and duty to Mrs. Bowden, and my kind love to all the officers!"

Eight or nine pounds a year are the wages I have always given to the female prisoner-servants at first, raising them afterwards, if deserved. Free women expect much higher terms, are not a whit better, but often worse than the prisoners, and are under less control. *All* are certain of marrying, if they please; *proposals* are plentiful, inconveniently so, indeed, sometimes, to masters and mistresses, when tidy handmaidens are wooed, won, and married in such quick succession that new servants have constantly to be sought, and their passage paid. But a suitable marriage is so probable and legitimate a means of reformation, that we never place

obstacles in the way of such good intentions.
Those prisoner-women who settle in the country,
with few exceptions, behave well and industriously.
I know many wives of this class who keep their
husbands' little cottages as clean and tidy as any
honest English village dame could do, and wash or
sew, to earn a little money themselves. An addiction
to *drink* is the chief temptation to be feared; if
they resist that, all goes well. Many of them have
no family, and the spare shillings and pounds are
only too likely to go to the publican or the " sly
grog seller," which is still worse, being illegal as
well as wrong. The temperance-pledge and the
savings-bank seem to be the two most efficient life-
boats, in such chances of moral wreck; but it is
only the naturally determined and resolute among
the well-meaning who have courage to adopt them.
Religious instruction, if adequate, would do much;
the beneficial influence of really conscientious,
sincere Christian ministers would be immense,
among the lower classes in the country here—those
who would go among the poor and ignorant, and
win them back to the right path by earnest gentle
counsel and kindly admonition; whose own lives,
pure and simple themselves, should be ever before

their erring brethren as a living testimony of the
great Example they preach; those who would be
seen more often on the poor man's threshold than at
the rich man's table; who would practise charity as
well as preach it, and watch that no beam obscured
their own eye, whilst spying out the mote in their
brother's. I have, I know, before alluded to this
subject; but the lamentable inadequacy of the
means of instruction for the lower classes in this
colony is so great, that the fact can scarcely be too
often reiterated. The deficient number even of
professors of religion, and the sad apathy and
indifference of some among them, ask most urgently
for a change.

POYSTON.

CHAPTER XVI.

Return Home.—Route over Badger Head.—The Asbestus Hills.—
The New Cottage.—Goats and their Kids.—Garden.—Bees.—
Native Wasps.—Flies versus Spiders.—Wasps' Nests.—The Dark
Avenger.—Rose-Tree Cuttings.—Wasp-Stings.

In January, 1846, we returned home by the coach
as far as Launceston, passing through, on our way,
the populous settlements and towns of Brighton,
Bagdad, Green Ponds, Cross Marsh, Oatlands,
Ross, Campbelltown, and Perth, all containing
good churches and inns, and the greater number
displaying shops of various kinds, and many sub-

stantial houses; whilst nearly the whole length of
the road traverses inclosed and cultivated land, and
constantly leads us past comfortable country houses,
farms, and cottages, proving a far greater amount
of improvement and change from a wild state than
our beautiful island is credited with at Home.

Pausing but a day in Launceston, we proceeded
in the steam-boat to George Town, expecting to
find our little friend the " Hope " there, and in
three or four hours more to reach Port Sorell.
But a perverse westerly wind, which had been
blowing for some days, still continued, and after
waiting idly two days at George Town, without a
symptom of any change, Mr. Meredith was obliged
to return home; and, as I decidedly declined the
alternative of remaining with the children and
maid at a dull little inn, we determined to make
our way across, over Badger Head, a track which
was described to us as all but impassable.

A kind settler at Kelso Bay, opposite George
Town, to whom Mr. Meredith applied for assistance,
promised us the loan of a horse-cart and two riding
horses, and on the third morning of our reluctant
sojourn we took a boat, and crossed over Port
Dalrymple, to the pleasant home of our new friend,

and shortly set forth on our route, the servant and children occupying the cart. I had not even put on a shawl, knowing so well the torment of any dispensable encumbrance in a fatiguing scramble like the one we contemplated.

A very rough road led us for some miles through bush and swamp, and finally brought us near to the sea-beach at the foot of the dreaded Badger Head. Here we found two of the constables and our groom awaiting us, Mr. Meredith having sent a foot messenger to them the day before; but we could not have our own horses brought to meet us, there being no safe means of crossing them over the deep broad channel of Port Sorell, on the western shore of which lay the settlement and our house, whilst Badger Head was some dozen miles eastward from it. The cart, which had brought the children so far, now went home again, and the men carried them onwards up the steep ascent. The horses were led up, with many a perilous plunge and desperate effort, scrambling like goats to keep a footing; and I clambered and climbed along, brave in the resolution of well accomplishing the task I had voluntarily undertaken, and antici-pating a succession of such difficulties, if not greater ones. On gaining a tolerably level space, I inquired of our servant, " How much more of the road is as steep as the last bit?"   And I began to think how much good heroism had been needlessly aroused in me, when he replied, " Oh! ma'am, that's all, except one ugly gully, a few miles further on."

The brow of the hill we had gained commanded a most glorious sea-view; east and west of us lay broad smooth sandy beaches, stretching away for miles, with the long white ridges of the in-coming tide breaking in five or six successive lines of snowy spray; and the deep sea beyond, blue as the heavens, lay heaving and sparkling in the sunshine. Several distant vessels were in sight, looking not half so big as the gulls and red-bills that circled and screamed beneath us. It was a Tasmanian version of Edgar's gaze from Shakespeare's cliff, only lacking the samphire gatherers.

The wild wide moorland tracts of the Asbestus Hills, which we now passed over, were but thinly wooded, the chief growth being the lesser kind of grass tree, with its tall clubs sticking up like a vast assemblage of long rusty pokers, with the handles downwards. A great part of the land had been recently burned, and the beds of light ashes made a most unpleasant dust as we passed along.

The " ugly gully" was easily passed. Mr. Meredith, choosing to avoid the precipitous descent commonly known, explored a new way for us higher up, the only obstacles we found being the dense, strong, interwoven masses of tall shrubs and ferns which completely occupied it, and through which we pushed our way on foot, with some exertion certainly, but with perfect success; and again walked on, over grass-tree moorlands, as before.

On reaching a bright little spring of fresh water in a ravine near the beach, about three in the afternoon, we rested to eat our sandwiches, and determined to send back from thence our good friend's horses, as it was then early enough for them to reach home by dark, and if we had taken them on to the shore of Port Sorell they must have been tethered all night in the Bush, a very sorry guerdon for the good service they had done us!

We rested about an hour, and had then five miles to walk to the point where the police boat would meet us; and, so long as we continued on

the hard smooth beach, our progress was easy and
pleasant, but an abominably rough, scrubby, soft
sand-bank of a mile wide, which we were wrongly
advised to cross, instead of following the course of
the beach, was a sad fatigue and difficulty at the
end of our journey: a right gladsome sight, therefore, was her Majesty's trim boat, lying off " Dead
Man's Point," just at twilight, ready to receive our
weary party.   Crossing to the police office, we took
up our abode for the night in Mr. Meredith's
private room, every member of the establishment
being ready and eager to assist and serve us; and
our good old servant soon came down from our
unfinished cottage, with such a wonderful basket of
cold roast wild ducks, chicken, ham, eggs, bread,
butter, and " sundries," as proved that the new
kitchen had well begun its duties by preparing for
our reception.

The next morning we breakfasted at Poyston,
our new home, named after my husband's birth-
place in Wales.   Since I had last visited it, the exterior had been completed, and the trees cleared away
towards the sea, opening a most lovely view of the
port and its fairy islands, the bold bluff of Badger
Head, the grand Asbestus range of mountains,

and the open sea; the western end of the picture
being closed by some wooded rocky points and
intervening sandy beaches.

My old longing for a home on the sea-coast
was now realized; and, rough as everything necessarily was at first, we enjoyed the change from
the dark forest to the bright sea-shore too intensely to feel any trifling discomforts. Nearly
all the furniture was packed and stowed away
in one room, so the first breakfast was spread on
the hall table, with packing-cases and trunks for
seats.

Our house, which contained large good rooms,
was built of wood, with chimneys of brick; the
tall thick " slabs" were weather-boarded on the outside, and wholly bare within, as, had they been
lathed and plastered at once, their inevitable warp-
ing and shrinking would have cracked and destroyed the plaster. The ceilings were all done
in a corduroy pattern, being neatly boarded, with
a narrow batten over each joint, and all well
whitewashed; a method much more expeditious
and durable than plastering, and, in a country
cottage, by no means unsightly.

Our inner walls, of the bare, rough, split timber,

full of gaps and crevices, maintained a more universal system of ventilation than even those of
" Lath Hall;" yet we all remained wholly unvisited
by colds of any kind during the autumn and winter, which passed before the cottage was finished,
although, when the wind blew from the north-east
(our only exposed quarter), we could scarcely keep
candles alight in the house.   Strong westerly gales
are very prevalent on this coast, but from these our
cosy nest was completely sheltered by an amphi-
theatre of high wooded hills behind.

We kept some goats and their pretty mischievous
kids, purposing to have a large herd of them in
time, both for milk and meat, cows requiring better
pasture than our sandy scrubs yielded, and the Port
Sorell mutton having a particularly unpleasant
flavour, probably from some prevailing plant eaten
by the sheep.   With goats for neighbours and play-
fellows, it was perfectly useless to make any attempt
at gardening, until a strong close paling-fence was
put up; and this being done, and a stable, fowl-
house, and goat-shed built, we began to look quite
civilized and settled in our new home.   An old
gardener in the neighbourhood resolving to go to
Port Philip, we purchased his whole stock of trees,

flowers, thyme-edging, raspberry canes, strawberry plants, pot-herbs, &c., and so gave our young inclosure a two-years old aspect at once.

We also commenced keeping bees, which thrive well at Port Sorell, the abundance of sweet wild flowers there affording them most dainty food, judging from the quality of the honey they make; some of which, from hives kept in the Bush, far from all gardens and ill-flavoured flowers, exceeds in fine delicate flavour any other I ever tasted, the famed honey of Narbonne not excepted. Such portions of the virgin honeycomb as become candied, and cut solid, like cheese, are the nicest of all sweetmeats. Numbers of bees are now wild in many parts of the island, and hollow trees are frequently found in the bush filled with honeycomb.

Several species of wild native bees or wasps are also numerous; and, some time ago, I wrote Home a few observations I had made on their ways and habits, which, as they do not seem to have crept into print, I shall insert, rather than recast the substance of the paper anew.

In the warm summer days, during our residence at Port Sorell, and more particularly in the evenings, we had often noticed a large kind of black fly darting in and out of the house with a loud, sharp, whizzing noise; and, on a more attentive observation, we found a most tragic addition made to our list of antipodean contrarieties—nothing less than the discovery of a savage and sanguinary war carried on by flies against spiders, and pursued with such vigour that one would believe the Tasmanian flies were bent on avenging the tyrannies and grievances suffered at the hands of the spiders by the whole winged-insect family all the world over.

We had observed the forcible and noisy abduction of many an unlucky web-spinner, before I could satisfactorily make out what became of them, as the frequent seizures made, apparently by the same fly, forbade the conclusion that they were forthwith devoured; but, by dint of sundry watchings and pursuits of the flies, and by eking out and piecing together my various small scraps of information and discovery, I at length acquired a tolerable knowledge of the habits and practices of my busy black neighbours.

In size and shape they exactly resemble a large English wasp, but are wholly black, and possess

formidable stings, a quarter of an inch long.   They
build very remarkable cells or nests of earth, finely
tempered, and formed in layers of tiny mud-pats,
like a swallow's nest.   Many of these were placed
in a small wooden out-house, between the upright
studs and the weather-boarding of the wall; several were formed on a shelf in the porch, where
some small pieces of wood lying heaped together
offered convenient nooks; and one wasp, resolving
to have a more costly lodgment than his friends,
took possession of a meerschaum pipe-bowl which
lay on the same shelf, and very snugly laid out
his house in its interior.   All the nests I have
examined are arranged in the same manner, the
whole fabric being from two to four inches long,
and rather less than an inch broad; the external
shape of the mansion, whether square, triangular,
or pentagonal, depending a good deal on the site
chosen.   When completed, no aperture is left; but
on being opened, three or four cells are usually
found, two or three containing each a soft white
chrysalis in a cocoon of white web, and the largest
apartment of the mansion is devoted to the purposes of a larder, and is always found full of
spiders, of all varieties of size, colour, and kind,

all closely and neatly packed together, with their legs trussed up, so as to occupy the smallest possible space.   The strangest part of the affair is, that the spiders are not dead, but remain perfectly soft and flexible in every part; and, on being exposed to the sun and air, and stirred, a feeble movement is evident in them, as though they were paralysed or stupified in some manner, so as to be unresisting victims and good fresh meat at the same time. The store-house is thus well supplied, doubtless for the benefit of the chrysalis tenantry, on their awakening to the knowledge of life and appetite.

I have rarely been more interested by any new insect than by these black wasps, ungentle and ferocious though they be; for there is a daring dashing energy and · brisk industry about their ways and doings that is very amusing and perfectly original.   The bee—dear little hard-working persevering fellow that he is—can still afford time for many a coquettish peep into blossoms and buds that he deigns not to taste; and, even when arrived at home with his two pannier-baskets loaded with their heaped-up golden treasure. can stay for a few moments' friendly hovering to and fro, and pleasant exchanges of hum and buzz with his helpmates. The ant—whose ways of thrift and industry even Solomon bids us to "consider and be wise"—never takes a straight road, but with a lump of plunder in her nippers thrice her own size, runs hither and thither, up straws and round sticks, or may be into a labyrinth of a violet root, where she plays at bo-peep with you for ten minutes before going forward again, and seems to get on in such a perversely round-about way, that I have only been cured of my inclination to put her straight, by the conviction (after many trials, when anxiously striving to trace out the marauders of my bee-hives) of the utter hopelessness of such attempts.

But the black wasp has none of these wandering weaknesses of character: solitary, stern, ruthless, and resolute, he goes about his work of cell-building and spider-catching. If you chance to be near his chosen place of abode, you may see him dart past with a bit of mud or a victim, and a shrill sharp *whizz-izz-izz* is continued for some seconds or a minute, during the operation of packing away his load, when forth he darts again, straight and swift as an arrow, and the next moment very probably invades the peaceful retreat of some cobwebbed recluse, who until now, safe from brooms and housemaids, has meshed and devoured his flies in comfort, but is at length seized, trussed, and packed up half-alive, by the dark avenger.

The varieties of wasps or wasp-like flies, which we noticed around Poyston, were very numerous. One is marked with alternate black and golden stripes, very similar to the English wasp, but more soft and downy-looking. Another is red, long and slender, with four long wings and a prodigious sting, which it can protrude nearly half an inch from a kind of double sheath beneath the tail. Another species, partially red, frequented the sandy paths of the garden, where several of them were generally seen darting along, flying straight up and down the walks. I have often followed them nearly round the garden, without their ever quitting the path, or rising more than a foot from the surface. Sometimes they would stop at a hole in the sand, possibly their nest, and after poking down into it, head foremost and tail up, for a minute or more, they made a great skurry of dust over the opening, so as entirely to conceal it, and flew on again.

L 3

Without enumerating many more members of this family, of whom I know little more than their outward aspect, I shall mention one more, which has interested me nearly as much as the architect wasp first described, and has caused me to waste infinitely more time in vain attempts to pry more narrowly into its domestic privacy.

At "Lath Hall" I had been annoyed to find that the multiflora rose-trees which adorned the veranda, had, towards autumn, become quite disfigured, by having large round pieces scolloped out of nearly every leaf; five or six great scollops being made in each, leaving the middle fibre entire. First I attributed the mischief to caterpillars, and then to grass-hoppers, but never found any on the treees. At length the frequent buzzing of a large bee-like fly attracted my attention; and on watching its movements I detected it in the act of snipping out a piece of rose-leaf, rolling it up, grasping it in its legs, and flying off. After this I observed the work going on in the same manner daily for some time. Plants, raised from cuttings of these same rose-trees, grew around the porch at Poyston, and these were used by the same busy workmen in the same manner, besides other kinds of roses, and the

leaves of the cherry, acacia, and other trees. This
wasp or bee has a pair of forceps, acting precisely
like scissors; and very many times I have closely
observed him snipping out, with a quick clean cut,
the piece of leaf, which is usually about the third
of an inch broad and long. Six or eight seconds
suffice for the cutting, when the piece of leaf
is most nimbly and adroitly rolled up and clasped
by the feet and legs, as the wasp flies away. I
have frequently started off when the wasps took
flight, and given chase to them, hoping to find out
whither all the leaves were carried, and how they
were used; but the depredators always proved
too clever for me, and glanced out of sight, leaving
me to come panting back again, vainly vowing to
be more agile and sharp-sighted next time.

Having often found these insects busy gathering
honey, I imagined they must have a hoard or
nest somewhere near, but never found any. An
intelligent young person who lived with me at this
time as nursery governess told me she had often
found the nests, which were holes in the ground,
filled with bits of leaves, in which small portions
of some sweet sticky stuff were folded up and
stuck together, only one or two wasps seeming

to inhabit each hole. This species, like all my other acquaintances of the wasp-kind here, has a long sting, and precisely the head and antennæ of the English wasp.

A totally different species from any of these frequented the wide sandy sea-beaches at Port Sorell; these latter were large bulky formidable insects, with great stings like the others, and were often seen on a warm day, darting about in twos and threes, just above the surface of the sand. One of them would sometimes hover over the same spot for a minute or two, when another would suddenly dart to the place, and the first wasp instantly took up his station at some distance, hovering as before, until he either displaced another, or was superseded in his turn; and the same dance of " change sides and back again" went on as long as we watched them; but what they were doing, or how they got their living, remained an undiscoverable mystery to me.

It is only just to all these long-stinged wasps, to add, that neither we nor our children nor servants were ever stung by any of the fraternity, although we frequently chased and captured them for examination; but always with a due dread of their threatening weapons of defence, and a careful restoration of their liberty when our curiosity was satisfied.

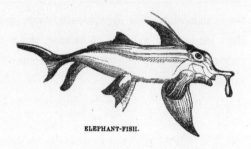

ELEPHANT-FISH.

CHAPTER XVII.

Fish. — The Blue-head. — Sting-ray. — Bathing. — Crabs. — Shells. — Echini. — Starfish. — Sea Anemonies. — Handsome Cuttle-fish. — Jelly-fish, &c.—A Marine Mrs. Gamp.—Elephant-fish.

ONE luxury which we enjoyed at Poyston was an abundance of excellent fish, with which the old fisherman supplied us twice or thrice a week, to our mutual advantage, for he had few good customers besides, and the impossibility of obtaining even tolerably good meat or poultry rendered the addition of fish to our bill of fare a great acquisition. Excellent flounders (of a much better kind than I remember at Home,) a few soles and guard-fish, plenty of fine bream, and quantities of flat-heads, composed the general assortment, which now and then included a few oysters, but not any cray-fish.

Mr. Meredith and George often went out fishing in our own nice little boat, the " Sea Egg," but they seldom found wind, and tide, and time, and all other marine influences so propitious as to do much injury to old Donald's trade, a few flat-heads or blue-heads, or a young shark, being their usual booty.

The blue-head is among fish what the rose-hill parakeet is among birds, a miracle of gay colours. It is a large thick fish, with patches of the most vivid blue and orange about the head, and touches of crimson, green, &c., in other parts. It is not very good eating, being, when cooked, almost as soft and watery as mashed turnips.

Great numbers of small sharks were often seen in the port, close in-shore, in such shallow water that we have thought they must be soon aground; and legions of the great ugly sting-rays were always gliding about, now and then turning up their finny elbows as they passed by us or hur-riéd after their prey. Some of them were of an enormous size, and once our boat grounded on one, and it was only when the living island swam away that it was discovered not to be a shoal. We frequently watched numbers of these great fish in the clear channels, looking, when lying motionless, like black rocks, or masses of kelp, and sometimes moving so slowly as still to deceive the eye, whilst at other times dozens and scores of them would come close by us, in water only deep enough to cover them.

The long barbed bone or "sting" in the tail of these unsightly creatures is from three to six or eight inches long, and capable of inflicting a fearful wound, each of the numerous barbs being jagged at both edges like the teeth of a saw, and lacerating frightfully where it strikes. No savage warrior ever invented a more horrible weapon, and I think some of the hideous implements of destruction brought from the South Sea Islands are made upon its model. A poor man near Port Sorell, in trying to catch some sting-ray by driving them on shore, had one of the stings struck through his thigh, and broken there, and it was with considerable danger cut out, having passed close to one of the great arteries.

Fortunately, neither sharks nor sting-rays ever visited us when bathing, a luxury we enjoyed to

perfection here. Mr. Meredith had a large rustic
bower of wattled boughs built for my use on a
great flat rock, which made an admirable 'tiring-
room, in a sheltered and retired nook of our pretty
bay, where we could almost pluck flowering shrubs
with one hand, and fish out sea-weed with the
other. At first I fear the sea-gulls, as they flew
over, must sometimes have been scared by piteous
cries from within of " Don't put *me* in, mamma,
please don't!" but these vain remonstrances soon
ceased, and the plaintive voices changed to joyous
shouts, as my young ones splashed about like wild
ducks, to the grave amazement of the baby, who
watched such terrible proceedings with evident apprehension.

Many a pleasant day was spent in long walks or
rides, or boating expeditions in the neighbourhood,
and scarcely one passed without our rambling on
the beach. The three children spent half their
days there winning bright eyes, rosy cheeks, and
untold baske of ocean treasures—shells, corals,
and kelp, which were afterwards strewn around
the house in all directions. The ever faithful Dick was their constant playmate, and also
a black Newfoundland dog, named Pluto, who

at first, when a soft fat puppy, used to ride down to the sands with Charlie in his little carriage, and after growing a great powerful dog, would good-naturedly insist on helping to pull it himself, and a rope was tied on for him, which he took in his mouth, and trotted along with great satisfaction.

At certain times of the tide, the broad beach used to be covered with little purple crabs, as busy stuffing sand into their waistcoat pockets as my old friends of the Homebush drains; and after the crabs had finished their odd repast, the surface of the beach was seen thickly strewn with tiny round pellets of sand, the size of duck-shot, showing how vast an amount of labour the busy little things had accomplished, to be all washed out again by the next wave. We were all careful not to crush the poor crabs, and often they were so thick as to make it difficult to avoid them. Pluto, who was not troubled with philanthropy, used to distress the children by squashing the little animals with his great paws, or picking them up in his huge mouth to play with; whilst our beautiful Dick kept us in constant alarm lest, with his indefatigable nose, he should hunt out the sea-birds' nests, that we knew were close around, and disturb or kill the young ones, which it was our great delight to have safely reared, and added to our beach companions.

One most noble shell is sometimes found on this coast, a species of volute or *Cymbiola,* ten inches or more in length, and five or six in diameter, of a shaded buff colour, beautifully marked with zigzag lines of brown, smooth on the outside, and highly polished within, with three plaits on the columella, and the outer lip thin and sharp. I have only seen five of these shells, three of which I procured myself. One had been dead some time, being covered with serpula inside; the other two had not so long parted from their inhabitants as to have also lost the odour which their remains had left behind, and were fresh handsome shells.

Sometimes we found a few smaller volutes of the same kind as at Swan Port, but usually more perfect, being alive; occasionally we captured a lovely Venus, in a marvellous array of ridges and spikes. At some seasons the beach abounded with fine brown date-muscles, alive also, and the *Haliotis, Sigaretus,* and *Stomatella* were also found, the former abundantly, and often very large.

A delicate species of *Terebratula* lived on the

reefs, some distance below low-water mark, and I obtained a few live shells, but never found any cast on the sands.   One most beautiful *Trigonia* was given to me, as having been picked up on the Badger Head beach, but I was never so fortunate as to find another there.

Coralines abounded, the same as those of Swan Port, and a far greater quantity of the delicate lace-coral, in pieces from two to six or eight inches broad, but too brittle to bear packing. Occasionally, but only rarely, a piece of beautiful pink coral appeared among the common kinds.

Several species of *Echini* frequented the reefs around us, and in the summer we often invaded their bright rocky pools, to make acquaintance with them.   At low tide we could run across the wide sands on to several of the reefs, with merely wetting our feet (which no true sea-side scrambler ever pauses to think about, albeit a fearful extension of shoemakers' bills is the result); and then most delightful was it to peer down through the clear water of the countless basins and hollows in the rocks, and see whole families of *Echini*, all unconscious of our alarming presence, rolling to and fro on their ever-moving *chevaux de frise* of

spines, and various species of star-fish, some with
short arms, some with long ones, and many with
no arms at all, but with merely obtuse corners to
their pentagon or hexagon shapes, all most brilliant in colour, and shining amidst floating kelp
and through the sunny water, like great marigolds,
poppies, and purple anemones; whilst the real sea-
anemones, of many bright colours, clustered up and
down the rocks, those above water closed up, and
looking like the transparent red lollipops which
children call " cherries," and the submerged ones
spreading out their filmy rays like starry flowers,
the mimic petals or arms of which clasp tightly
around an intruding finger, as if believing it to be
some dainty jelly-fish or other pleasant comestible.
I have often watched both these Actinia and the
star-fish eating soft jelly-like sea creatures, and
have marvelled at the celerity with which they
dispatched their meal.

Mr. Meredith and George once found some very
beautiful *Asteriæ* on one of the reefs, and carried
one home to me; but, despite all their care, it was
very much broken before it arrived. The body,
hexagonal in shape, was not larger than a shilling,
but the arms were at least twelve inches long, and

not more than an eighth of an inch broad, consisting of one series of small shelly scales or plates, with two short feelers to each scale; each arm looking like a very long centipede. Although so much injured, it moved when touched, and then emitted a bright pale blue phosphoric light, which trembled all over it for several seconds, but became gradually fainter, till it was no longer emitted. We never found the same species again.

Very many of the black sea-slugs, or sea-hares, whose shell is known as the *Parmophorus Australis*, also dwelt in our reef-pools, and dead shells were often thrown on the beach. The airy shells of a beautiful *Spatangus*, as thin and white as cambric paper, were also very plentiful, but I never found the creature within them, though very curious to see the animal which could inhabit an abode so fragile that I could scarcely breathe upon it without wafting it away, although some were the size of a good orange.

During one of our boating expeditions to the islands, we found a very handsome individual of a very ugly family, being a species of cuttle-fish, in a coat of bright salmon-colour, profusely trimmed and embroidered with brown, and the multitudinous

arms each dotted with two lines of buttons (*i. e.,*
suckers) as thickly as the jacket of a lady's page.
We tried to send this creature out from his bower
of kelp into clearer water, to gain a better view of
him; but his extraordinary arms always reappeared
where we least expected them, and seemed to be
many feet in length, gliding and writhing amidst
the kelp forest like a colony of snakes. Some time
afterwards I found a smaller specimen of the same
creature washed ashore on the sands, and, as it was
still alive, I carried it to a deep rocky pool that it
might recover; but the horrible sensation of all the
strong suckers fastening round my bared wrist and
hand was only just endurable, and I gladly felt it
loosen its tenacious hold, and glide off into the
water.

At some seasons the beach used to be thickly
strewn with what are called "jelly-fish," left by the
receding tide; most of them being the size of a
large dinner plate, and not unlike a great mass of
encrusted glass, with a large star pattern within, of
pink or purple. When seen swimming they resemble an expanded umbrella, with a cluster of long
fringed arms extending from its convex centre.
During a short voyage in Bass's Straits, the my-

riads I have seen of these jelly umbrellas were
perfectly astonishing; every wave passing the vessel
contained five or six, and their bright soft irridescent colours of pink, purple, blue, and crimson,
seen glancing in the rapid water, were most beautiful.

Several species of curious bony fish are found
at Port Sorell. One, about four inches long, is
called the dog fish, from the accurate resemblance
which its head bears to that of a pointer. Another,
which we named the porcupine fish, is about eight
inches long, and is armed all over with sharp strong
spines. We preserved some of these excellently by
suspending them by a thread, near an ant-hill, and
in a short time all the skin and form of the fish
became dry and hard, whilst the busy little insects
had disposed of all the more perishable matter.

One very singular fish, the size and shape
of a large egg somewhat compressed at the sides,
was arrayed in a complete suit of white bony armour, beautifully embossed and engraved, with sharp
fins and tail, and a mouth like a small whistle. It
is sometimes found dead and dry among the heaps
of old kelp and shells on the sand banks, but I
never saw one either alive or fresh.

A large skeleton of a hideously ugly fish, which none of us knew, was brought me by one of the constables (all of whom used to do their best to contribute to my heterogeneous collections of oddities). Its heavy bony head was more than half of the whole fish, with a large under-jawed bull-dog mouth, and the body tapering sharply off from it, being altogether about two feet long. Mr. Meredith said it somewhat resembled a fish called by whalers "an Old Nurse," and then we decided that it must be the Mrs. Gamp of the ocean. If my lame description is unintelligible to the ichthyologically learned, I can direct them to an admirable portrait of my ugly friend, in Cruikshank's Comic Almanack for 1843, for he has drawn it to the life, in the astonished fish which rushes full in the light from his submarine steamer, to gaze upon the portentous visitant with supercilious indignation.

On passing our fisherman's hut one morning, we found him quite busy, wheeling in a quantity of unsaleable fish to enrich his little potato garden, and we detained one, of a kind new to us, to examine. It was a large fish, nearly three feet in length, and about five inches deep, with a singular

bony head, from which a narrow bony process
extended in front, like a very prominent Roman
nose, with a turn-up at the point of it; from the
end of this hung, outspread, a soft fleshy heart-
shaped membrane, three or more inches long.   The
mouth was placed at some distance behind this
pendulous apparatus, which looked like a bait, with
which this odd fish was perpetually angling for
himself.   A long, strong, sharp spine proceeded
from the front of the dorsal fin; and the vertebræ
continued through the upper lobe of the tail, tapering finely to the end.   I have rarely seen a more
singular fish.

BADGER HEAD, AND THE SISTER ISLANDS, FROM POYSTON,
PORT SORELL.

CHAPTER XVIII.

Improvements at Poyston.—The Harriet.—A New Bird.—Diamond
Birds.—Dragon-flies.—Green Frogs.—Rabbits.—Great Owl.—
Small Owl.—Mawpawk.—Bush Fires.—Providential Escape.

WE continued to improve our pleasant sea-side
home in various ways, by enlarging the house and
garden, by having our rooms plastered and papered,
by making some log-bridges across watery hollows
in the sand bank, for our winter walks to the beach,
and by marking an avenue through the wood, in
the direction of the police station, which was partly
cleared at our own expense, and partly by the

M 2

occasional labour of watch-house prisoners; and, when completed, opened a beautiful vista, ending in a distant view of the station, and the woods and mountains behind, as shown in my little sketch from our garden, given at page 258.

The arrival of the Port Sorell vessels (small schooners and cutters of from fifteen to forty tons) added considerably to the life and interest of our sea view, especially when any friend or long-expected package was known to be on board; and as the reefs and channels of the entrance to the port are rather intricate, we frequently watched the little craft with great anxiety.

We took great interest in a small schooner, which the builder of our cottage (a generally useful native genius) commenced after nearly finishing our house; *perfect* completion of a task we found was impossible to him.

The "Hope" cutter, which I have before mentioned, was also the work and property of our worthy neighbour, but she had been sent to sea at first without a rudder-case, and sailed without that apparently indispensable appendage ever afterwards. His new schooner was very cleverly and accurately modelled after the brig "Scout," formerly a slaver, and the fastest sailing vessel in these colonies. We could readily distinguish her from all the other ships seen passing through the Straits, bound for, or leaving Launceston, by her superior speed, and were much grieved lately to learn that the beautiful vessel had been wrecked.

We often visited our ingenious neighbour to see how his vessel got on, and anticipated the launch with great interest; but, as I fully expected, something was left undone, or was not done quite enough, in the laying down of the "ways," and instead of dashing boldly into the water, when we were all assembled to see her, the gallant "Harriet" stuck fast, and was unsatisfactorily and ingloriously shoved off in the evening tide, with no one to look at her.

Having by means of the "Mosquito craft" of the vicinity constant opportunities of communication with Launceston, we commenced subscribing to a library there, which, although not very extensive, seemed to promise us a twelvemonth's supply of reading; but after exchanging our books about four times, and sending in vain for more, I discovered that our supply was finally cut off; the whole collection of books having been sold by auction! and we were once more reduced to the chance volumes we could borrow, and our own rare and scanty acquisitions from Home.

When living in a new country, and in great measure apart from the advantages of civilized life, it is no small solace and pleasure to possess the habit, apparently so natural, but in reality very rare (at least *here*), of deriving interest and amusement from the perusal of whatever page of the great book of Nature lies open to us; and strange indeed must be our destiny, if we are ever without some instructive and wondrous passage before us, telling of the beneficence and wisdom of Him who alike hath fixed the track of the mysterious comet through the illimitable immensity of space, and decreed the shape in which the little bees shall make their tiny cells!

In old countries, where every change of season, every successively-opening flower, and every insect that flutters the frailest wing in the sunshine, has attracted the study of naturalists and philosophers for centuries, we can always refer to books for information respecting all that interests us, or excites our curiosity. But here, if we would learn from Nature, we must strive to read her own untranslated

history, and no one who has not tried can tell how
pleasant a book it is.   Sometimes, it is true, we
should like a book of reference, when some quite
new bird or flower proves too profound an enigma
for our small acquirements.   Such was a lovely
little creature like a large humming-bird, which
came daily to suck honey from the trumpet-flowers
of the *Ecremocarpus* creeper round our porch and
garden fence.   It never perched, but remained on
the wing, hovering and sipping the honey with its
long hairy tongue, and uttering a low murmuring
sound as it skimmed about.   Its plumage was
chiefly brown and fawn colour, with a long beard-
like shadow on the throat.   I was quite glad to see
the *Ecremocarpus* honey made useful to something,
for I had often thought it a pity that the mouth
of the flower was too small for the entrance of a
bee, whilst so well stored with sweets; and the little
bird came as if on purpose to show me that all in
Nature must be right and good.

A pair of little gems of diamond birds had their
nest in the bank near our cottage.   Mr. Meredith
found the hole one day, and thought it belonged to
a snake, but whilst peeping about it, one of the
alarmed little birds flew out, almost in his face.

We visited it several times afterwards, and, on look-ing steadily into the dark little nest, could just discern the baby-birds within, and often saw the beautiful little parent pair flying or creeping in and out.

Some gigantic dragon flies, larger than the diamond birds, often visited us ; and had, I imagine, emerged from their former more humble condition of existence in our fishpond, as we saw many in its vicinity. I always admired their handsome tribe, but was rather shocked one day to see a very large one snap up a poor heavily-laden bee, and fly off with it. Had I seen many such captures, a declaration of war against the great dragon flies must have followed, but it was a solitary outrage, so far as I know.

Numbers of my old favourites, the gorgeously-attired green frogs, also abode in our pond and brook, and in warm summer days were wont to bathe luxuriously in the sunshine, with their moist gold-threaded heads and backs, and great calm eyes, gleaming like jewels ; and as they sit thus, they keep up a kind of friendly conversational croak with each other, each exclamation being apparently the result of great effort. The speaker suddenly collapses his portly body, and at the same instant inflates a large white speckled pouch beneath the under jaw, which expands to the size of a small hen's-egg, whilst the croak is going on—the sound and the inflation ceasing together; and in the space of a minute the process begins again. The appearance of a party of frogs thus conversing, seated a few feet apart, over a pond or lagune, is most gravely ridiculous; but a spectator must wait for some time, motionless and silent, before the discourse begins, the approach of any noise or movement, however slight, causing the whole solemn assembly to plop under water.

To our favourite household troops of goats, horses, dogs, cats, tame swans, and poultry, we had now rather a droll addition in a flock of tame rabbits, the progeny of one pair given to the children by our gardener. These had for some time been kept in a hutch, but we decided on giving them their liberty, and had a capacious cage made of paling for them at one corner of our paddock, and put them in it, with a daily supply of food, intending that they should burrow out into the Bush and go free, but still have their safe cage as a retreat from dogs or other molestations. They

very soon availed themselves of the liberty we gave
them, and scratched their way out, but, instead of
going into the Bush, straightway came back and
took up their abode under the kitchen, burrowing
an entrance beneath the massive wooden sleepers,
and no doubt finding a warm and roomy apartment
ready for their reception, as the floor of the kitchen
was raised above a foot from the level ground.
Here they continued to live, and bred numbers of
young ones, which were of all colours, though the
old pair were black, and in the evening, a troop of
all sizes, black, brown, gray, buff, and white, used
to come out and frolic all about us: the old ones
were so tame as to jump into our laps as we sat
down; and very often used in play to scratch the
children's faces, who had taught them to take
bread from their lips. The young ones very
rapidly spread abroad, and colonized the whole
neighbourhood. We, or rather our spaniel, Dick,
found several at one or two miles' distance from
home. Our garden was so well fenced that only
very juvenile bunnies could gain admittance there,
and as we had not anything else they could possibly
injure, and abundance of food for them, we greatly
enjoyed our novel kind of rabbit-warren; the only

trouble connected with it being our constant fear lest strangers coming to the house should inadvertently tread upon our bold little favourites, which were always trooping about.

The poor old doe fell a victim to the kittenish propensity for play of an Arab colt we had; he used to run after everything, and pawed over dogs, fowls, or anything he could overtake, as a kitten would a ball, and in an unhappy hour, with one playful stroke of his fore-foot, broke a hind leg of our old bunny, so that we were compelled, after ineffectual attempts to set the bone, to let our poor pet be killed as an act of mercy. We never before kept tame rabbits, but these free and sociable ones were exceedingly interesting, and their evening gambols, when the whole family party was assembled, were most graceful and diverting.

I had one day a most unwelcome present brought to me by one of our constables, who, poor man, had taken infinite pains to obtain it, but had wofully mistaken what he conceived to be my wishes in the matter. Hearing that I wanted to procure an owl, he brought me a most magnificent one, but alas! it was dead, and my wish was to have one, or, still better, a pair, alive, to put them

in undisturbed possession of two great lofts in the
gabled roof of our house, where they and their
progeny might benefit us and themselves by carrying on the mousing business, and gratify us occasionally by a glimpse of their ghostly shapes
winnowing silently around in the twilight.

The poor dead bird was a most noble specimen of
his order, about fifteen inches in height, and of a
broad comely figure, with the proper great heart-
face, and very large eyes; the plumage gray and
fawn-colour, barred with brown, beautifully soft
and downy.

I since had one of the small Tasmanian owls
alive, and kept it for some months, feeding it on
mice, birds, and raw meat, but I could not tame it
in the least. It tore and bit any one it could reach,
and always greeted our approach with a savage
chop-chopping of its beak, that sounded most
defiant and ferocious. It was a very handsome
bird, six or seven inches high, with dark plumage,
and very quick, savagely-bright eyes. Finding I
could not by any means render it sociable and
friendly, I determined to set it free, hoping it might
possibly remain about the house or garden; but
the emancipation, so kindly meant, proved fatal.

Unaccustomed to procure food for itself, and teased and attacked by crowds of other birds, it sat moping in a high tree, for a day or two, until pecked blind, and almost in pieces; and I only recovered my perverse pet in time to see it expire in its old cage.

The Mawpawk, More Pork, or Mope Hawk, is common in most parts of the colony, and utters its peculiar two-syllable cry at night, very constantly. Its habits are those of the owl, and its rather hawkish appearance partakes also of the peculiarities of the goat-sucker tribe. The bird is ten or twelve inches long, and the head forms more than a third of this; the mouth, bristling with strong whiskers, opens to the very back of the head, and displays a cavern, apparently capable of accommodating a whole family of mice at once. The eyes are large and hawk-like, the plumage dark and dusky, and the bird's flight is silent as that of the owl. We often listen to them at night, as they answer each other's cry, sometimes from a tree close beside us, and then from the distant woods. The sound does not really resemble the words "more pork," any more than "cuckoo," and it is more like the "tu-whoo" of the owl than either.

The summer bush fires in these forest regions sometimes rage to a fearful extent, from the great masses of dead wood, bark, and scrub which accumulate though successive seasons. During our abode at " Lath Hall" I once suffered great alarm from the very near approach of the bush fires, which, in those dense and lofty forests, have a most terrific appearance, as the volumes of lurid smoke come rolling onwards, and tree after tree bursts into flame ; whilst the frequent thundering fall of some mighty trunk, and the crackling and hissing of the blazing mass, are as terrible to hear as to behold. By anticipating the approach of the great body of fire, and carefully burning and beating out the low scrub, ferns, and grass beside fences, or for a considerable breadth in the probable track of the conflagration, any serious mischief may frequently be prevented ; but when a high wind prevails at the same time, immense flakes of fire are carried along by it, and falling in distant places, or perchance on thatched roofs, spread the devastation with terrible rapidity.

We had on one occasion a fearful drive home from the house of a friend with whom we had spent the day, and during our stay one of these tremendous forest fires had traversed the road we had to repass in returning, leaving the whole country in flames.   As we drove along, great burning trees came toppling and crashing down on both sides, and some fell directly across our track, compelling us to make a détour in the Bush, where we feared the horses would burn their feet in the hot ashes, the terror of the poor animals increasing our own peril not a little.   The air was like a furnace and thick with smoke, and fiery fragments of leaves, sticks, and bark were falling around and about us.   I have not often felt more awed by any impending danger than during that scorching drive, nor more devoutly thankful for our preservation than when at last we emerged from the terrible dominions of the tyrannical Fire King, into the cool olive-green avenue of our forest road, and once more breathed air instead of smoke.

Mr. Meredith was absent from home when the bush fires in the near vicinity of Poyston seemed to me threatening its speedy destruction, and my intense terror was consequently uncomforted by his better experience; nor was I aware at the time, that he had, before leaving home, taken the wise precaution of burning the ferns over the whole of a

wide span of forest land around us, although I
knew it had been partially done. The appearance
of the rapidly-advancing fire was indeed such as to
appal a stouter heart than mine, when at last, after
many disregarded entreaties from my frightened
women servants, I went out to look at it. Overhead, a thick black rolling cloud of fire-speckled
smoke shut out the sky; and behind, the mighty
array of flames whence it came rose high over the
tallest of those giant trees, in tongues and spears
of red blaze, bright even at noonday, and wreathed
about the trunks and branches, devouring every
leaf and fragment of bark as it went crackling on.
The wind blew the fire directly towards our apparently devoted house, which, almost wholly composed of resinous wood, dry as tinder after the
summer's heat, would have burnt like touch-paper.

I began to count up our carpets and blankets,
intending to have them all soaked in the brook,
and laid over the roof to prevent its becoming
ignited by the falling flakes, and I had our small
stock of gunpowder ready to bury in the garden,
under the camp oven, if the danger increased.
The two men servants went to beat out the fire so
as to prevent its crossing a narrow gully at the

back of our inclosure, and I dispatched George and the nurse-girl to the police station for more men to help them, the fire meanwhile evidently making rapid progress, and the horrid crackling becoming louder and nearer.

A reinforcement from the station, of the district constable and two others, enabled our party to spread out so as to keep a wide extent of the ground-fire under control, but not without having their clothes burned in the effort, and I had my share of active business in serving out tea, grog, and flannel shirts. A sudden shift of the wind providentially aided our endeavours, and, before night, the body of the fire was raging onwards in a different direction, but still leaving so much behind as to render a night-watch requisite; nor did we feel quite safe until the following evening, when the alarming appearances had to a great degree subsided.

These extensive fires must no doubt destroy great numbers of snakes; and if they were of no other service, that alone would plead their pardon for many mischievous deeds. The poor opossums, too, I fear, must suffer martyrdom in crowds, and quantities of small vermin and insects; but the

chief service of the bush fires is, the rapid and
wholesome consumption of heaps of vegetable
matter, that would otherwise accumulate to excess
on such rich damp soil, and, in their slow process of
decomposition, fill the air with unhealthy vapours.

VIEW FROM THE GARDEN, POYSTON.

CHAPTER XIX.

Resignation. — Removal. — Voyage. — Contrary Breeze. — Great Peril. — Anchor at George Town. — Overland Journey to Swan Port. — Riversdale. — Improvements. — The Veranda. — Pigeons and Fowls. — Plenty without Profit. — Arrival of the Harriet. — Conclusion.

THE apparently uncertain continuance of all police appointments in the colony, and the strong inducements we had to return to Swan Port, at length decided us in favour of a removal from Port Sorell. Mr. Meredith sent in his resignation of the police magistracy accordingly, and had the gratification of receiving, both from his Excellency Lieutenant-Governor Sir. W. T. Denison, and from the Chief Police Magistrate, flattering testimonies of their high estimation and approval of his past services, and kind expressions of regret that they were to cease.

As we had to transport ourselves, children, and servants, together with our furniture, horses, dogs, bees, favourite fowls, and other matters—a very

menagerie of clanjamphry—Mr. Meredith engaged
our graceful friend the "Harriet" schooner to
convey us direct to Swan Port, all but the horses,
which were sent overland with the groom; my own
especial gray Arab and her pretty foal having been
carefully taken across previously.

Mr. Meredith's successor at Port Sorell gladly
agreed to purchase our house, land, &c.; our
preparations for departure were, therefore, very
speedily effected, although not without many
regrets at leaving our comfortable home, and its
most beautiful sea-view, which, so far from becoming indifferent to us, by long use, seemed ever to
acquire some new charm.

Yet, having once rooted ourselves up, ready
for a transplantation, delays became provoking, and after waiting two days on board, and
receiving more "last visits" from the few valued
friends we were leaving behind, we finally set sail,
on a day universally considered of ill omen—in
seafaring matters, at least—on *Friday* evening,
February 22, 1848. Our good neighbour, the
builder and owner of the vessel, had at the
eleventh hour suddenly relinquished his intention
of going with us, and left the command to a very

unworthy representative, a careless, lazy fellow, lately hired, whose chief vocation seemed to be dozing and smoking, and who could not even rouse himself enough to get out of the port at high water, but dawdled about on shore until we very narrowly escaped another night's detention, and, by some mismanagement in the narrowest and most dangerous part of the intricate channel amongst the reefs and islands, were, for a short time, in considerable peril.

The following morning, when Mr. Meredith went on deck, hoping to find that we had made good progress during the night, as we had had a fair breeze the evening before,—what was his annoyance to discern that our lazy "skipper" had afterwards hove the vessel to, and gone to sleep, during the greater part of the night, and so lost us at least thirty or forty miles of our voyage.

By the time I thought of rising we were making tolerable way through the Straits, and the vessel's motion had become so unpleasantly lively, that I found it desirable to make my ascent to the deck as quickly as possible, and try to ward off the approaching return of indisposition. My nursemaid, as a matter of course, was totally useless, having

given herself up a voluntary, or at all events an
unresisting victim, to sea-sickness, and lay on the
deck refusing all aid or remedy; so Mr. Meredith
and our good old servant-man made their first
essay in the nursery department by putting George
and Charlie into their respective garments, but
with an ingenious variation of back and front,
tapes and buttons, which did infinite credit to
their powers of invention. However, I was very
thankful even for such aid, baby Owen's toilet
being quite as much as I could safely undertake
myself. The poor children were all very ill, and
nothing but a most resolute determination saved
me from sharing the same fate. I sat on deck
all day, facing the fresh breeze, nursing the baby,
and endeavouring to keep every thought busy with
the passing clouds, the distant shore, the shoals
of strange jelly-fish sailing along beside us, or
anything, rather than suffer myself to admit
the real truth, that I felt very far from well;
and thus I continued all day without becoming
worse.

The wind had been veering round for some
hours, and at last settled to a strong breeze from
the north-east, the most directly adverse point

for us. We passed "Tenth Island," and "Ninth,"
or "Gun-carriage Island," both of them barren
and rocky, with low scrub and sand; and we
were very anxious to reach "Waterhouse Island,"
where we could anchor safely, until a change of
wind enabled us to weather Cape Portland, and
then a breeze from any point of the compass,
except due south, would carry us down the east
coast to Oyster Bay. But the contrary breeze
grew yet stronger towards night, and the vessel
pitched and rolled horribly; the children suffered exceedingly, and poor Charlie, who had
only recently recovered from a dangerous illness,
became seriously ill and exhausted. The vessel,
perfect as were her form and sailing capacities,
had she been properly rigged, had only her fore
and aft canvas, without square sails, and could
not therefore be properly worked, even by skilful
hands, whilst those we had on board were ignorant
and helpless in the extreme.

A thick dark night, a contrary wind blowing
half a gale, and a rocky reefy lee-shore, added
to these disadvantages, made me petition my husband most earnestly for a run back to George
Town, whence we could proceed overland with

our children; and, about eleven o'clock, I had the great, but I must confess unexpected, satisfaction of hearing that the order had been given, and we were soon hurrying back most rapidly, bounding before the gale towards the Tamar.

Knowing the inattention and recklessness of the "Master" (and which knowledge alone induced him to turn back), Mr. Meredith went on deck frequently to see that all was right. Once, as he stood gazing at the lighthouse, the point for which we were steering, he suddenly lost the light for a long interval, much longer than its period for revolving; then it reappeared, as if from behind some dark body, and again vanished. He then thought there must be an island which intervened, and asked the master if he knew how "Tenth Island" bore from us then?

"Oh, yes, sir!—We're leaving Tenth Island two or three miles on the port quarter."

Still my husband's suspicions were not at rest, and he took the man forward with him to look out again. By this time the vessel had rapidly approached "Tenth Island"—for such it was— the roar of the heavy surf was distinctly audible on the rocks, and there remained barely time to alter our course, ere we swept close past the white gleam of the breakers on the cliff.

Had we driven onwards another two minutes in the direction we were going, not one of us had survived to tell the tale:—and with a devout and grateful heart did I most earnestly thank God for our signal deliverance from such a fearful death! I knew nothing of our danger until it was past, yet even then it was horrible to think of, and a right welcome sound was the rumble of the cable as we cast anchor at George Town, about one on Sunday morning.

Leaving our servant as our supercargo on board the "Harriet" to proceed to Swan Port when the wind served, we exchanged our cabin accommodation for snug apartments in a quiet little inn, and took our passage from thence on Monday afternoon in the steamer for Launceston. Her Majesty's ship "Rattlesnake" had also arrived on Saturday night, and several of her officers and midshipmen were fellow-passengers with us in the steamboat.

A very pleasant voyage up the Tamar brought us in the evening to Launceston and our old hotel; whence, the following afternoon, we proceeded in

the mail to Campbell Town: and here began the
real difficulties of our progress; our own good
horses were comfortably grazing at Swan Port, and
our peerless tandem cart lay dismembered in the
hold of the "Harriet;" Mr. Meredith consequently
made a voyage of inquiry the next morning in
search of some strong vehicle that could be hired
to convey us across the tier, a weary journey of
nearly sixty miles, over the same rough track
described in our pilgrimage *to* Port Sorell. A
spring cart was at length obtained, and in it we
proceeded on our slow and weary way. On the
third evening of our journey, we arrived and halted
awhile at our old home of Spring Vale, where we
pressed one of our own stout horses into our
service, and had the pleasure of being welcomed
with a shout of delight from some of our old
servants.

Our pretty cottage and the garden we had made
and cultivated with so much care and pride, were
unworthily tenanted by people who kept cattle and
horses tethered to our choice fruit-trees, and had
even erased the very form of the garden. Ragged
disreputable sheds were set up in front, and
slovenly brush fences behind; but I am happy to

say, it has since, in the occupation of our servants, under our own care, recovered much of its old neatness.

We made a pleasant sojourn at Cambria, our father's hospitable home, where we joined a right patriarchal assemblage of our own " kith and kin," then visiting there, and contributed our triad of boys to the merry group of grandchildren already met. We waited in anxious expectation for the " Harriet's" arrival, and as one week after another went by without intelligence of her, began to fear the worst for our valued old servant and our goods and chattels ; but at length, after being driven about the straits in every direction but the right one, and paying involuntary visits to Circular Head, and other out-of-the-way localities, they contrived to cast anchor at Waterloo Point. As soon as our goods were landed, we took up our abode once more at Riversdale, where the commencement of a garden and orchard had brought a pleasant altera-tion on its former appearance and comfort, and where we have happily passed the last two years, busy in all farm matters, and in effecting every practicable improvement in all around us.

If these unpretending chronicles of our Tasma-

nian life seem to have lingered long in the recording, the perpetual enticements and beguile-
ments of pleasant country occupation must bear
the blame.

I could not possibly sit down quietly to write
whilst I had my new garden entirely to remodel;
and my anxious wish to leave all things in their
places that were growing luxuriantly, so as to
prevent too much evidence of newness, and at the
same time to turn all the straight dirt-walks into
gracefully curved turf ones, and to have a nice
grass plat in front, was not very easily fulfilled, and
cost me many runs up stairs, to contemplate the
effect of my plans from the upper windows, before
my clever old gardener and I could finally accom-
plish our task, the result now being highly satisfactory. A rustic wooden bridge leading to the
orchard over a long fishpond in the garden is also
one of our useful embellishments, and a thatched
octagon summer-house, nicely placed beneath a fine
old lightwood tree near the pond, will, when covered
with creeping roses, ivy, jasmine, and passionflowers, be very ornamental too, though at present
the popular opinion of my taste in erecting it
seems somewhat divided. A spacious veranda,

erected this summer along the front of the house, is the most important and essential addition of all; in this country, a good veranda is like an extra sitting-room; and, as an airy play-place for children on a warm or rainy day, is invaluable. We hope that some of our numerous families of swallows will take, or rather make, apartments in it next summer. Last year we were prevented from using our little boat for some months, although the Swan River is a delightful place for sailing, because a pair of confiding little swallows had built their nest in it, as it lay on the cross beams of a shed in the yard; and we could not dream of disturbing them till the young ones were grown up; then the boat was removed at once, lest another brood should claim our forbearance. Our veranda also forms my only substitute for a green-house, and in this climate such partial shelter is sufficient for the cultivation of most plants which must be wholly protected during an English winter.

From the front window of our dining-room, where I now sit, I look through the veranda over the grass plat and flower borders, now past their summer beauty, but still gay with noble hollyhocks, carnations, tiger lilies, and other autumn

N 3

flowers. A hawthorn hedge, and some graceful white-blossomed acacias, overhang two ranges of beehives, and conceal the paling fence, behind which passes the public road; and beyond its other hedge, which is of gorse, lie sweet fields of clover, where the children's five pet lambs, and some favourite horses or cows, lead a luxurious life. Beyond these, again, is another gorse hedge, and other larger meadows, also fenced with a grand *chevaux de frise* of gorse, with some emerald bright English willows, forming lofty clumps on one side; and in spring, giving us a pleasant home-like interest in marking their gradually deepening green, amidst the unchanging, dull, olive natives of the soil. Still again beyond flows the Swan River, a noble broad stream, sixty yards or more in width, but only visible to us from the house when a heavy flood spreads it over the meadows. On the opposite bank of the river lies a small farm, some of the whitewashed buildings just showing through a fine belt of trees; and, bounding the whole, rises a woody ridge of steep rocky hills, only used as a sheep-run, and a very poor one.

From our side-window, through the passionflowers, roses, and jasmine trained round it, and over

a gay little flower-garden below, we look up the
public road, through the district. Opposite the
entrance to our farm-yard stands our blacksmith's
forge, whilst the mill, barn, stack-yard, cow-sheds,
stabling, dairymen's cottages, and other buildings,
fill up the side-view, and complete the extensive
farm homestead. A dovecote on a high wooden
pillar, safe from cats, but alas! not always so from
hawks, is the abode of a large and handsome family
of tumbler-pigeons; and a capacious yard beyond,
well stocked with portly porkers, if not adding
much to the ornamental character of the scene,
gives by no means an unsubstantial promise of
creature comforts. The common barn-door fowls
are our most profitable kind of poultry, being more
hardy and requiring less tending than most others.
Turkeys were apt to wander away into the bush,
where they are killed by the native vermin; Guinea
fowls generally become wild; geese do not commonly thrive so well as at home; and ducks, very
successful on some farms, are on others always
carried off by disease.

From the two hives of bees which survived
the long confinement of the voyage from Port
Sorell (one hive died entirely, not having enough

honey to maintain them so long), we have now twenty-three, besides five that I have given away; and as we always drive the bees into a new hive when we take the honey, instead of smothering the swarm with brimstone, &c., our stock will soon be much larger. Whether the system of driving them into an empty hive would answer in the severe winters of England, I am not aware; but here, we perform the operation early in February (which answers to August at Home), and the bees collect a good store again before winter, and are even then rarely kept prisoners three days together without fresh food. Here the wide extent of English clover fields, and the long, long lines of glorious gorse edges, added to all the usual bush and garden flowers, seem admirably suited to the good little honey-makers. At Poyston the young swarms always gave us great trouble to hive them, from their tendency to fly swiftly away, and we lost many in this manner; but here we have now even left off performing the usual tin-dish-and-key concert, on the rising of a swarm, for without any interference they settle within a few feet, or at most a few yards, of the parent hive. One little bush of Chrysan-

themums has had four swarms light in it within a
month, and an old peach-tree has been similarly
favoured; so that we have come to the conclusion
that our bees are of peculiarly domestic and
contented habits. The honey-comb of this year is
much of it, not figuratively, but literally, as white
as snow, and the honey colourless as liquid crystal,
and of most delicate flavour.

Our fine dairy of beautiful cows, and our busy
hives of good little bees, fully realize to us that
scriptural picture of rural luxury — " A land
flowing with milk and honey;" the only alloying
drop of gall being the absence of all possibility of
turning any of our surrounding abundance to
pecuniary profit. Our fat grass-fed beef and
small delicious mutton—equal to any "Welsh" ever
tasted—sell at *two-pence halfpenny* a pound; our
wheat at 3s. the bushel; oats scarcely saleable
at 1s. 6d.; and barley not in demand at all,
most brewers here concocting their compounds
from damaged sugar. Were colonial distillation
permitted by the Government, it might become
a profitable means of disposing of the surplus
grain; but the fear lest the finance department
should suffer by any diminution of the duties now

so largely paid on imported spirits, prevents that boon being accorded to the colonists; and they, unable to make the business of grain-growing pay its own expenses, must soon do generally, as so many have already done, lay down their luxuriant corn-fields in grass and clover, for the production of wool, cheese, and butter, and cultivate no more corn than their own establishments require to consume; and this in a country suited beyond most others for the production of excellent wheat and other grain. Wool seems the only staple commodity of the colony that can be made to pay even its expenses, and a short time since the prices for that were exceedingly low, nor have they yet become adequately remunerative to the sheep-farmer.

I have now retraced my Colonial life from first to last: from the period of my leaving England in 1839, to the present month of February, 1850; and as I fold up the last leaves of my Tasmanian chronicle, and wish my little book a safe voyage to dear old England, I cannot ask or desire a more cordial welcome for it than that which greeted its predecessor; and I heartily hope it may be deemed deserving of one as kind.

THE END.